GIVING AN ACCOUNT
The Life and Ministry of
Richard H. Vigneulle

Richard H. "Dick" Vigneulle

GIVING AN ACCOUNT
The Life and Ministry of Richard H. Vigneulle

By Bruce R. Peters

To order copies of this book:

www.givinganaccount.com

or

www.dickvigneulle.com

Portrait Photo on p. ii: Courtesy of Brittany Moore

Library of Congress Control Number: 2009927279

ISBN 1-59421-053-5

Printed in the United States of America

Published by Seacoast Publishing, Inc.

Birmingham, Alabama

"Thou wilt show me
the path of life:
in thy presence is
fullness of joy;
at thy right hand there are
pleasures for evermore."

Psalm 16:11 / KJV

Preface

God created each of us for fellowship with Him, and only in surrender to Jesus Christ as Savior and Lord can anyone find eternal peace and purpose. This book is the account of one man's path of life as he made this discovery and then helped others to do the same.

Each life should be a purposeful journey. In telling the life story of Richard H. (Dick) Vigneulle, I am paying tribute to the pastor who became a mentor and friend as I pursued God's call on my life as a believer and minister of the Gospel. I was first asked to write this book nearly ten years ago, but the task seemed too daunting. When the opportunity again presented itself to me nearly two years ago, the Lord gave me the courage and conviction to accept the challenge.

This book is the culmination of countless hours of heartfelt conversation and prayerful reflection with Pastor Vigneulle. In addition, there were many interviews with members of the Vigneulle family as well as Dick's former co-workers (at the bank and church), church members, and other friends. This circle crosses generations, genders, and the globe.

From the outset, I kept in mind a list of objectives prayerfully compiled, written out and kept in my manuscript notes. First and foremost, I want this project to glorify God. Second, I want to honor God's man, Pastor Vigneulle. My third aim is servanthood and inspiration. As a young Christian I found encouragement in the biographies of Christian men and women from generations past and present. May this book aid a new generation of believers as they follow their own "path of life." Finally, in transcribing Dick's life and gifts to paper, I identified convictions and principles that distinguished him as a godly leader in both secular and sacred arenas. His story presents a worthy model of Christian faith in the business world and sound business practices in the church house.

Under Pastor Vigneulle, the founding and development of Shades Mountain Independent Church resulted in the prolific creation of ministries. All were significant, appreciated, and fruitful. For the sake of containing the expansive story of this amazing pastor and church, I narrowed my focus to two primary areas of ministry: evangelism and missions. Both were at the heart of the pastor and church and became the focus of all other SMI ministries, from tireless volunteers in the church kitchen to enthusiastic staff in the Christian Book Store.

There are many significant men and women who are part of this story, and Pastor Vigneulle would be the first to want to acknowledge their invaluable contributions and eternal impact. More voices are heard in this book than identified by name. In fact, in deference to the larger theme, I chose not to include my own name in the chapters telling the story of SMI and its pastor, though certainly my voice is heard. Likewise, I deferred emphasizing my personal ministry areas in Christian education to maintain the overarching emphasis on evangelism and missions. The point is that many names and ministries are left out or narrowly covered, including my own.

This book addresses homage and heritage, and so my intent is inspirational more than academic. Even so, I have strived for accuracy while compiling information and constructing the story's telling. My subject's life now spans nearly eight decades, and so too do the memories and recollections of many who contributed to my fact gathering. I have taken some artistic liberties, for example, in re-creating long-ago conversations. Sometimes the interchanges are written as they were told to me by the person recalling them. Other times, to unfold the story, I created them based on information given me, and then in such a way as to reflect the character and intent of the people and events described. On occasion, it may be that minds have been clogged by time passed or hearts enlarged by gratitude.

BRUCE R. PETERS
Edgewood, Kentucky
April 7, 2009

Contents

Chapters

Acknowledgements

The author, along with Dr. Vigneulle, wish to thank the amazing team the Lord called out to bring this book to reality.

"He who calls you is faithful, who also will do it" (I Thessalonians 5:24).

GLENDA MASSENGALE and BETH MASSENGALE, an inspired mother-daughter team, served as research assistants and editors with diligence and grace.

Their talents and spiritual gifts inspired their vision for this book, with grateful hearts for the pastor who touched their individual lives and family.

TOM MASSENGALE, husband and father to this amazing duo, gave limitless practical and prayer support. As the manuscript neared its deadline, he donated countless hours of technical support.

―――――――――

DANIEL A. MOORE, nationally acclaimed sports artist and founder of New Life Art, has won acclaim for his paintings which commemorate historic, even legendary, sports events. A Birmingham native, he was a high school student when he first heard Dick Vigneulle preach, eventually becoming a Christian and member of the SMI family. Mr. Moore has carried out a labor of love for the man who led him to the Lord. He devoted his artist's eye and heart to this book, serving as a photo consultant and art director.

―――――――――

JANIS BAILEY, Publisher, Seacoast Publishing, Inc., quickly became a valued and respected member of our team. Her quiet voice spoke warm-hearted encouragement and professional counsel. Her input as well as her publishing company assured a quality product that honored not only the team's labors but also the man behind the story.

Finally, Dr. Peters wishes to thank two authors who provided strategic critical evaluations and personal encouragement for this biography, his first book. CECIL MURPHEY, whose scores of titles include *90 Minutes in Heaven*, said, "Professional writers write even when they don't feel like it." JANIE BUCK, author/editor of biographies of Dr. Frank Barker, Elizabeth Newbold, and Dr. D. James Kennedy, sweetly said, "Bruce, just tell a story." Their voices coached the author to completion.

Dedication

First, this book is dedicated to my loving wife, Nancy, whose devotion to Christ and her husband helped make this book possible. She continues to fulfill the promise of our wedding day: "Oh, magnify the LORD with me, and let us exalt His name together" (Psalm 34:3).

Second, this book is dedicated to the men and women with whom I served at Shades Mountain Independent Church and Shades Mountain Christian Schools (1976-1984). Their testimonies and lives—pastors, teachers, staff—helped make SMI for me "The Place Where the Love Is."

Foreword

Someone asked my friend Dick Vigneulle how it felt to know God used him to bring thousands to Christ—not just in Alabama—but all over the world. Without a blink, he answered, "It's very humbling. I've never forgotten who I am—just a sinner saved by grace."

Few attain the upper echelon of business success, let alone walk away from it to become a pastor, but that is just what Dick Vigneulle did.

Dick Vigneulle is the founder of a great church, Shades Mountain Independent Church in Birmingham, Alabama. He is the founder of a great school, Shades Mountain Christian Schools, a ministry of SMI. He is the founder of a great missionary organization, World Reach, Inc.

I regard him as one of the South's leading pastors of his era including his stand for family values—his influence reaching all the way from Alabama's State Capitol to Washington, D.C.

Dick and I have been friends for many years, first crossing paths in ministry travels and later sharing in ministry after his invitations for me, along with my wife Beverly, then President of Concerned Women for America, to speak at SMI. A special season of ministry came in 1988 when Dick invited me to preach a thirteen-week series on Sunday nights at his church. I had continuing preaching duties in Texas that carried me from my then home and headquarters in Washington, D.C., on a weekly basis. At Dick's urging, I made Sunday night stopovers in Birmingham. Those visits connected me to the dynamic SMI congregation and the great-hearted man who founded the ministry.

As a pro-life leader and outspoken pastor for family values and responsible government, Dick led Moral Majority of Alabama in the 1980's. I was so impressed with his stand that I invited him to serve as the Director for the Birmingham area of my American Coalition for Traditional Values. He served with distinction.

This successful banker and distinguished pastor has led multitudes to Christ—he is a great soul-winner and missions statesman. In the world of finance and later for the kingdom of God, he mentored men and women to succeed as leaders. This book contains the lessons he taught. I feel this book—the inspiring story of Dick Vigneulle's amazing life and ministry—is a must-read for Christians, but especially for those who are leaders in God's work, and for those who have holy aspirations to make a difference in their generation.

One of the evidences of Dick and Peggy's Christian lives is the great Christian family they have raised.

Beverly and I regard Dick and Peggy Vigneulle as dear friends whom we want others to meet and be inspired as we were. This book will give the reader just that opportunity!

TIM LAHAYE
Author, Pastor, Teacher

Introduction

Many a man claims to have unfailing love,
but a faithful man who can find?
Proverbs 20:6 / NIV

A faithful man is rare. The wise man of the Proverbs recognizes the abundance of those who claim fidelity but bemoans the rarity of such men. The story to follow is the story of a rare man. In a culture full of those who "say one thing and live another," it is an honor to introduce the story of someone who has lived what he has preached and modeled what he has taught. For over 20 years as Pastor Dick's successor, I have known Dr. Richard H. Vigneulle to be one of those "few" faithful men. For decades he served as a faithful pastor, church leader, and community influencer. Pastor Dick was faithful to the Word of God. He was faithful to the mission of the Son of God. He was faithful to the people of God. He remains a faithful husband, father, grandfather, great-grandfather, and friend.

Though unusually gifted and inspirational, though admired and highly regarded, Pastor Dick displayed the daily commitments of a man who knew his strength was God's. He sought to faithfully lead his staff and faithfully fulfill his pastoral duties. In all my years of ministry association I have never known him to be unfaithful in his calling or the principles that defined it. It is with my highest expectation that someday he will be the recipient of those precious words from the most faithful of all, "Well done thou good and faithful servant."

The writer of Proverbs has also declared that "***a good name is to be preferred above great riches.***" After serving with Pastor Vigneulle for 7 years and ministering to his people and in his city for over 20 years I can say that for sure, and for certain, that Dick Vigneulle has a "good name" in the city of Birmingham, in the state of Alabama, around the nation, and throughout the world! It is my privilege to bear witness to the fact that Pastor Dick has truly been a priceless treasure to this church and to this community. The story that follows will help you know why.

HARRY F. WALLS III
Senior Pastor, Shades Mountain Independent Church
March 2009

CHAPTER ONE

Final Sunday

On July 2, 1995, Shades Mountain Independent Church celebrated its Silver Anniversary Sunday. Since its founding twenty-five years earlier, Dick Vigneulle was the only pastor the church had known. In turn, SMI was the only church the banker-turned-minister had ever pastored. And it was his final Sunday.

The first Sunday in July, known as "Birthday Sunday" at SMI, marked the annual celebration of the church's founding. In 1969, a small band of believers who were meeting in an insurance building in Hoover, Alabama—an Over the Mountain suburb south of Birmingham—invited a City Federal banker to share his testimony. After repeated requests for this dynamic speaker to return, he reluctantly consented, and so began an incredible journey for both the little group and the layman.

By the next year, on July 5, 1970, sixty-seven charter members formed "Shades Mountain Methodist Church (Independent)" with the banker as its

Typical church service inside SMI sanctuary

1

Pastor. Despite his repeated reminder "I'm a banker not a preacher," that same year, to appease his tiny flock, the confirmed businessman consented to ordination. Now in 1995, the church and Dick Vigneulle celebrated twenty-five years of ministry together. By God's grace, the church now occupied an expansive campus on Shades Mountain and touched the world with the Gospel.

The present-day congregation, meeting in a sanctuary holding 1,500 worshippers, maintained the zeal of SMI's founders. As if spirited by the words of the old hymn *Onward Christian Soldiers*, the church marched to the end of the twentieth century "with the cross of Jesus going on before."

Birthday Sunday traditions in tact, a giant cross-shaped birthday cake would be on display in the sanctuary, eventually decorated with hundreds and hundreds of burning candles, each one placed by a man or woman, boy or girl, who had come to Christ through the ministry of SMI. On the first Birthday Sunday, the cake measured 2 feet by 2 feet. Now twenty-five years later the gigantic confection measured 10 feet by 12 feet.

But in 1995, the milestone event warranted special measures. One month earlier Dick surprised the congregation with an announcement that everyone knew was looming—the time had come for him to step aside as the church's Pastor.

Dick's preparation for the church's inevitable transition in leadership began years before, but even so, knowing just when to make the hand-off was difficult. Dick wrestled with the timing for months. Mounting health problems made the rigors of a pastor's life not only difficult but threatening to his stamina and well-being.

"Dad, you need to back off," his twin sons advised him.

Peg long encouraged her husband to slow down, but that was like asking a hurricane to move in slow motion.

After much prayer, comforted by the counsel of family and dear friends, Dick found God's peace. The time had come to end his pastorate.

As he confided to the congregation that June morning, from the very start of his ministry on the mountain, Dick prayed for divine wisdom to guide the start as well as the stop of his pastorate.

"Folks, I asked the Lord, if it's a year or fifty years, give me enough wisdom to know when it is time. The Lord has answered that prayer and has told me that now is that time. Even though this is probably the most difficult thing I've ever done, it is the right thing."

Months of planning anticipated a weeklong celebration culminating on Birthday Sunday. Special services featured dignitaries and noted guests. The roster included giants from the evangelical world, all long-standing personal friends of Dick and Peggy Vigneulle: Jack Taylor, Wales Goebel, Jerry Falwell, Brom Cowser, Sumner Wemp, Tim LaHaye, and John MacArthur.

Not a surprise to those who knew him, Dick Vigneulle opted to sing not preach on his final Sunday. Lyrics not sermons were always his most natural medium to celebrate his faith, and besides, his well-known preacher friends arrived with sermons and challenges they were eager to share.

As a special keepsake, members of the congregation received copies of a commemorative publication issued just for the event: *25 Years of Ministry and Miracles: SMI—Celebrate the Silver 1970 - 1995.* An opening key verse heralded the theme of Dick Vigneulle's life and ministry: "Where there is no vision, the people perish" (Proverbs 29:18). The booklet opened with tributes from Alabama Governor Fob James, as well as letters from local mayors. All honored "The Man with a Vision."

Church historians chronicled SMI's first quarter-century of ministry, recounting eight miracles, one after another, that documented the once tiny church's numerical growth and property expansion. The impact of the church's very existence testified to what God could do through people of faith, led by a man of vision.

Years before, in the early years of unfulfilled dreams and even adversity, SMI's Pastor rallied the faithful with a prophet's voice: "Call unto Me and I will answer you, and show you great and mighty things, which you do not know" (Jeremiah 33:3). Today, on this special day, the congregation knew the promise was true—they had proved God's faithfulness time and again.

One friend suggested, with reverent humor, "Well, now folks not only know our Pastor's name—they know how to pronounce it! Everyone knows Dick VIN-YELL!"

The occasion fitted an homage paid years earlier by Sumner Wemp, famed evangelist, educator, and author. A longtime, loyal friend to Dick and Peggy as well as the church, he wrote a congratulatory letter on Dick's tenth anniversary as SMI's Pastor.

Dick, A couple of verses came to my mind concerning you and your ministry. I Samuel 9:6 says, "Behold now, there is in this city a man of God, and he is an honorable man; all that he saith cometh surely to pass..." Thank God, Birmingham has a man of God in its city and look what has come to pass. Then in Nehemiah 2:18, Nehemiah tells that "the hand of God was upon me" and they built the work of God. It has been evident that the hand of God is upon you and your ministry there...You and your people should be honored and humbled at all God has done. May this be only the beginning until He comes.

Dick and Peggy both would be the first to testify that Shades Mountain Independent Church, the Miracle on the Mountain, was not the work of man—it was the work of God. To bring home the point, in his final message to his flock as their Pastor, Dick chose to sing *My Tribute*, a song which opens with a humble exclamation of praise: "To God be the glory!"

Dick arrived on the platform with a surprise or two of his own for the congregation. As a fitting trophy of grace, the former banker, and soon-to-be retired pastor, had one more "miracle" to announce. The church had recently received the largest gift ever bequeathed to the ministry.

AGNES GAINES

SMI's Prayer Room ministry carried on wherever a praying church member went. But just off the sanctuary was a small room in an out-of-the-way corner organized and designated for an intercessory ministry. Prayer was a core value and practice in Dick's life, so naturally prayer would be a vital ministry for the church's growth as well as its congregation of young believers. Dick adhered to the old adage "Little prayer, little power; much prayer, much power!"

The story is told that Charles Haddon Spurgeon, the soul-winning pastor of a huge church in Victorian London, ended a tour of the church with visitors by asking a question.

"Would you like to see the furnace room—the source of all the power that keeps this church going?"

The eager guests nodded their approval and followed Spurgeon as he descended into the basement. When he opened the door, set before the visitors was not some big mechanical device, but scores of Christians on their knees praying.

"There, my friends, is the source of the power to all that goes on here!"

SMI needed just such a "Furnace Room." The Prayer Room was simply outfitted with a chair and prayer bench, along with myriad literature and books on prayer. On the prayer altar was a large notebook that contained countless prayer requests sent to the church, some from mission fields across the globe, some from strangers and neighbors in the community, many from the church family and SMI staff itself, and yet others right out of the news and headlines of the day.

Supporting the Prayer Room was a team of volunteers recruited and organized from the congregation, each with an assigned day and hour to be in the Prayer Room. The team was as diverse as the congregation. This prayer ministry gave a place to many who wanted to serve but did not feel equipped for public or platform gifts. It excited the staff to see the unfamiliar faces of the congregation show up eagerly and faithfully to carry out their prayer assignments. They became behind-the-scenes spiritual commandos.

One such person was Agnes Gaines. An older woman with tall, gaunt features, Agnes suffered health disabilities that limited her church attendance and restricted her means of serving the Lord in a public way. The Prayer Room gave her a place to serve. But even on her assigned day, Agnes would sit in a chair in the hallway just outside the church offices. Narrow steps to the Prayer Room made that prayer chamber difficult for her to access. But she wanted to be a part of the intercessory team, so she came faithfully week after week and perched in a shadowy, out-of-the-way alcove. One of the church staff would dash to the Prayer Room and bring the book of requests down to Agnes.

She would balance the book on her lap, bow her head, and pray. As quietly as she arrived, Agnes would slip away, never calling notice to herself. But Agnes was a person hard not to notice. Her wardrobe never seemed to change, wrapping herself in a gray cloth coat which she never removed. She wore stockings, but her legs were so thin that the nylons bowed and crinkled all the way down to her loafers as if never touching skin. Agnes had pretty auburn hair, even in old age, and she always wore it up, twisted in a chignon. Even with little or no makeup, her strong, classic profile was striking. It was whispered that in her youth Agnes had been a fashion model.

The elderly saint seemed to be surviving hard times with a meek spirit and *quiet faith. Few knew about her public ministry on the prayer team, but she inspired the staff who watched, week after week, as Agnes appeared and disappeared.*

In her declining months, she could no longer keep up her prayer ministry, but no one doubted that she continued to intercede for her Pastor and the church. The dear woman who seemed to live on the brink of poverty found herself the recipient of elder care by her loving church family. Not a matter of special treatment, this ministry typified New Testament church compassion, the kind of care SMI afforded many over the years.

When Agnes went to be with the Lord, it would surprise many if not all the congregation to learn that Agnes Gaines actually left behind a sizeable estate—one that included a bequest to her beloved church—a gift of one million dollars.

One announcement on this 25th Birthday Sunday came as no surprise— the introduction of Shades Mountain Independent Church's new Pastor, Harry F. Walls III.

As Dick had shared with his church family just weeks before, "I've always felt that a pastor has a responsibility never to leave his people without a shepherd. That has always been a major priority of mine, and about ten years ago I began to pray, 'Lord, send us that individual.'"

On his last day as Pastor, Dick consoled the congregation with the reminder that loving Pastor Walls did not mean they no longer loved Pastor Vigneulle. In fact, honoring the new pastor would pay tribute to the one who prepared the way.

"Folks, he is God's choice for SMI to take us to the next level….I love him and he will have my wholehearted support."

After much prayer, Dick had hand-selected his successor. Harry Walls, in turn, faithfully waited, serving a seven-year apprenticeship. Dick delegated pastoral duties and authority in stages. By 1995, Harry already had held the administrative helm for a year. After mentoring his own "Joshua" and readying his congregation for momentous change, Dick knew the time was now right. Today the transfer would be completed, as SMI's new Pastor would be welcomed by the Pastor *Emeritus*.

Beyond all the day's festivities and personal accolades, Dick had to admit to himself that his "Final Sunday" was painful. The letting-go moment was harder than the day Tom, his last child at home, went off to college, or even the day he had walked Diane, his only daughter, down the aisle to take another man's name. Solomon's wisdom described this season of life now settling on a veteran pastor and his people: "To everything there is a season, A time for every purpose under heaven" (Ecclesiastes 3:1).

Dick's life had long been energized by change, and the miracle of SMI unfolded because a congregation embraced change. Today would be the same—charge ahead!

Looking back, a friend observed, "Make no mistake—Pastor Vigneulle was not quitting the ministry. He was retooling or transitioning, if you like."

As he recently reminded the congregation, "Peg and I will be right here. We are not going anywhere. This will continue to be our church too."

Dick's statement of fidelity testified to his support of the new Pastor and hopefully aided a stable transition. SMI would not only continue to be his church home, it would be the home base for his wider ministries in God's vineyard.

Dick looked forward to carrying on his ministry as Chairman of the Board of World Reach, Inc., the missions organization birthed out of SMI. Likewise he would continue to serve on the board of his twin sons' ministry, Rick and Mick Vigneulle Ministries. Lingering from his days as the head of Moral Majority of Alabama, Dick still felt a compassion for the unborn. He would remain an outspoken pro-life voice. Invitations would multiply from home and mission fields. There would be more sermons to preach, of course, and certainly plenty more songs to sing.

As he prepared his farewell, Dick gave a closing charge.

"I just want to say this, folks—I LOVE YOU! And I challenge you and charge you to keep on keeping on till Jesus takes us home!"

———————

No one believer had been molded by SMI's ministries more than the church's Founding Pastor. After twenty-five years, the public knew him as one of Alabama's most influential pastors, but had to be reminded of his early career as a prominent businessman and banker. His spiritual gift for evangelism and a midlife call of God took Dick from the City Federal executive suite to the SMI pulpit.

Nearly three decades earlier, the business world rocked at the news of his resignation from one of Alabama's premier financial institutions. Like

Levi leaving his money tables to become Matthew the Apostle, it was a stunning career path change that led to a life transformation.

His business background served him well, and Dick remained foremost an evangelist. But through his years of pastoral ministry, God gave Dick a shepherd's heart.

Along the way, even he struggled with the transformation. For example, in the throes of ministry struggles—whether with people or issues—there was a refrain often repeated, almost under his breath and to himself, spoken with a heavy heart and burning frustration: *"It was not like this at the bank!"*

Why not? What was the difference between standing at the helm of a bank versus a church? Business life trained Dick Vigneulle to bring a practical savvy to ministry life, but there were times and situations when the business world and the church separated. Rules of the marketplace did not always apply.

One staff member, who heard Dick repeat the phrase over the years, tackled the question for himself: "Why is a church different from a bank or a business?"

"I concluded that a bank is an ORGANIZATION but a church is an ORGANISM. One is mechanical, the other living. It amazed me to see how people who will submit to earthly authority, sometimes rankle at spiritual authority. Organizations have goals, but people have expectations. You can kick a machine and it won't yelp, but wound a living thing and it will bruise or cry out."

As Dick reflected on his final Sunday in the pulpit as SMI's Pastor, there was another irony not lost on many of the onlookers. When City Federal's Executive Vice President left the bank for a newly

The City Federal Building as it appears today, now site of downtown condominiums founded church, in some people's opinion, he went from prestigious banker to obscure pastor. The move, for the earthly-minded, was a comedown, turning his back on the secure for the unknown.

After all, City Federal was a front-line financial institution in all of Alabama not just the city of Birmingham. The bank's name, emblazoned in giant neon red letters, rose on the rooftop of the city's premier skyscraper. The tiny church on the mountain, not even affiliated with a denomination, faced an uncertain future. The congregation, after all, was largely made up of teenagers ("Jesus Freaks" to some). Dick's step of faith seemed risky, even to some professing believers. Now, twenty-five years later, City Federal Savings and Loan was no more, the banking institution gone in the Savings and Loan debacle of the 1990's. On the other hand, the little church on the mountain grew to a large fellowship of believers with a continuing national reputation and an international impact.

Dick often reflected on the words of missionary martyr, Jim Elliot: "He is no fool who gives up what he cannot keep, in order to gain what he cannot lose."

The promise that fueled his ministry now testified to the wisdom of Dick's choice so long ago.

Ministry as with life is measured more by people than events. So many people, early pioneers and long-standing co-laborers with Dick and Peggy, were now with the Lord. Although they were not sitting in the SMI pews on this very special morning, their presence was felt. Dick missed one man most of all—his first and best teacher—his father, Harold Vigneulle. "Pop" was still his hero. And Dick had come so far from his boyhood days in Wilmington, Delaware.

CHAPTER TWO

Delaware Kid

Sixteen-year-old Dick Vigneulle—or "Rich" as his family called him in those days—was about to be packed up and shipped off from his home in Wilmington, Delaware to a youth camp in the Pocono Mountains. His parents, devout believers and no-nonsense disciplinarians, had become exasperated by their strong-willed son. A good boy at heart, he needed a strong hand to guide him. They hoped the Bible preaching and fellowship at a Christian camp away from Rich's hometown and the influence of unruly friends would reach their son.

In a twist on the traditional "3 R's," his life so far was defined by Religion, Regimen, and Rowdiness. His parents' pious training established the first two, but the third "R" came from Dick's seemingly limitless physical and emotional energy. The son of a well-known music evangelist and a church secretary, Rich sometimes disappointed the expectations of his family.

Harold Vigneulle was a widower with one daughter when his evangelistic ministry brought him to the Union Methodist Episcopal Church in Wilmington where he met the pretty and efficient church secretary, Irene Marjorie Stevens.

A native of Cleveland, Ohio, Harold was converted as a teenager in an Assembly of God revival meeting. His musical gifts matched his love for song as a medium for sharing the Gospel. In 1923 the Calvary Baptist Church of Cleveland, Ohio licensed him—in the words of his licensing document— "to exercise his gifts in preaching the Gospel of Jesus Christ."

For many years Harold partnered with an evangelist named George W. Cooke, and together they traveled the Delmarva Peninsula, covering Delaware, Maryland, and Virginia, in extended preaching campaigns. Oftentimes a planned three-week meeting would extend to eight. Evangelist Cooke preached, and Harold sang and led the choir and congregation in hymns.

When the team reached Wilmington to conduct a campaign at the Union Church, Marjorie as church secretary played a key role in organizing the meetings and assisting the guest evangelists. Both her parents had died when she was a girl. For a time, she lived in an orphanage until an aunt took her in. Marjorie began attending church all by herself. Her aunt was an unbeliever and wanted nothing to do with religion. When Marjorie came home one Sunday and announced she had been saved, her aunt frowned and told her never to speak of it again. By the age of sixteen she had moved in with a Christian family named Abbott who provided a nurturing environment and encouraged the teenager in her faith. After high school graduation, Marjorie attended the Moody Bible Institute in Chicago before joining the church staff in Wilmington.

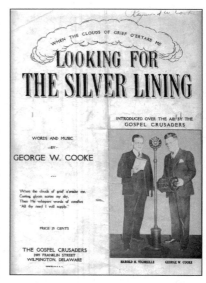

Sheet music written by George W. Cooke (evangelist) – 1926. Shown with songleader Harold H. Vigneulle, Dick's father. Traveled as an evangelistic team.

Dick's parents – Harold and Marjorie Vigneulle, 50th Anniversary –1975

Committed Christians in a shared mission, Harold and Marjorie enjoyed working together. Quickly their friendship bloomed into romance. On their first date, the music evangelist took the pretty secretary to a nice restaurant. When the meal was over, he reached for his money to pay the bill. But his pocket was empty. He had forgotten his wallet at home.

The young woman orphaned as a girl continued to be courted by the widower evangelist with a three-year-old daughter. Despite their youth, both were mature and levelheaded in their approach to life, no doubt seasoned by the serious losses each survived in earlier years. Strong faith enabled them to be overcomers, not just survivors. Their Christian faith shaped their relationship. After a careful, prayerful courtship, the two were married in the very church where they met. The Vigneulles made Wilmington their home, and for many years Marjorie continued her work at the church. Harold, on the other hand, found extended absences for revival meetings too taxing for his growing family. He left the road and became sales manager for a local firm. He remained vitally committed to Gospel outreaches, singing in churches, and leading the musical program in the Union Church which was now his church home.

Harold Vigneulle was respected in his community and recognized as a moral leader, even making a bid for the office of Governor on the Prohibition ticket in 1944. When Dick was in college, his father was honored in *Who's Who in Delaware*, a publication naming distinguished leaders from various fields. While home from school, Dick read the publication's biography featuring his dad. Only then did he learn his father had been married before.

In addition to Harold's daughter, Eva Lee, the family grew with the addition of two more daughters, Ellen and Esther. When Richard Harvey Vigneulle was born, July 24, 1931, parents and sisters alike were delighted by the arrival of a boy. Another son, Bill, followed two years later. The two sons were named in honor of Harold Vigneulle's brothers, Harvey and William.

Dick as a young child (almost 3 years old) in front of his house in Wilmington, Delaware

Raising a large family required organization and efficiency, almost natural life skills for the Vigneulle parents. Marjorie's institutional upbringing in the orphanage as well as her keen business and administrative sense, made her a natural in formulating schedules and job assignments for her children. She lived by a schedule, and they would too.

Dick later described some of the routine expected of the five children. Up at 6:00 a.m., he would be the first to practice piano—a requirement met with mechanical obedience. At 6:30 a.m. Bill would take his turn

13

Dick's love for music began as a young boy – January 1951

at the piano while Dick set the breakfast table. Bathroom rotations allowed time to wash and groom, and then everyone met at the breakfast table. Appearance mattered, and so too did punctuality. Before oatmeal was spooned from a pot or eggs scooped out of a skillet, the Vigneulle family worshipped first. Bible reading and prayer came before mealtime, a regimen sometimes resented by hungry, sleepy siblings. Faith matters and family matters seemed stitched together by the disciplines of schedules to be kept and duties to be fulfilled.

Harold and Marjorie believed the motto "The family that prays together stays together." The Vigneulle children respected their parents as vigilant prayer warriors. The parents prayed regularly and often. While respecting their family prayer times together, the children also knew that both father and mother kept private, personal prayer vigils. Marjorie had her prayer closet in her room. Harold often found a quiet refuge on his back porch in summertime and in the kitchen during wintertime. When the kids spied their folks bowed or kneeling, they knew heaven was being showered with their names. Years later, Marjorie's children would discover another of her spiritual disciplines when they found the journal she kept, chronicling her daily spiritual insights.

One of her most charming entries, however, was written not in a private journal but rather in her son's baby book. It records a mother-son washday routine that showed Dick's gift for song, even as a five-year-old boy. He would sit on the basement steps and look down at his mother standing over the washing machine, pulling laundry from the washer tub and feeding it into the wringers. One morning she made a special request. In her own typewritten hand, Marjorie told the story. It was Dick's first solo.

We were having revival meetings in the Union Church in the fall of 1936, with Dr. Burke Culpepper as the evangelist. During these meetings we had a twenty-four hour prayer circle, round-the-clock. I had one-half hour in the morning from 9:30 to 10:00 a.m. Richard knew about it so he would watch the clock for me and tell me when the hands would get around to the time. He would tell me when the big hand was on five, and he would say, "Mother, it's almost there" and that would give me five minutes.

One morning I was in the basement washing and I heard him upstairs in the kitchen singing a song he composed all by himself. He came to the top of the stairs, and called out to me with a little song of his own. He sang in perfect tune to the melody of a church chorus titled *No Night There*. His little song went like this:

> It's almost there. It's almost there.
> Hallelujah! It's almost there.
> You'd better come upstairs,
> And go and say your prayers.
> Hallelujah! It's almost there.

This little boy's melodic call to prayer pictures two great forces in the Vigneulle household—music and prayer. Both would shape family values and practices. The family delighted to sing together, each child's musicality making the harmony a rewarding experience for building faith and family bonds. Melodies seemed to hum inside little Rich. He could sing and play the piano, more from ear than disciplined practice.

One of Dick's fondest childhood memories was singing with his family around the piano – mid 1940's (Dick at far left)

15

Harold Vigneulle modeled an unbending work ethic, and he expected all his children to follow his example. All his sons and daughters, from an early age, learned to work and work hard and without complaint. His children's childhood memories are of a father always working, never allowing himself time to play, even with them.

Most of Harold's free time was spent on repairing or improving the family home. The house, in a respectable area in Wilmington's suburbs, was situated on a lot surrounded by big poplar trees. On the first floor were the main shared areas, including a living room, dining room, and kitchen. There was a tiny back porch off the kitchen, but the big front porch was the children's favorite gathering spot. On the second floor were three bedrooms and one bathroom. The house was comfortable but tight for a family of seven.

Their neighborhood was idyllic and as pretty as a Currier and Ives print. The children could walk to school, and a grocery store was close. A nearby hill became a popular sledding spot. A close-by pond iced over in wintertime and became the neighborhood's ice skating rink.

In a different era and circumstances, Harold would have excelled in studies and a career as an engineer. It was more than the necessities of life during the Great Depression that forged his skills, whether constructing his own radio from a simple piece of glass and wire, or methodically installing a copper heating system in all three floors of the family home. No task was too large or too complicated for Pop Vigneulle to tackle single-handedly. He dug out a two-car garage underground, hauling off all the dirt in a wheelbarrow. If he needed a special tool, he crafted his own. Harold was as skilled at inventing as Marjorie was in organizing and baking.

The Vigneulle home became the gathering place for their children's friends. All were welcome. Marjorie was popular for her ample provision of homemade snacks—cookies, cakes, and root beer. While Mother cleaned, baked, and canned, Pop worked. Much to his daughters' embarrassment, even while their boyfriends were visiting, Harold would be in his work clothes, hammering or sawing or hauling, sometimes recruiting his girls' beaus to lend a hand.

Dick was his father's son in his readiness to sing or to work. Industry may have been expected, but his natural enthusiasm for work was a bonus. After-school hours offered prime time for money-making opportunities. Dick created opportunities if none existed, and took the ordinary and made it extraordinary. He recalls his first job—a salesman. As an elementary school boy, he walked door-to-door selling magazines such as *The Saturday Evening Post* and *Ladies Home Journal*. Later he delivered newspapers for the *Wilmington Home Journal*, building his route from 30 to 100 daily deliveries.

While in high school, he took an after-school job at the local grocery store, stocking merchandise and delivering groceries. The boy mastered his father's lesson: work, work hard, and work well. That work ethic stayed with Dick all his life.

Harold Vigneulle diligently taught another primary life skill—money management. Income was not necessarily for immediate consumption or self-indulgence. Hard work would result in profit, but that blessing must be shared.

For every dollar Dick earned, ten percent was set aside for a tithe for the church, ten percent was to be put in savings, and the rest was his to spend.

Just as all the family gathered at the breakfast table every morning, so too the whole brood would reconvene at the dinner table. Mealtime together was an expected

Dick's parents, brother, and three sisters
L-R: Esther, Bill, Ellen, Harold, Marjorie, Dick, Eva Lee –1975

pattern. Clean-up chores followed, and then came the family's one bit of shared free time—an hour or so around the floor model radio in the living room. This was the golden age of radio, and the Vigneulle family had their favorites—*The Lone Ranger* and *The Shadow*. When the western and the mystery shows ended, homework had to be done and then bedtime routines fell in place.

Dick's home church preached the Gospel, his parents prayed diligently for him and all their children; but contrary to expectations, he became their problem child. Years later he would look back on himself as the family's black sheep.

Dick loved the outdoors. As a boy he would organize his neighborhood pals whether to play ball or to forage in the woods surrounding his neighborhood. He assigned players to their positions or organized the work crew building a fort. Even as a young person, his high energy and winsome smile won followers.

Envious of Dick's popularity, the local bully picked a fight with the wrong guy. The tough guy felt threatened by Dick's growing influence on the other boys. Trying to hold on to his turf, he raised his fists. Dick was never one to run from a fight, especially when his pals stood by cheering him on. When the scuffle ended, Dick walked away bloodied but with his honor in tact.

In time, however, the local gang's play gave way to pranks, like cutting down all the neighborhood clotheslines and stowing away the useless booty in a clubhouse. A summertime caper found the boys skinny dipping in a river spot near railroad tracks. When trains passed by, unsuspecting passengers would be shocked at the sight of all the boys jumping up high in the air and waving at the surprised onlookers.

After attending Richardson Park Grammar School and then moving on to Conrad High School, the willful little boy had grown to be a temperamental adolescent. Harold Vigneulle was a strong and forceful man in voice and presence, but his son's surly attitude grew bolder as his misbehavior became covert.

Harold Vigneulle was a man of THE Book—the Bible. All that he believed, all the man did was guided by the Word of God. In raising his children, whether teaching them or disciplining them, Harold Vigneulle looked to the Lord for direction. He strongly held to a principle from Proverbs 13:1, "A wise son heeds his father's instruction, but a scoffer does not listen to rebuke." Concerned for the bent of Dick's character and life, Harold looked for a teachable spirit in the teenager. But he could not demand it. Only God could change the young man's heart—if he would let Him.

Still praying fervently for their son, the Vigneulles put feet to their prayers. They kept Dick busy, using work to occupy the teen's time, hoping to funnel his energy in constructive ways. More effective than the rod for corporal punishment, work became a useful disciplinary tool for Dick's parents. Good deeds might forestall bad ones. Despite a defiant mood in many other ways, he always seemed ready to meet the challenge of a hard job. The schedule and rigors of hard work gave him a means of self-control otherwise beyond him. Even more significant at heart, even in his most troubled years, Dick deeply admired his father as the one true hero in his life, a man he delighted to please.

Once in high school during school breaks, Dick began working at various farm camps in Delaware. With many men away in World War II, youth propped up a depleted work force. The workers were lodged in tents, fed well, but worked hard. Dick loved the Spartan, military-like regimen of camp life.

The camp workers could make five cents a quart picking peaches or strawberries. One summer Dick worked cutting asparagus for ten cents an hour. As his pocketbook grew fatter, his palate for asparagus grew weaker. To this day, he hates asparagus and most vegetables in general. He swore to his friends that in the darkness after lights-out, as he tried to sleep, he could hear the asparagus growing during the night, ready to be harvested again the next morning.

The Vigneulle's first son was growing up quickly. Already several inches taller than his father, Dick could not resist pointing out that fact. Harold Vigneulle may have been shorter than his son, but he was not intimidated.

"Hey, Pop! I'm *bigger* than you now," said the strapping youth, with a lighthearted grin.

Sober-faced, Harold stepped toward his son, sharply tapped his son's chest with a forefinger, and looked up into Dick's eyes, without a glint of humor in his own. Then to correct his son's perspective, not just his vocabulary, the father said three never-to-be-forgotten words:

"*Taller*, NOT bigger!"

His rapidly increasing stature and independent spirit, however, signaled urgent measures must be taken. Soon he might be totally beyond their ability to control. But it was concern not fear that prompted a generous offer from parents to son.

Despite the family's austere finances, Harold and Marjorie were quite willing to spend money to send Dick to Christian camps, an offer repeated with all their children. But in Dick's case, as concerned parents, they hoped a change of scenery, as well as life in the great outdoors that he loved so much, would do Dick good. Perhaps through the influential teaching of godly youth workers, their son might make a connection with God that would be life changing. Bottom line, more than anything else, Dick Vigneulle needed the Lord.

The summer of Dick's sixteenth year, an opportunity opened to attend Pinebrook Camp in Stroudsburg, Pennsylvania. The Vigneulles sacrificially but gladly sent their lovable rebel off to the Poconos.

The camp was directed by renowned evangelist Percy Crawford. He was a vibrant preacher with the charisma sure to attract his young audience to the Gospel message. Crawford was a visionary in adapting ministry to modern technology. He pioneered in utilizing radio to broadcast the Good News, over the years building a radio network that still ministers today.

Dick knew his heart was not right toward his parents or God. Any authority exercised over him only roused anger and resentment that sometimes erupted in confrontations. His parents' goodness did not rub off on him, nor could he find peace in the religion that brought comfort to his parents.

His home church did preach the Gospel, but Dick got lost in the congregation of 400. As a boy of twelve he had been baptized, following the church ritual expected of him. But even that holy moment ended in hilarity. When the minister sprinkled the baptism water, some trickled down Dick's neck and he started giggling, much to his parents' chagrin.

His pastor, always formally attired in religious garb, preached sermons that were more morality tales than expositional sermons. Church made little impact on Dick.

But now a teenager, away from home and settled into Pinebrook Camp, Dick felt a reprise from inner conflict, not just family chores. He was alone and on his own, or so he felt.

The open air would always be his favorite cathedral. Camp life afforded his favorite pastimes from fishing to athletic games. His ever-ready people skills quickly won new friends. He delighted in camp life camaraderie until it was time to gather under the tent for the nightly preaching meeting.

Percy Crawford's preaching was electric. His lively delivery style was a far cry from the formality of Dick's pastor back home. Even more unfamiliar to the teen was Crawford's clear call to make a decision about Jesus Christ. Night after night he challenged his young audience to make a personal decision to receive Christ. Desperate for release from his guilt and a means to harness his angry spirit, Dick grew under greater and greater conviction.

One night, as the invitation was given, his struggle became obvious to the fellow camper sitting next to him.

Four stanzas of the invitation had already been sung, and on the last one, Dick's buddy offered, "I'll go forward with you, if you want to go."

How can a lad express his longing for God? What did he need to do to be forgiven? In an act of faith, Dick stepped forward, accompanied by his faithful friend, eager for the evangelist to explain what he needed to do and, if only with a pat on the back, give the assurance that he was right with God.

But to Dick's dismay, when he reached the front, the famed evangelist only looked his way and said, "Son, you got saved, didn't you!"

And with that the preacher turned and walked away. Dick felt rebuffed, and spiritual confusion would linger for many years to come. Questions would linger and doubts haunt him.

Years later, Dick would determine to mark all his evangelistic efforts by intentional one-on-one communication with seekers. A clear presentation of the Gospel would lead to an invitation to accept Christ. Those who responded positively would be given resources for follow-up. These tracts and Bible studies nurtured new Christians, hopefully building up the assurance of any new believer.

When camp ended, Dick returned to Wilmington befuddled by his new faith, not empowered by it.

In high school, Dick's high jinx became more brazen. Cutting classes became routine. He and his pals would skip school and spend the morning at the empty home of a schoolmate whose mother worked, passing the morning and early afternoon playing poker, wagering cigarettes. When the local movie theater opened later in the day, the party moved on. For a lad from a religious family steeped in conservative habits, Dick now hit a triple play of unacceptable behavior: cards, tobacco, and Hollywood movies.

Sometimes a mark of God's hand in a child's life is a sensitive conscience. If that tenderness is lacking—and certainly it was with young Rich Vigneulle—often God's next move is to expose the sin and let the culprit get caught! That is exactly what happened one afternoon.

Once again skipping school, the boys stood in line for their movie tickets when a passing car pulled quickly to the curb and then came to a screeching halt. The driver was the high school principal. The rogue truants were caught!

He rolled down his car window and called out to the red-faced teens, "See you in my office in the morning, boys!"

Rich Vigneulle was without excuse, so the next day's meeting with Conrad High School's principal meant his doomsday. Just how severe would be his punishment, and just how quickly would his parents be informed?

To his surprise, the principal offered a choice.

"Rich Vigneulle, you have two options. Either is acceptable to me. You will have to choose. I can call your father and notify him and your mother of your truancy, and they can meet out their own family discipline. Or you can accept ninety demerits and serve after-school detentions. But with so many demerits, young man, you are going to be staying after school for the rest of the year!"

It was a no brainer—Dick opted for the demerits. Each demerit would require one hour spent after school. Christmas vacation was around the corner, and second semester would soon follow, so there did not seem to be enough school days remaining to make up all the hours his punishment required. Even worse, detentions conflicted with his after-school jobs.

Just as God was working through crushing circumstances in their son's life, so too the Lord was stirring his parents' hearts.

Camp had not made the difference the Vigneulle parents hoped for, or at least there was no outward sign of change. Worse than Dick's brash manner or overconfident speech was his growing indifference to any spiritual instruction his mother and father offered. Dick's sister and her preacher-boy husband had enrolled in Bob Jones University, a Christian school in Greenville, South Carolina that included a high school academy on its campus. The faculty and staff were born-again believers committed to educating youth with a Christ-centered world view. The doctrine was sound and the rules strict.

But the prospects of a Christian school, in a new town, with his sister nearby to provide family support, seemed not only like the best option for young Dick Vigneulle, it was his parents' last one. With much prayer, Harold and Marjorie resolved to present the idea.

To their utter surprise, Dick immediately agreed to the plan. No noble spark ignited his acceptance. He simply saw the new school as the means to sidestep 90 hours of detention at his old school. Only years later did his parents learn about the detentions that motivated their son's eager compliance.

Dick was ready to escape Wilmington, even if it meant leaving home and family behind. Like an outlaw heading out of town before a showdown, the "Delaware Kid" was ready to move on.

CHAPTER THREE

New Man on Campus

$\mathcal{A}$s the Pennsylvania Railroad train pulled out of the Wilmington station, on board was a teenager excited about his new beginning. The train snaked through winter landscapes, passing snow mounds and barren trees, traveling toward Baltimore, next on to Washington, D. C., and then farther south to Richmond, Virginia. Finally, the locomotive whistled its final stop in Greenville, South Carolina, home of Dick Vigneulle's new school, Bob Jones Academy. Despite chilly temperatures outside and his midyear transfer, Dick was flush with excitement.

His father's parting words still rang in his head. Just before he stepped aboard the train, Dick turned and shook his father's hand. In an unexpected show of affection, and for the first time in the boy's memory, he heard his father speak the words, "I love you, son."

Harold Vigneulle may have felt he fell short in transferring all the values he had hoped to impart to his son, but one of his many successful imprints on Dick's spirit was confidence. Dick seemed hyper with excitement, and there was no fear in his heart. With each passing mile, it seemed the rhythm of the tracks steadied his courage, just as each jostle of the train car, shaking him in his seat, only quickened his self-assurance.

Before the train finally pulled into the Greenville station, Dick found the home values he so long fought against now quickening his spirit. As the miles between son and parents increased, so too did the young man's resolve to make his family proud.

His sister Ellen was at the train station, waving and smiling as she greeted her little brother. Ellen and her husband, seminarian Howard Van Sice, loaded up her brother's things and drove out to the expansive campus that would be his new home.

Bob Jones University, eventually billed as "The World's Most Unusual

University," was founded in 1927 near Panama City, Florida by a Methodist evangelist named Dr. Bob Jones Sr., a younger contemporary of Billy Sunday. During his years in evangelism, Dr. Jones counseled many young people shaken in their faith while attending secular colleges and universities, and even students in religious institutions where biblical Christianity was compromised by liberal theology. With savings from his meetings, Dr. Jones purposed to build a school that would be known as a "citadel of biblical Christianity."

From the outset his vision was to draw students from around the world to a training center for world evangelism, equipping young men and women for professional careers as well as ministries. Academics would be high and standards strict, all in a refined cultural environment. The fledgling school relocated to Cleveland, Tennessee in 1933, and then finally moved to its permanent campus in Greenville, South Carolina in 1947, after a welcoming invitation from city leaders opened the door to a 200+ acre site within the city limits.

In time Bob Jones University could boast a beautifully landscaped and gated campus, with expansive grounds and buildings, including a world-famous museum of Italian art and Holy Land antiquities, and a Christian film production company. But when Dick arrived in the winter of 1948, the recently relocated university was undergoing explosive growth and construction, so there were few buildings and acres of red mud everywhere. After the university's founding, the school's mission spawned a preparatory school to provide a Bible-based education for high school students (grades 9-12). The Bob Jones Academy reflected the university's education and discipleship values. BJA students were housed in the same dorms as college students, where the older roommates afforded discipleship and watchcare for their young charges.

The school's mission focused on building Christlikeness in each of the students. God used the dedicated faculty to mold character by precept and example. For the new man on campus from Wilmington, old habits and bad attitudes were not tolerated. In his first semester, Dick's greatest lesson was self-control, one learned not only in a classroom but the gymnasium. In the first days at the Academy, his quick temper was easily provoked and often, especially on the basketball floor.

Dean of Students in those days was Dr. Monroe Parker, affectionately known by his students as "Monk Parker." He was a powerful preacher and a gifted athlete, often working out in the gym with students. Dick was impressed by his Dean's powerful build and the ease with which he lifted heavy weights. He looked like Charles Atlas, so his physique commanded as much respect as his title.

Dick's "chip on the shoulder" attitude showed itself once too often. Dean Parker summoned the hot-head to his office for a crash course in anger management. The charge was clear and straightforward, and so too Monk Parker's ultimatum.

"I am not going to have any more of these heated outbursts from you, young man! I know your father, but I am not going to call him."

As the humbled student listened respectfully, he felt chastened by so powerful a man. Monk Parker had the Bible and the biceps to back up his authority.

"The next time you step out of line, I will deal with you myself. Do you understand?"

Dick nodded in agreement and managed to utter a quiet, "Yes, Sir!"

The transformation in Dick's attitude was almost immediate. With God's help, he learned to harness his bully spirit and to take personal responsibility for his response to life. The attitude correction led to an easier removal of other barriers hindering his growth as a man and as a Christian. The recent arrival from Delaware was indeed becoming a new man!

The Academy provided many opportunities for Dick that motivated him to succeed. The classes were interesting, and teachers integrated the Bible into their instruction. He began to grow spiritually as well as intellectually. A variety of sports occupied his free time as well as student-life activities, and

Soccer team at Bob Jones Academy – 1949 (Dick standing second from right)

soon he made a self-discovery—he was a leader. Others probably saw his potential long before, but campus life stirred his awareness and confidence.

Shortly after arriving at the Academy, someone recruited Dick to lead songs, and he was elected chorister by his classmates. The Vigneulle family sing-alongs and the countless hours watching his father lead song services made him a natural. Standing on the platform before hundreds of schoolmates, his voice loud and commanding and his arms moving in perfect rhythm to the music, Dick held great sway as he roused the student body into one mighty Gospel choir.

One of the great musical experiences of his life was Student Day in Chapel when he directed 4,000 students in singing *Peace Be Still*. Though not a trained musician, he was an exact one. When standing before groups large or small, he showed a spiritual force that many technically proficient musicians lack. He empowered his musical audience.

By the fall of 1948 and the start of his senior high school year, Dick settled happily into Academy life. The rules that some students found difficult to live under were no bother to Harold Vigneulle's son because the standards were no different from home. Besides, with a student body numbering in the thousands, Dick easily understood the need for guidelines to keep order.

God still worked to refine his spirit, but Dick had grown into a tall, good-looking young man made all the more attractive by his wide smile, confident stride, and boundless energy. His enthusiasm for life filled any room he entered. His many friends would gather around him, and strangers hoped for an introduction. When he stood before the student body, leading in hymns and Gospel songs for chapel, he won a ready following.

That same fall, a young lady transferred to the Academy from West End High School in Birmingham, Alabama. Her name was Peggy Haley. As she sat in the chapel for the opening service of the new school year, she was taken by the strapping young song leader.

Nudging the classmate sitting next to her, Peggy whispered, "Who is he?" a smile giving away her growing interest.

"Forget it!" her friend said. "He's taken!"

Within a few days the lively senior song leader discovered Peggy, sitting in the front row of his history class. In any competition—academic, athletic, or social—Dick was quick-thinking and determined to win. The new Southern belle on campus may not have known who he was, but he would soon change that. Dick gave up his seat in the back of the class and sat directly behind the new girl. His advances were thwarted by the history teacher who took a dim view of students socializing during his lectures. Repeatedly he warned the two to take their courtship outside the classroom.

Dick was not the only young man on campus with a fancy for Peggy. She was a stunner, always beautifully dressed and made even more attractive by her happy spirit and kind demeanor. When Peggy Haley walked by, heads turned. She enrolled in Bob Jones Academy at her own request. Led to the Lord at age six by her mother, a tireless worker with Child Evangelism Fellowship, Peggy was brought up in a strong Christian home.

Her father, James Pleasant Haley Sr., was Admitting Supervisor at Birmingham's Tennessee Coal Institute Hospital (later renamed Lloyd Noland Hospital). He was a hardworking man with a quiet temperament. His commitment to provide for his wife and three daughters and one son was tireless, despite disabling health problems. He survived three serious stomach operations with death-defying recoveries.

During one of those illnesses, Mr. Haley had become a Christian. His wife was a devoted church worker and respected Bible teacher. At best, he seemed to hope to get to heaven on his wife's coattail. During a hospital emergency, he turned to his wife and asked her once more to pray for him.

She quietly answered, "Oh, Honey, I have prayed for you for so long, but tonight you must pray for yourself."

It was a short sermon with an eternal impact. From his hospital bed, the weak man rallied strength and courage to talk to God. He prayed the Sinner's Prayer, asking the Lord to save him, and asking for forgiveness for a wasted life.

Louise Haley had the inner strength of Birmingham steel, all wrapped in the personal grace of a Southern lady. She loved God, she loved her church, and she loved her family—in that order. From the Haley home in the West End, she would bundle up her children for the streetcar ride to downtown in order to attend The Birmingham Gospel Tabernacle.

Her pastor, Dr. Glenn Tingley, was a stirring preacher impacting the whole city and state with crusader zeal. Health hindered Mr. Haley from attending church as faithfully and frequently as his wife and children. After his conversion he would attend sometimes, and years later when his son and namesake became a pastor, he was eager to attend Jimmy's church. Even if homebound, however, Mr. Haley delighted to hear Pastor Tingley on his Sunday radio broadcast.

This loving father demonstrated his support with a Saturday night ritual faithfully carried out every weekend: he would polish all the Sunday School shoes of his children and wife, and he would carefully lay out on the kitchen table coins to provide the exact streetcar fare for each of them. The family's means were modest and at times hard, and at one point he balked at the expense of transporting all his family downtown to attend church.

"Louise, there are good churches right here in our neighborhood. We need to save our money! From now on, there will be no coins for streetcar fares."

His wife said nothing until bedtime Saturday night.

"Dear, will you be sure to have all our shoes ready extra early in the morning? If you meant what you said about no more money for the streetcar, then we will have to get up extra early to walk the five miles to church. Good night."

In the morning, the coins were again on the table.

In a church known for strong preaching, Mrs. Haley was also widely followed as a gifted Bible teacher. Young Christians and even preacher boys would visit her home, seated at the kitchen table or gathered in the living room, to be taught by her. She loved to study prophecy and developed a great love for Israel and "God's chosen people."

Despite her mother's godly pursuits and her father's steady presence, Peggy Haley flirted with the world, as she would later describe it. As a teenager, Peg wanted to be popular and go to parties.

"I will be a 'silent Christian,'" she told herself.

Sometimes her unsaved friends would wait in the church parking lot until Peggy's church meetings ended and she could join their outings to a movie or a restaurant. Through her mother's prayers and Pastor Tingley's preaching, a revival swept through the church youth group, and Peggy re-dedicated her life to the Lord. Her heart was tender toward spiritual matters now, yet she recognized how easily influenced she could be by her worldly friends.

"I knew I needed to be around Christian young people, and so I asked my mother if I could go to a Christian high school," Peggy would recall.

One of her sisters attended Bob Jones, and that is where she wanted to go. Louise Haley was delighted—both her parents in fact supported her decision. To pay for the boarding school, Peg's mother sold Bibles and

Christian literature and cards. Once on the Greenville campus, Peggy Haley wanted new friends, and the confident lad from Delaware in her history class wanted to be one of them.

Once he met the Birmingham belle, Dick lost interest in any other girl. He began asking Peggy out on dates and often, but too frequently her dating calendar was already full.

Not used to being put off, he complained, but Peg only smiled and said, "I am sorry, but I only accept dates one week at a time."

He persisted and won. Their dates were simple and usually confined to campus. Most students frequented the university's dating parlor. Nicknamed "the furniture store," it was a huge room filled with sofas, chairs, tables and lamps, and patrolling chaperones. Dating students could go there freely and spend time together, as long as the boy sat opposite from the girl, never beside her, as Dick would recall.

The Vigneulles faithfully sent their son $4 a week to cover all his expenses. On one special

Dick Vigneulle and Peggy Haley dating at Bob Jones University. They dated from 1949 to 1952.

occasion, to buy books or something, Dick's father sent him twenty dollars. He stashed the bill in his gym bag while he played basketball, and later when he gathered up his belongings, the money was gone.

"Losing that money was one of the worst experiences of my whole school life. My folks did not have money to waste, and I dreaded telling my dad the money was lost or stolen. With a really heavy heart, I made the necessary phone call and told Pop. To my amazement, he did not get mad at me. In fact, he said something that would stay with me all my life. 'Son, the Lord will provide.'"

Sometimes the Lord's provision meant ordering one Coke with two straws in the snack shop. The two became a regular dating couple, and Peg's interest in the Delaware chorister was serious enough that she needed to tell her mother about him.

"Mom, I have met a really special boy, and I like him a lot. His name is Dick Vigneulle."

The phone line seemed to go dead, but after a long silence, Peg's mother spoke up and asked only one question, "What nationality is he?"

In the spring of 1949, Dick graduated from Bob Jones Academy, and that fall would begin his college studies at BJU. His parents traveled down to South Carolina to attend their son's high school graduation, taking their place near the front row of the 3,000-seat auditorium. When they picked up the graduation program, to their amazement, their son was listed as a special feature in the ceremonies. Dick had been invited to give a reading. It was a lengthy monologue he committed to memory, even perfecting different voices for the story's characters. Perhaps even more meaningful than seeing their son receive his diploma that night was witnessing the transformation of the churlish teenager who now stood alone on the platform and spoke with perfection. The crowd, mesmerized by the young speaker, followed each line he spoke. If Dick could take command of an audience, surely he was ready to take command of his life.

When he returned to campus that fall, he knew which registration line to get in—the school of business. Not sensing a call to ministry nor a pull to any particular course of study, Dick had sought his father's advice.

"Son," Harold urged, "you would be wise to major in business because that will prepare you no matter what field you pursue later."

The rest of Dick's life would prove the wisdom of his father's inspired direction.

Discipline began to shape the man, forming character and reputation that would bless him all the rest of his life. Punctuality marked his routine and became a virtue he expected in others. A red bicycle was his mode of transportation, as he hustled from his dorm to a classroom building or the gymnasium. His pursuit of Peggy Haley intensified into an earnest courtship. By his sophomore year in college they dated no one else, and by Peggy's own account, every date that year included a marriage proposal before the evening ended. He carefully managed his money not only because his resources were meager but also out of a sense of duty to his parents who sacrificed for his education. Dates with Peg were limited to campus events and locations: the dating parlor and snack shop, sports events and concerts, church services and campus special events.

As much as he loved sports and time with his sweetheart, Dick made prayer a priority, a spiritual discipline enriched by prayer partnerships he formed with buddies, a practice he would repeat later in life. God was working a life formula in this young student which would ignite his future: PRAYER = FAITH + PLANS. Seek God in prayer, and let prayer build faith and birth plans for the future. Dick would follow this precept the rest of his life.

It shaped his counsel to others, even years later with one added insight.

"Step out in faith! What God calls for, He will underwrite. Even if you make a mistake, if your intent was right, God will bring you back to a place of safety and blessing."

Life seemed to be coming together in a winning way, as he became increasingly aware of his God-given gifts, and thrilled to use them. Yet there was a yearning in his heart and unsettledness in his spirit, as he found himself beyond the giddiness of youth but short of the full independence of manhood. Like a youth who prefers the company of adults in the living room over the rowdy revelry of children on the porch, Dick wanted to hasten his steps and quickly move his life forward.

By the end of his college sophomore year, life took an unexpected curve. Happily, Peggy accepted Dick's marriage proposal, but their blissful plans to be married that summer were stymied when their parents withheld their blessing. Each set of parents delight-ed in their child's choice of a life partner, but all four parents felt it was too soon.

Though disappointed, Dick and Peggy respected their parents' counsel and purposed to wait, delaying the wedding date for one more year, in accord with their folks' wishes. Peggy left the University and then returned to Birming-ham and went to work to save money and make plans for an August 1952 wedding.

Dick applied himself to school and work. His junior year in college proved to be his busiest and most reward-ing. He missed Peggy terribly and wrote

Dick voted "Mr. Versatility" by his Junior class at Bob Jones University - 1952

31

a letter to her every day, but campus responsibilities kept his calendar full and the hours fleeting. He was president of his class and active in sports. All single students were members of a literary society which met regularly for entertainment and fellowship as well as prayer meetings. Dick was a leader in Nekonium, his literary society. By the time he graduated, his BJU classmates would vote him the yearbook superlative "Mr. Versatility."

In the spring, he made a quick trip to Birmingham to visit Peggy. The Dean refused his initial requests, but Dick's persistence prevailed, and he was finally given permission to accompany a married couple from BJU who was traveling home to Birmingham. They were old friends of the Haley family and glad to take him along. His arrival was unannounced and unexpected. The couple went up to the Haley home and greeted the family, and then as a ruse insisted that Peggy come out to their car to see the new big dog they had just purchased. There was no dog in the car, but there was one excited fiancé.

Dick won Peggy's family on earlier visits, especially capturing Mrs. Haley's admiration when he sat at the family piano and began playing hymns. The reunion was a happy one all the way around. That evening, after finishing the supper dishes, Peggy and Dick sat alone in the kitchen. As he held her hand, he kept twisting and fidgeting with the senior class ring she wore on her left hand. Almost without notice, he slipped it off and replaced it with a diamond engagement ring.

With the end of his junior year, Dick spent the summer as he had every one since he was ten years old—working! Jobs were few and underpaid in his hometown, Wilmington, and so each summer after his freshman, sophomore, and junior years, Dick found employment elsewhere. His BJU classmate Milton Enbean invited him to go home with him to Detroit, Michigan to find work after their freshman year.

Both young men were hired by the Standard Tube Company. The work was hard but paid well. They loaded boxcar after boxcar with company shipments. Dick earned enough to pay room and board to Milton's parents, and there were other Bob Jones University students in his pal's home church to fellowship with. By summer's end he had saved enough money to pay for his entire sophomore year's tuition expense. Harold Vigneulle delighted to receive the news when his son wrote home, not just because a financial burden was eased but also because it proved Dick was frugal and hardworking.

The summer following his sophomore year, he again took an out-of-state job. This time he accompanied classmate and prayer buddy George Clark to his home in Tallahassee, Florida. But the job market in the Southeast did not compete with an industrial center like Detroit. Both young men found jobs with a sheet metal company. The work was hard and gritty, often requiring them to belly along crawl spaces to install metal ducts in houses, a finger-slicing chore as they snipped and slid metal pieces into place.

The summer temperatures in the Panhandle soared to unbearable degrees, but worse than the hot weather was the pay scale. The rate was $1 an hour, but after three weeks, noticing that they were the top two performers in the whole crew, Dick and George insisted on a raise. The supervisor listened quietly and then rewarded them with a pay increase—now they would be making $1.05 an hour. Hard work and persuasive speech earned only a nickel raise and no more.

By summer's end, Dick barely broke even after paying boarding expenses to George's parents. The previous summer taught him the financial rewards of hard work and good financial planning, but this summer's benefits, though not monetary, would prove to have far-reaching value. Beyond learning technical skills, he now could give authoritative direction to workers following his command.

The next summer, following his junior year, Dick secured a job with the Atomic Energy Commission's Savannah River Project. Because he could type, Dick was assigned to be the personal assistant to the project manager who oversaw six thousand workers. This Georgia assignment was a long way from the noisy Detroit boxcars or the sweaty crawl spaces in Tallahassee. Here was a job that taxed his brain not his back, and it afforded practical insight to management styles and corporate operations. The job ended just days before Dick's wedding day and only weeks before he began his senior year at BJU.

August 21, 1952 was the hottest day of the summer, or so it seemed to the bride and groom. Dick and Peggy's big day finally arrived, and the happy couple would walk down the aisle of The Birmingham Gospel Tabernacle to the beaming smiles of approving parents on both sides of the aisle. Dr. Tingley, the Haley family's beloved pastor, officiated, and the reception followed immediately at the bride's home. Peggy looked beautiful in the wedding gown she worked many hours to pay for. She found the perfect dress at The New Ideal, a shop that was the dream destination for generations of Birmingham brides. The princess-style dress, with a peter pan collar, was made of an expensive

Dick Vigneulle and Peggy Haley's wedding day, The Birmingham Gospel Tabernacle, Birmingham, Alabama - August 21, 1952.

satin adorned with lace, and featured a long train. Years later, Dick would tell every bride who stood before him that she was about to become the queen of a home, and on that day Peggy Haley Vigneulle certainly looked like royalty.

Back in Greenville after a short honeymoon, the newlyweds settled into their new home, a mobile home located in a park near the campus. Dick would have a short walk for his senior year.

Dick saved enough from his summer job in Georgia to pay for his entire school year. With great pride, the recently pronounced "Mr. and Mrs. Vigneulle" walked into the bursar's office and wrote the biggest check of their young married life. Harold informed Dick earlier that since he had taken a wife, he must also assume full financial responsibilities for himself. There would be no more monetary aid for schooling.

Dick joyfully accepted financial responsibility for himself. Paying the whole year's bill in one swoop was an act of independence and commitment. He called his father.

"I've got good news! I paid off all my tuition!"

Dick would never again ask his father for any financial assistance, and he and Peggy committed themselves to his graduation from college by year's end.

With a full course load, Dick also worked full time. He found a job selling carpet in a department store. His co-workers, coarse in their speech and off-color in their jokes, mocked the Christian college salesman in their midst. After weeks of enduring their profane bullying, Dick confronted the men.

"You may cheat on your wives and make fun of sin, but I am going to be true to my wife and live for God. From now on, stop hassling me! I am trying to do right and you should too!"

Here was a holy assault that even Monk Parker would approve. From that day on, the co-workers respected Dick's testimony, and later several of these men came to him privately with spiritual questions.

Several months later the Lord opened the door for a new job selling "Memory-O-Matic." In that pre-computer era, this innovative filing and organizational system revolutionized the office and research habits of students, teachers, and preachers. Dick worked out of his home primarily, inviting students for a home-cooked meal and a presentation. As his sales record soared, Dick became the sole breadwinner, enabling Peggy to quit her secretarial job.

In just a few years, the feisty teen from Delaware had grown into a spirit-filled husband, worker, and student leader. The transformation was awesome. Praying parents and a devoted wife were God's blessing and heaven's instruments to mold a man of God, but an equally influential force in Dick's life was his school's president.

Dr. Bob Jones Sr. singularly shaped Dick's values and nurtured his faith. Especially through his frequent chapel messages, seasoned with his famed "sentence sermons," Dr. Bob preached the Word with a fiery conviction that insisted on results.

"Do right if the stars fall!"

"Duties never conflict!"

"The greatest ability is dependability."

"It is never right to do wrong in order to get a chance to do right."

The result was sound doctrine, moral character, and a vision to change the world. From its founding, BJU aimed to translate a student's love of God into a mission to serve others, whether working in secular or ministry vocations. What a Christian believes should shape his life, and his life should shape his generation.

As a result of his Christian education, there were three primary results for Dick. First, he grew in assurance of his salvation. A lingering spiritual struggle for assurance left him unsettled for a long time. Doubts persisted, perhaps because of his sloppy introduction to faith matters at the camp in the Poconos. Most soul-stirring that night long ago at camp was the warning that God has no grandchildren. Dick's standing before God was not based on his parents' Christian commitment. He recognized his own need for God's forgiveness and his personal acceptance of Christ and His death on the cross as his substitute.

A claim to heaven was not based on family connections, denominational attachments, or even good works—not even the religious kind such as going to church or getting baptized or confirmed. The Apostle Paul likened salvation to a gift paid for by God and offered because He loves all sinners (Romans 6:23). All that remains is to recognize one's need and to turn from sin and accept God's free gift.

Dick's confidence built slowly, but Bible teaching led to a clear understanding of what actually happened that night at Pinebrook Camp when, in his heart, he had called out to the Lord. After hearing the Word of God preached semester after semester and seeking the counsel of trusted fellow students, Dick grew more and more confident in his faith and the desire to share it.

As a second outcome from his Christian education and Dr. Bob's preaching, Dick became an ardent soul-winner, delighting to share his faith with others. Dr. Bob in his heyday on the road as an evangelist preached to huge crowds, even numbering up to ten thousand. Now when he preached to his student body, also numbering in the thousands, he still spoke with a down-home humor and the speaking skills of a Southern orator that captivated the audience.

The strength of the founder's Christian convictions gave authority to his voice and message. Just as he called sinners to repentance on the revival trails, now Dr. Bob called his Christian university students to evangelize. Go out and tell others—fulfill the Great Commission! Winning the lost to Christ was every believer's duty now. There was no reason to delay until graduation or on the field of service. Soul-winners today will be soul-winners tomorrow.

Neither calendar nor distance gives an excuse for delay. Dick heard the call.

As a single student and then as a married one, there was always time for soul-winning and preaching missions. Brom Cowser was an upperclassman who knew Peggy from high school in Birmingham and became Dick's friend at BJU. One summer, Brom accepted the invitation to preach a revival at a Methodist church in Berry, Alabama, and he invited Dick to partner with him. Brom would preach and Dick would sing and lead the congregation in hymns. It meant a delay in Dick's summer employment before college resumed in the fall, but Harold Vigneulle delighted to see his son following his steps in music and evangelism.

Years later both Dick and Brom would recall that week of meetings as a spiritual highpoint in their lives, a time when they witnessed "revival" as a spiritual reality and not just a calendar event. The pastor, perhaps weary in his field, seemed indifferent and slow paced, but the young revival team charged into town, excited by their mission. Dick and Brom would pray for hours each morning in the sanctuary. In the afternoons they would visit the homes of church members, urging the pastor to accompany them.

One family opened the front door, delighted to see the visiting young preachers and their own pastor, exclaiming, "Why, Pastor, this is the first time you have ever visited our home!"

News spread of the team's door-to-door canvassing. One family gathered with Brom and Dick in their living room. Before the young men could speak, the husband spoke up.

"We hoped you would come!"

God's Spirit poured out on the tiny congregation. A deep feeling of conviction swept over the people, and when the invitation was given each night folks came forward by the dozens, weeping and calling on Christ for forgiveness.

The third influence and end result from Dick's Bible college training was a proactive Christian worldview. The heartbeat of Christian educators is to teach students not just how to make a living but how to live. Although strengthened by the faculty's instruction and his classmates' fellowship, Dick learned "how to live" from Dr. Bob's chapel messages. His mentor imparted a value system that secured his character and instilled a life strategy that would guide Dick whether building a bank or a church.

His Christian worldview recognized God as the center of his life and the Bible as his guidebook for life. Even as he anticipated a career in business, Dick wanted to live by the same standards directing his buddies entering ministry as pastors and missionaries. God's Word and God's people refined Dick's character. The moral strength his father modeled and Dr. Bob preached vested in him stamina to build a life and career without compromising morals or goals. Wherever life took him, Dick purposed to be God's man, and no matter the obstacles or temptations, by God's grace, he would indeed "do right even if the stars fell!"

CHAPTER FOUR

Pathways

*L*ife can be like a drive to the airport. The driver en route may follow twisting interstate highways and dodge intersecting access roads that make the way seem convoluted, even confusing. But once the traveler is in the air, the view from the airplane looks down on the perfect order of roadways configured in purposeful patterns. As years advance, life too can gain a retrospective view of the past that now seems more orderly than when living out those days.

As Dick's senior year neared its close, he had a wife and soon would hold a diploma, but this mix of responsibility and achievement left him clueless about his future.

What next?

What job would open?

What did he want to do?

What did God want him to do?

The young man-about-campus who assaulted life with confidence now found his spirit as uncertain as his future seemed to be. Faith and desperation met when he fell to his knees and prayed.

"Lord, I do not know what You are doing. I need an answer."

God answered, not with an audible voice, but with the certainty of Scripture.

Dick opened his worn, brown leather King James Bible. Its dog-eared corners bore the wear of countless classroom and homework sessions, street preaching and mission assignments. His finger traced the lines to a verse from the Psalms. The passage voiced his prayer to God and spoke God's assurance in response to him.

Thou wilt show me the path of life: in thy presence is fullness of joy; at thy right hand there are pleasures for evermore.

(Psalm 16:11/KJV)

Like a map charted in heaven, God already had a plan for Dick's life, and He would reveal it. Time and time again this Bible promise would be God's formula for unfolding a business career and later a pastoral ministry— all part of the Master's plan.

Dick kept repeating the promise to himself, sometimes in words spoken out loud and other times in unspoken prayers from his heart: "Thou wilt show me the path of life."

God's promise gave Dick confidence even though circumstances had not changed.

When would God's open door appear?

Days later, Dick took his place on the platform in the university chapel to direct the songs for the morning service. That day a very special guest came from New York City to the Greenville, South Carolina campus to speak to the students. But he was not the only one with a divine appointment that day. The man was Dr. John Wimbish, Pastor of the famed Calvary Baptist Church in New York City. The church was one of America's most distinguished for its imprint on the great city it served. Not only was the congregation large, its approach to ministry was as dynamic as its location. Booksellers and innkeepers for the Lord, this metropolitan church sponsored a large Christian bookstore and operated a huge hotel—the Salisbury.

When Dr. Wimbish came to the Bob Jones University campus that day in 1953, he was a man with a mission for his church. BJU in the 1950's ranked among the nation's best schools for its business department, standing with prestigious Ivy League schools. Calvary Baptist Church needed a manager to lead and rescue its bookstore because continuing losses jeopardized its future. Church leaders wanted to close down the bookstore in order to stay the financial drain on Calvary's budget.

As Dr. Wimbish took his place at the podium to speak that April morning, he looked out at the student body. Before preaching, he shared the story of his church and its urgent staff need, finally issuing a challenge.

"We need one of you to come and lead Calvary Christian Book Store in New York City!"

Dick's heart started beating rapidly.

As Dick would recall, "Electricity went off in me and I thought, 'Lord, for the first time you have something You would have me do!'"

He heard nothing else the guest preacher said. God's promise once more flooded his mind, "Thou wilt show me the path of life...."

Once the chapel service ended, Dick pushed through a throng of students in a vain attempt to meet Dr. Wimbish. Once he reached the platform, to his dismay, Dick learned the speaker had already slipped out a side door and left for the airport. Fired-up with the conviction that this was the job for him, Dick borrowed a friend's car and rushed to the airport.

Once inside the terminal, he anticipated a long line of students ahead of him vying for the job, but then he spied Dr. Wimbish standing alone!

Dick hurried up to him and said, "Sir, you mentioned a need for a manager for your bookstore, and I am interested."

Before boarding his plane, the pastor handed Dick his business card and invited Dick to come to New York City for an interview. The pastor in search of an employee met the student in need of a job: each was God's gift to the other.

Soon afterward Dick and Peggy traveled up the coast to the Big Apple. He met with the church leadership, and the meeting ended with an offer—the job was his!

After the couple's move to New York City, they joined Calvary Baptist Church, intent on being a part of the ministry not just the managerial staff. Dick was baptized by immersion. The moment was more solemn than his boyhood sprinkling when he giggled through the ceremony.

For the Vigneulles, life in a mega-metropolis, fast-paced and demanding, was buffered by their benevolent apartment building manager and his wife, affectionately known as Mom and

Outside of Calvary Bookstore in New York where Dick and Peggy worked for over 2 years.

Inside view of Calvary Bookstore in New York.
Dick and his dad Harold

Pop Caminiti. Living quarters were modest, a basement apartment in a neighborhood near the Triborough Bridge.

Dick and Peg both held jobs. She made $25 a week and Dick's position as bookstore manager earned $50 a week. Far from family, the Vigneulles enjoyed their friendship with the Caminitis, who loved and cared for the young couple as if they were kin. True to her heritage, Mom Caminiti excelled at Italian cooking. The pungent smell of spicy tomato sauce and the sweet aroma of home-baked bread often filled the apartment building hallways. Often Mom and Pop invited the Vigneulles to share home-cooked meals.

By the end of his first year as manager, Dick led the bookstore to financial freedom and so insured the ministry's future. All outstanding debts were paid, and the store continued to operate in the black.

Not only did the store prosper that year, so too did the Vigneulle

Dick and Peggy's first wedding anniversary – taken at Calvary Baptist Church to announce that Dick & Peggy were new bookstore managers! – August 21, 1953

family—Peggy was pregnant! In the ninth month of his wife's pregnancy, Dick's delight doubled when they learned Peggy was expecting twins! The news was an answer to maternal prayers because Peggy had asked the Lord for twins.

Imminent parenthood brought Dick a whole new understanding of "the path of life" and God's provision. Mom Caminiti, proud as a grandmother, gave the Vigneulles a baby shower. When news reached Calvary Baptist that twins were on the way, church ladies duplicated all the baby gifts. In recognition of Dick's financial turnaround of the bookstore, church leaders awarded him a bonus, which paid medical expenses for the twins' delivery. With no medical insurance, Dick knew God's provision was one more blessing for following the Lord's path.

The day the twins were born played out like a television episode from *I Love Lucy*. When Peg gave the word—"The time has come!"—Dick hurried out to the street to hail a cab. But the 8:00 a.m. rush hour blinded the NYC cabbies to the frantic father-to-be's waving hand. Mrs. Caminiti took charge and telephoned a cab order. But once the cab arrived, the unintended comedy routine only continued.

Swelled by her pregnancy, Peggy could not climb the steps from the basement apartment up to the street level and the waiting cab. Dick hopped behind her and began a gentle, steady push till husband and wife reached the cab door. Act 2 of the comic sketch began. Peggy was too big to fit into the cab. Quicker than Prince Charming reaching Cinderella's coach, Dick ran to the opposite side of the cab, climbed in and crawled across the back seat. Then he reached up and began pulling on Peg until she was inside the cab. The cabbie reached the hospital in time, and within a few hours, Richard Harold and Michael James Vigneulle arrived. On May 26, 1954, the "Rick and Mick Show" began!

Home life changed drastically overnight, as the Vigneulles went from a couple with two jobs and no children to a family now with one job and two kids. Motherhood meant Peg would now be a stay-at-home mother. The church raised Dick's salary to $75 a week to compensate for the loss of Peggy's income. Dick kept long hours at work, and Peggy did the same in the nursery caring for her two babies. New York City's nickname as "the city that never sleeps" took on a whole new meaning.

As much as the Vigneulles appreciated their friends and his job in

NYC, it was an expensive city. Their dollars and energies draining, Peggy began to yearn for home in the Southland, a longing that was practical, not merely nostalgic. Her extended family could provide hands-on help with the twins.

Dick knew he needed to increase his income. The Apostle Paul's admonition applied here: "But if anyone does not provide for his own, and especially for those of his household, he has denied the faith and is worse than an unbeliever" (I Timothy 5:8). After much prayer and husband/wife pillow talk, despite his success and opening doors at Calvary, Dick decided to begin a job search. Sometimes God uses need to stir hearts and direct paths. Once more this young husband and father would test the promise "Thou wilt show me the path of life." Dick claimed the verse in prayer over and over.

God brought an old friend from college days in South Carolina into Dick's life in New York City. Dr. Kells, an executive with the Mt. Vernon Foundation, had hired Dick as a college senior to promote his Memory-O-Matic system with pastors and teachers. Earlier efforts to lure Dick back to his company failed, but when Dr. Kells returned to NYC with a job offer, Dick was now ready and accepted.

News of Dick's resignation disappointed leaders at Calvary Baptist because they planned to make him manager of their eighteen floor hotel. But Dick and Peggy experienced God's peace and recognized the Lord's provision. Besides they did not want to raise their sons in a big city. As further proof of God's hand at work, charting their path, Dr. Kells transferred his Southeast Regional Manager to the Northeast in order to create a position and location that appealed to both Vigneulles. Headquarters for Dick's new job was in Birmingham, Alabama—Peggy's hometown.

Dick purchased plane tickets for Peg and the twins to make the journey quicker and easier for his wife and babies. While still in New York, Dick bought his first family car. For the move, he attached a small trailer and packed it with their few possessions. With his family as well as a new job waiting, the long drive began. Dick was Bama bound.

CHAPTER FIVE

Coming Home

𝒫eggy's hometown now was Dick's home, one where he would come to make such an impact that he could easily be mistaken for a native son. Once settled in Birmingham, life for the Vigneulles, now back in the genteel South, still moved at the rapid pace of New York City traffic. Their first home, an apartment in Central Park, was only two blocks from Peggy's mother's home. Proximity to family aided Peg with the hands-on care of twins and provided ample companionship to fill many lonely hours as Dick traveled for business. Dick excelled at the Mt. Vernon Foundation, and his diligence on the job won even more responsibility. The company now led the nation in sales, and he managed forty men in a territory spread over nine states.

Advancement enabled Dick and Peg to buy their own home. They chose a house in Belview Heights, one with a vacant lot beside it where the twins could roam and play football. The Vigneulle home became a neighborhood gathering place, and Rick and Mick were spirited players in neighborhood antics.

One afternoon, as Dick arrived home, the boys suddenly appeared

Dick and Peggy's first purchased home in Birmingham, Alabama
Terrace M (Belview Heights), circa 1955

as he climbed out of the car. Without even a greeting, the twins announced to their father that there was a contest with their buddies to find out whose father was the strongest. Dick rallied to the challenge with a smile and mock heroics. He dropped his briefcase on the driveway, lifted his arms in the air, and flexed his biceps.

"Why boys," he declared, "your daddy is so strong he could lift two elephants!"

Rick and Mick's eyes grew large, and without uttering a word the boys disappeared to spread the news. Dick laughed and dismissed the whole episode as he went into the house for dinner. The next evening, as he returned home and pulled his car into the driveway, a mass of children crowded around him as he emerged from his car. Taken back by the large but silent crowd, Dick went on inside.

Looking out the window to the gawking little eyes still standing in their yard, Dick asked his wife, "Peg, what's that all about?"

"Oh," she said, "they've come to see the man who can lift two elephants!"

Dick's work for the Mt. Vernon Foundation required more and more travel as he spread the wonders of the Memory-O-Matic system. His territory expanded, meaning business trips became more frequent and required longer and longer stays away from home. His twin boys grew and changed so quickly that Daddy missed out on too many of the wonders of his children's growing years.

In 1955, the Lord had blessed Dick and Peg with a daughter, Diane. Family joys and pressures intensified. Now with three young children at home, road trips became a greater struggle. Dick grew more unsettled with his position. He began to pray and once more claimed the promise, "Thou wilt show me the path of life."

God soon opened a door, and Dick accepted a position with the Remington Rand Systems Division. With an office in Birmingham and a more localized territory, this job suited him personally and professionally. Now he could get off the road and eliminate extended absences from home. Family life was happier. On the professional front, the Remington Rand position introduced Dick to financial institutions and the banking world, a part of the business world that fascinated him. As a Rand sales representative, Dick helped monetary institutions set up financial systems. He worked with the city's leading banks, such as Birmingham Trust Bank, Exchange Security Bank, and First Alabama Bank.

The Lord's hand still moved. The Remington Rand Corporation would prove to be a bridge, transporting Dick from a life in corporate sales to a prominent position in banking and real estate. As his interest with the banking world grew, Dick determined to follow his heart. Again he sought the Lord's help, and God affirmed Dick's pursuits by bringing into his life a "patron saint," that is, a fellow believer who could intercede by opening a door of opportunity with banking bigwigs.

Frank Hembry was a godsend. One of a succession of patron saints God would bring Dick's way, he was a family friend from their church, The Birmingham Gospel Tabernacle, and he worked in the accounting department of the Bank for Savings. Dick confided in him his heart's desire and asked for his prayerful counsel. Mr. Hembry directed Dick to meet with Mr. Mark Hodo, the Chairman of the Board and President of City Federal Bank. He was one of the city's prime movers and shakers in the business community, and Mr. Hodo had recently been saved. Going the extra mile to help his young friend, Mr. Hembry himself called Mr. Hodo and arranged an appointment for Dick.

Mark Hodo – President of City Federal Savings and Loan Association in Birmingham, Alabama 1941 – 1966, Chairman of Board 1966 – 1974

The meeting with Mr. Hodo would prove to be a golden hour in Dick's burgeoning business career. In time, Mark Hodo would become a father-like figure in Dick's personal and professional life, as well as his mentor and boss. But this first meeting met a disappointing end. There was no opening for Dick in his bank. The bank President must have seen promise in the eager young man sitting across from him. While he could not offer a job at the present time, Mr. Hodo would provide Dick with an introduction to another bank executive who was in search of a person with his skills and interest.

The Exchange Bank in Birmingham had recently merged with Security

47

Commercial to form The Exchange Security Bank. The new bank's President was Mr. Bob Russell, and his son-in-law, Norman Pless, was the Executive Vice President. With Mr. Hodo's recommendation, Mr. Pless agreed to interview Dick. The bank needed a leader in its Business Development Department. The position required business acumen and a full measure of people skills. The job meant securing new customers among emerging businesses. Entertaining prospective customers would be a big part of the job.

The opportunity before him was a heady one. The executive suite surrounding them, the dignity of the would-be boss, the thrilling challenge of a big job with a new company—it all made Dick feel as though he was riding a wild roller coaster. When the job description hinted at social drinking, Dick balked and the roller coaster took a deep plunge. Mr. Pless did not understand Dick's concern at first. Dick's Christian convictions ever in command, he asked outright if the job would require drinking alcoholic beverages. Misunderstanding the nature of his prospect's reticence, Mr. Pless sought to sweep aside his concern by assuring him that the bank would cover all expenses.

Dick responded with a clear explanation that the issue was not money but rather personal convictions. As a Christian businessman and local church leader, he would not compromise his beliefs. The banker, trying to appeal to human reason, argued that he knew Christians who drank liquor. As much as he wanted the job, Dick stood firm. He would not take the job if the company would require him to drink or provide alcoholic beverages. The interview soon came to an awkward close.

The short drive home seemed longer than the one a few years before when he hauled a trailer from New York City to Birmingham. If his convictions were so strong, why did he now feel so weak? When he arrived home, he confided to Peg that he had just walked out on the greatest job opportunity he could ever have. A restless and sleepless night followed, but not just for Dick. Early the next morning the phone rang. When he answered, Dick was surprised to hear the voice of Mr. Pless's secretary.

Her greeting was followed by a simple question, "Mr. Pless would like to meet with you again this morning at 10:00. Are you available?"

God can instruct and direct His children using humble instruments: tablets of stone, a shepherd's staff, a little boy's lunch of loaves and fish. In Dick's life that day, the Lord used a telephone call to change his life. When he reached Mr. Pless's office for the unexpected follow-up interview, Dick looked in the face of a man with a changed countenance and a changed opinion.

"Dick, I could not sleep at all last night because I kept thinking about our exchange of opinions. The more I thought about your words, the more convinced I became that you are just the kind of leader our bank wants. We need employees who are completely honest, people of integrity who will stand up for their convictions—even if their job is on the line. We have a spot for you!"

A firm handshake sealed the deal, and Birmingham now had a new banker in town. Dick began his new job at The Exchange Security Bank on August 1, 1961. He readily remembers the date because his son, Tom, was born a week later.

CHAPTER SIX

City Federal

*A*fter Mark Hodo commended Dick Vigneulle to his new employer, The Exchange Security Bank, Hodo's position as a member of the bank's Board enabled him to keep Dick on his radar. He tracked the young banker's steady advance, often asking Mr. Pless, the Vice President who hired Dick, for updates on his performance. For two years Mr. Hodo kept watch, and then one day invited Dick to his office for lunch, a rare opportunity gladly accepted. Dick assumed all his peers from Exchange Security had been invited, so it came as a surprise when he walked into Hodo's office and saw a table set for only two. The office was plush and the host kind, though formal, as he pointed his young guest to the table where uniformed waitresses hovered over fine china and silver.

Dick's appreciation for Mr. Hodo, an almost reverential awe, was larger than his gratitude for the door opened at The Exchange Security Bank. The city itself held Hodo in high esteem. He was one of Birmingham's established business leaders, a financial veteran with old-world values but the heart of a new-world pioneer. His business interests were almost as diverse as his community service projects. Though a churchman all his adult life, Hodo had become a born-again Christian only a few years before, largely through the ministry of evangelist Billy Graham. He found in Dick Vigneulle a protégé who shared his two loves—banking and an evangelical faith. The lunch time exchange continued long after the meal was finished, as Hodo shared a personal dream. His savings and loan business was poised for growth, and so he was constantly on the lookout for young men to join his executive team. Dick's proven leadership ability was only one criterion.

The other was his unswerving Christian faith, as well as his gift for sharing the Good News naturally and without offense. Hodo confided his goal to build a "Christian bank," so to speak. He envisioned not just a bank guided by biblical principles, but one where Christian employees could freely live and share their faith in the workplace. Motivated to do something for his Lord, Mr. Hodo knew banking, and so the business arena would be his platform for spreading the Gospel. Dick could bring to his staff banking abilities and spiritual authority.

"Dick, how about coming to City Federal to work for me?"

At first Dick was complimented when the older man praised his performance, and even more so when he heard Hodo's vision for a faith-oriented organization. But when the conversation evolved into a job offer, Dick was dismayed. He stood before a general in the banking industry, feeling no more than a raw recruit himself. Usually a man ever ready with a quick response in any conversation—business or social—Dick now found himself speechless. The promising young executive could only answer with one word: "WOW!"

True to his keen ethical practices, Mr. Hodo would not pursue hiring young Vigneulle without informing Dick's present employer of his intention. Likewise, Dick requested time to pray over the offer with his wife.

The Exchange Security Bank's upper level rocked at the news that one of their up and coming managers might be lured away. Dick's positive performance was only exceeded by the bank's. Its future was bright too, and covert expansion plans included Dick as a key player.

Harry Brock, a top executive who rarely made even casual exchanges with trainees, unexpectedly dropped into his office one morning.

"Dick, let's go get a cup of coffee."

Down the block in a coffee shop, and beyond the ears of other employees, Mr. Brock made a counteroffer to Mr. Hodo's, only then divulging The Exchange Security Bank's promotion plans for Dick.

"What would it take for you to stay at this bank, Dick? Tell us what you want!"

Blindsided by the whole event, Dick was not prepared for this exchange.

Speaking more from exasperation than aspiration, Dick said, "I want a raise."

It took a while to get the request out, but the response was rapid, "You have it. What else?"

Shared, cramped quarters made the next reply easier to say, "My own office."

With a nod, it was his.

"Anything else?" his interrogator continued.

"My own secretary."

Another nod in agreement.

The offer was still open, "Anything else?"

Already on a roll, Dick reached higher and said, "I would like to become an officer in the bank."

That was a promotion only the Board could approve, but certainly Dick would be recommended for the title, the executive assured him.

Having faithfully discharged his assignment, Mr. Brock then shocked Dick with a personal disclosure. In the near future, Mr. Brock would be leaving the bank to start his own. Papers were being drawn up, even as they sipped coffee.

"Dick, how about coming with me, and I will make you an executive in my bank. I have a place for you."

Dick had not been reaching for the moon, and suddenly the stars were being offered to him. Now, after a four-hour coffee break with Harry Brock, three job opportunities beckoned him. The choices before him, staggering in their prospects, left him confused. Mark Hodo was one of Birmingham's leading businessmen and a sincere Christian. His present employer was one of the city's leading banks and faced an auspicious future. And now Mr. Brock offered a ground floor opportunity.

As a wise Bible teacher once cautioned, "God guides but Satan drives." Dick would not be driven by haste or even material perks. He needed time to make a decision, time to talk with Peg and to pray together with his wife. Every career change in Dick's life was launched by a test of his Christian faith. Before his hiring by The Exchange Security Bank, the Lord allowed a test of his convictions. Now it seemed like a test of his values. What would be the motive energizing his final choice?

Once more Dick hit his knees, as the familiar Psalm again became his prayer: "Lord, Thou wilt show me the path of life" (Psalms 16:11/KJV).

Church continued to be a vital part of Dick and Peg's life. They were faithful members and workers in The Birmingham Gospel Tabernacle. Dick enjoyed a warm, personal relationship with his pastor, Ronald Johnson, so it was natural for him to seek Rev. Johnson's advice regarding the career choices looming before him. After a careful review of his job offers, Dick waited anxiously for his pastor's reply. It came without hesitation. The opportunity to work for a banker who wanted to bring Christ to the workplace sounded like heaven's call to Dick's pastor. With the young executive's Christian college training, his love for the Lord and evangelism, as well as his career goals and accomplishments, the choice seemed obvious to his preacher. The answer now seemed clear to Dick too. He called Mr. Hodo to say "yes" to the City Federal offer.

The Bible promises that trials and tests position the submissive child of God to receive grace: "God resists the proud but gives grace to the humble" (I Peter 5:5b).

Dick certainly qualified for a heaping measure of grace because at the new bank, he would in many ways be starting over, leaving behind friends and sure opportunities. His new employer affirmed his potential, but as a wise old man said, "*Potential* just means you haven't done it yet!" Dick would have to prove himself anew. Just how far would God take Dick Vigneulle at City Federal?

Mr. Hodo believed in giving an employee the job first, and the title would follow if the work was well done. His new boss shared a vision for both the bank and the young banker just hired. Both knew Dick was destined to be an officer in the company: Dick had the desire and Hodo recognized his ability as well as his ambition.

City Federal's new executive-in-training began with a promise to fulfill to the Lord first and foremost but also to Mr. Hodo, his mentor. He worked hard and with the zeal of an evangelist. Dick was poised for great opportunities, but his eventual rise to the top did not begin in the bank's basement or its vaults, so to speak, but rather at City Federal's front door.

"Put him where the people are" seemed to be his overseer's aim. The world of finance engaged him on every level. As he pursued his career, Dick never lost sight of the "Great Commission" at the heart of Mr. Hodo's initial challenge when offering him a City Federal position. The goal was not just to build a bank but to build a "Christian" bank. The Christian faith served as more than the ethical standard of the institution, it defined the character of the leadership and directed the strategy of both bank and bankers.

Prayer had brought Dick to this lofty position, and staying on his knees not only gave him empowerment and direction to succeed, but also the humility to remain on an even keel before the Lord and his co-workers. City Federal's mission from the start included serving more than just the financial needs of people, and that commitment served employees as well as customers.

For employees who were born-again believers, the bank could be a house of prayer as well as a house of commerce. Every Monday morning staff could voluntarily gather in the lobby for Bible reading and prayer. These devotional meetings met with wide acceptance and participation, creating common ground as executives, managers, tellers, and janitors joined in one accord as a new workweek began. Likewise, prayer opened all committee and Board meetings, as well as any social gathering the bank sponsored. It was not unusual for Dick to pray with an employee or customer, readily affording spiritual counsel not just financial planning.

Indeed City Federal's mission to be a "Christian bank" was more than lip service.

Among fellow employees and customers alike, folks found Dick to be a caring person and a confident banker, making his company sought after and his advice trusted. His people skills, neither artificial nor learned in a seminar, seemed genetic—a natural trait he was born with like his eye and hair color.

One co-worker described him respectfully, "He was a warm, outgoing personality. Even though he held a high position at the bank, he made everyone feel welcomed no matter their position or temperament."

People took notice of his work ethic and his standard for excellence. When job demands multiplied so too did Dick's energy. He never seemed to tire, in physical stamina or emotional toughness. However long Dick's workday, his mind always remained engaged. His performance motivated others. Dick knew how to delegate and to inspire.

A former bank employee remembers a boss who led by example. There were rules, sometimes chafing a less inspired employee, but the staff's respect for Mr. Vigneulle made them want to please him. Those working directly under him appreciated a boss who gave the assignment and then trusted them to carry it out, without nagging or constantly looking over their shoulders. The result was high performance from a loyal staff with a huge sense of job satisfaction.

Dick and the bank's leadership purposed to enrich not just enlist employees. Creative and "extra mile" measures secured workers' personal welfare as well as their career paths. Employees received personal and practical demonstrations of encouragement and appreciation, carried out as part of the bank's distinctively Christian witness. For example, the bank gave a $20 a month bonus to any employee who would refrain from smoking cigarettes. A private employee dining room was installed with a staff of cooks who prepared Southern fare at its best. City Federal workers could eat lunch daily for free.

Also, Dick realized that a worker's appearance was important for self-confidence as well as projecting a professional look when serving customers. Under Mr. Hodo's direction, he instituted a policy at City Federal that for many years afterward won the favor of their bank tellers and other employees—the bank bought their clothes. Each year an allotment provided matching, stylish outfits for the workplace, purchased from one of Birmingham's elegant department stores.

The most important part of the bank's unspoken spiritual mission was sharing the Gospel of Jesus Christ. Dick's desk became a prayer altar for many. Employees and clients alike heard the Good News. His skill as an evangelist exceeded all his many gifts. Dick could present the plan of salvation with clarity. His good nature and winsome conversation style put folks at ease. He spoke with an authority born of heaven, not a bank board. He believed the message—anyone who turns from sin and in faith calls on Jesus Christ to be his or her personal Savior will be forgiven.

Years later, he recalled a couple who came to his office to apply for a loan. Sensing their spiritual need, Dick shared the Gospel with them. Sitting across his desk, they bowed their heads and prayed to receive Christ. The man and woman were jubilant. They thanked Dick profusely and then promptly left the office. Only after their departure did he realize the bank loan papers had been forgotten.

Dick's secretary, Sandy, was a recent convert who found her boss to be a spiritual mentor as well as an astute banker. She confirms Dick's enthusiasm as a ready evangelist even in his office.

"Although wise in the banking business, he never missed a chance to lead someone to Christ. Witnessing on the job received Mr. Hodo's blessing. Many men came to talk to Dick in his office. It was not unusual for him to call me in and say, 'San, I want you to meet your new *brother* in the faith—he just received Christ as his Savior.'"

Coming from Delaware for a visit, Harold Vigneulle, Dick's father, once accompanied his son to City Federal and watched Dick's workday unfold. At the end of the day, he said with approval, "Son, I don't know if you're operating a business or a soul-winning station here."

Loyalty to Christ never meant Dick lost sight of his professional duties as a banker. For himself and the rest of the staff, witnessing was not a substitute for doing one's job. Freedom to share one's faith was not to be abused by neglecting banking duties. One did not have to cost the other.

One early-on achievement particularly defined his success and secured his upward course to top management. City Federal purchased the historic, twenty-seven story Comer Building, then Birmingham's tallest skyscraper. The building suffered from neglect, and Mr. Hodo endured a great deal of ribbing for buying a "white elephant," a mocking nickname playing on the building's white-tiled façade. Newer sleek buildings vied for tenants with the staid old tower in the heart of the financial district.

Mr. Hodo gave Dick the assignment of finding tenants with a simple command, one he still remembers: "Fill it up!"

He eagerly accepted the challenge and began by renovating and remodeling the second floor, site of his personal office space. Dick's suite served as a model to "show off" to prospective tenants. The first con-

The City Federal Building, 27 stories, located in downtown Birmingham as it looked in the 1970's when Dick "filled it up"

57

struction phase included four floors. As new tenants moved in, painters and decorators moved up. Floor by floor, Mr. Hodo's "white elephant" became a showplace until all twenty-seven floors were transformed.

The skyscraper truly was a jewel that just needed polishing. Dick countered stark new construction with the restored elegance of the old Comer Building's exquisite craftsmanship and decoration: rich wood paneling, marble floors and columns, solid brass fixtures and hardware, and lush velvet draperies. The restored old-world workmanship gave the space unrivaled luxury. In this setting even new firms and young entrepreneurs took on the grand building's aura of "old money" prestige and security.

Dick enticed prospects with affordable rent, and new tenants appreciated added perks, such as built-in bookcases, lowered ceilings with recessed lighting, drapes, and carpeting. The vacant, box-like new spaces could not. City Federal's amenities combined functionality and aesthetics that so many prospective tenants found irresistible. With unexpected speed, the Comer Building—now re-christened the City Federal Building—was filled to capacity. New tenants moved in as Dick moved up!

When considering a commercial loan request, Dick often visited the applicant's business site to inspect not only the building's value but also its maintenance. The care of a building, he felt, divulges a lot about its owners and the future of the business that occupies it. Good leaders take care of their property. Commercial success depends on more than lucrative profits and accurate bookkeeping. Neglected or run-down structures tattletale on the management's shortcomings and the business's unsteady prospects. Dick practiced what he preached too. He was committed to the City Federal Building's preservation and continued development.

Much to the annoyance of some of the bank's maintenance crew, Mr. Vigneulle always carried a yellow legal pad whenever he walked through the building, jotting down notes as he walked. Memos would soon follow: a storage room needed cleaning, a stairwell light bulb needed replacing, a hallway had not been swept. Some of the men did not know how to pronounce his last name, and so Mr. Vigneulle became known as "the man with the yellow pad."

No space was too small or too grand for his inspection. He arranged the installation of the huge red neon letters, adorned with spotlights, on the bank's roof that spelled "CITY FEDERAL." Later, on the same rooftop, at Dick's direction, workers built a lookout point with a twenty-seven story view that awed those bank guests privileged enough to visit it.

When Dick one day urged Peggy to come to the bank to see his most recent project, she was excited as her imagination raced with possibilities. Expecting an elevator ride to the rooftop, she found herself following her husband down the lobby steps to the bank's basement.

"Here it is, Peg! Isn't this a beautiful piece of work?"

He was serious, as he opened the door to the basement elevator room and pointed to newly whitewashed walls and a concrete floor freshly scrubbed and painted. The "man with the yellow pad" wanted every inch of the City Federal Building to shine, top to bottom.

Mr. Hodo took notice. The executive trainee fulfilled the promise his mentor knew was there all along. Hodo also wanted hands-on instruction for this up-and-coming executive. The bank created an in-house mentoring program where Dick was apprenticed to City Federal vice presidents, who groomed their young charge for emerging leadership roles.

Within a year of his hiring, Dick rose from Assistant Cashier to Assistant Vice President and then later Vice President of the Loan Department. Eventually he was promoted to the bank's upper echelon, first as First Vice President and then Senior Vice President. Only two men ranked higher at City Federal: Mr. Hodo who was President and Chairman of the Board, and his son-in-law, Jesse Miller, Executive Vice President.

Dick's enterprise expanded into real estate for the bank and later for his own personal investments. Management of the bank's own office tower remained Dick's domain. Conference room negotiations and building site inspections and appraisals honed his skills and stirred his entrepreneurial zeal. In time he took the helm of Service Corporation of Alabama, a subsidiary dealing in insurance, mortgages, and land acquisitions and developments. He headed up myriad loan areas for the bank—VA, FHA, conventional, and commercial loans.

His work as head of Service Corporation kept him in contact with leading real estate developers, overseeing major developments from subdivisions to shopping centers. Titans of commerce, "Mom and Pop" businesses, and families from the full spectrum of social and economic standing—all called City Federal "MY bank!" Under Dick's direction, the bank expanded service to more and more individual residential customers until the City Federal home loan market reached out in a hundred-mile circumference from downtown Birmingham. With the flourish of a signature on the dotted line and the grip of a firm handshake, as deals closed, friendships formed.

Among Dick's business contacts were two men who became best friends. Bill Longshore, an attorney with one of Birmingham's leading firms, and Wales Goebel, a rising home builder in the Over the Mountain area. Their shared Christian faith, not just business interests, bonded the three men. They often shared coffee breaks in a downtown shop. Their wives became close too, and the three couples often socialized after work. The friendships have lasted a lifetime, continuing even after two of them eventually left the business world for ministry. Devoted to Christ and each other, these three business musketeers formed a triad of crusaders for the cross, holding each other spiritually accountable and stoking each other's lay ministry pursuits.

Wales recalls 5:00 a.m. Friday prayer meetings with Dick, usually meeting in whatever subdivision site Wales was working on. Huddled in a car on cold mornings or sitting on a stack of lumber on warm days, they would pray—praying for each other, praying for their city, praying for God to use them to make a difference. More than holiness united these men. They enjoyed a good laugh. Jokes and pranks offered a release from business pressures, as well as a natural expression of their personalities, especially for Dick and Wales.

Peggy and Dick, Wales and Jean Goebel –
Two businessmen became full-time ministers and lifetime friends.

Years later, while in Germany on a mission trip, they were taken into a town by their chaplain host. The two visitors became frustrated by the language barrier that cut them off from anyone they met. Shopkeepers and passersby seemed to ignore them, the isolation made worse by the swirl of foreign conversations filling their ears but never including them. Not to be outdone, right then and there in the town square, Dick and Wales concocted their own mock version of German and began speaking to each other in a hilarious exchange of Teutonic gibberish. They were delighted with each other's antics, and they finally had the townspeople's attention! Now the townsfolk felt like the excluded ones! To this day, when Wales and Dick get together and reminisce, they are apt to erupt into German gibberish again.

Years of hard work brought success for Dick and for City Federal, destined to become the largest Savings and Loan institution in Alabama, not just Birmingham.

One day as Dick left work, walking across the parking lot, he looked up, surprised by the voice of his boss.

Mr. Hodo smiled and greeted Dick with an extraordinary salutation.

"Hello, Mr. Executive Vice President!"

Dick was dumbfounded.

Hodo continued, "I have just come from a meeting of the bank's Board, and the vote was unanimous, Dick, to make you City Federal's new Executive Vice President!"

The asphalt pavement made a humble platform for so exalted an announcement. Dick was now third in command. This promotion, as Hodo would later explain, anticipated an even loftier one. In time, Mr. Hodo would step aside and make his son-in-law, Jesse Miller, his successor as the Chairman of the Board. Dick would then be elevated to the office of President.

To prepare Dick for his future role as bank president, the Board funded an executive training course at the University of Washington in Seattle. For one month, every year, he would travel to the Northwest, to be confined to classrooms for ten-hour weekday sessions. The intense study load allowed scant time to be a tourist.

One year during his Seattle stay, however, Dick rented a car and drove up to Mt. Rainier, one of the volcanic peaks in the Cascade Mountains. Reaching a remote site, he parked his car and began a long walk into the woods. He stumbled onto a fallen tree and climbed on top of it. The French have little chapel chairs which sit low so a worshipper can kneel rather than sit on the upholstered seats, and the chair's back provides a little rail upon which to rest the arms and fold the hands in prayer. Such a chair is called a "Pre-Dieu" or "Before God." The log resting on the forest floor became Dick's "Pre-Dieu," only he chose to stand to pray, and there he remained for several hours. Far from a bank office or university classroom, he relished the woodland's quiet and nature's reminder of God's presence. In this new place he found himself praying an old prayer: "Thou wilt show me the path of life." This woodland prayer retreat proved to be more than a busy man's spiritual respite. God refreshed him, certainly, but there was something planted in his heart that day, never to be forgotten. A few years later, the spiritual seeds sown that afternoon would bear fruit in a most unexpected way.

Dick reluctantly returned to his car and drove back to his duties at the university. Days later he flew back to Birmingham and the bank. The views from land and sky fascinated the traveler, but the roads and highways passing his view were nothing compared to the path God had waiting for the young man from Delaware. Life had already carried him a far distance from the South Carolina town where he once sold Memory-O-Matic systems.

God in His grace allowed great promotion that brought influence and material blessings beyond anything Dick ever hoped for, even as a young father rocking twin baby boys in a New York City basement apartment. Indeed, his path in life—as the Psalmist promised—was unfolding and his joy in full measure.

As a college student, Dick often heard Dr. Bob Jones Sr., as he preached in chapel, repeat one-line sermons, his signature maxims for his students to live by. Many of Dr. Bob's proverbs still hung fresh in Dick's mind, especially the charge to "Do right till the stars fall!" Dick long ago purposed to "do right" no matter what. In retrospect, however, it seemed each new opportunity in life was preceded by a test of his heart and conscience. For example, coming to City Federal meant being willing to start over, beginning a new venture only after relinquishing the perks and promises of his former employer. Mark Hodo's offer led to a much bigger ladder to climb, but even so Dick had to start climbing from the bottom rung. He consistently based his life choices on faith values more than career or wealth strategies. What might have seemed like a step backward became, in God's time, a big leap forward. The Lord's unfolding plan for Dick already was "exceedingly abundantly above all that we ask or think" (Ephesians 3:20b).

But would his resolve to "do right" face other challenges? Advancement and gain presented privileges he must manage without ever becoming corrupted or compromised. Dick's clear understanding of Biblical stewardship kept him centered. He understood that all that anyone holds comes from God—family and friends, opportunities and advantages, advancement and profits. It all comes from God's hand, entrusted to His servant only to manage, and that but for a season. Only the spiritually misguided presume success is self-made and lasts forever. Poverty and demotion have purified multitudes, but few can handle the weight of success. Many are eventually ruined by plenty and promotion.

Stewardship proves surrender, in attitude and action, by holding with an open hand all that God entrusts. If the servant's hand is truly open, and the heart surrendered, it does not hurt if God pulls the required thing from his servant's hand. If it does hurt, it means the grasp was too tight, the surrender incomplete. The amount of anger or resistance to loss is a Richter scale measure of yieldedness. Dick purposed over and over in his heart that all God put in his and Peg's hand would be held with an open hand. The Lord gave and the Lord could take away—blessed be the name of the Lord!

Nearing mid-life, Dick now approached the very pinnacle of his profession, but little did he realize that his ultimate assignment was still before him. His admirers probably thought he had arrived, but God knew that his servant had not yet begun the role that would ultimately define his life. The years at City Federal were merely the final semester in God's training school for the job that lay ahead. God would soon point to a new and unexpected path for His servant to follow.

CHAPTER SEVEN

Sceptor Lane

*I*f home is where the heart is, Dick's heart moved over the mountain in 1961, the year he and Peg bought a home on Sceptor Lane in Hoover. His position as a banker kept him in contact with most of Birmingham's builders and developers, many of whom were personal friends. A favorite pastime was to drive Peg around the city, passing through the many beautiful neighborhoods and parks, oftentimes pointing out various projects his bank partnered with.

The Over the Mountain area, outside the Magic City's industrial center, spread out over Shades Valley to Shades Mountain and beyond. Within its boundaries were some of Birmingham's most affluent neighborhoods. One day Dick, alone in his car, drove out of the downtown area and beyond Red Mountain, up into Shades Mountain and the little community called Hoover.

The area's namesake was William H. Hoover, a local insurance company owner. The woodsy area, still in its infancy and not incorporated until 1967, would later expand into one of Jefferson County's most fashionable communities. Dick's tour of the mountain led to a new development called Regent Forest. Only a few houses had gone up. The first one he inspected did not catch his fancy, but as he drove out the semicircle driveway, the house directly across the street immediately caught his eye. Like first love, he knew this was the one!

Dick later recalled, "My heart jumped, and I thought to myself, 'This is the house the Lord has for us!'"

2412 Sceptor Lane was a roomy split-level brick house with shutters and siding that gave it a homey, chalet look. A quick walk-through heightened Dick's interest. The interior was as pretty as the exterior, and the house's three levels would accommodate his growing family. The twins and Diane were now school age, and son Tom would be born later that year. The lower level held the garage and an apartment-like suite perfect for the twins. The main level included a foyer, living room and dining room, den and eat-in kitchen. On the upper floor were three bedrooms and an office. Always decisive, Dick wanted to move quickly. He brought Peg to inspect the house the same day, and she loved it as much as her husband. They made an offer, and within days the house was theirs.

Vigneulle's second home in Birmingham, Alabama – Sceptor Lane – lived there 25 years and the place where their children grew up

By God's blessing, here was an executive home Dick's bank advancements made possible. But more importantly, it was the Vigneulles' dream home where they would raise their four children. Rick and Mick, Diane, and Tom all trace their childhood memories back to Sceptor Lane.

The twins were seven years old when their younger brother arrived, so while Tom was a baby, the twins and Diane were lively children. They remember their father as a loving parent who made time for them. If their dad ever had a problem at the office, the kids never knew it. As easily as his necktie slipped off once home, so too did business cares. Home time was family time. Dick not only delighted in his children's playtime, he joined in and welcomed neighborhood children too. As soon as Rick and Mick could toss a ball, they were trained for competition. Dick would divide the twins and their buddies into opposing teams, basketball in the warmer months and football in the cooler ones. Football was the family's favorite sport. Dick quarterbacked for both teams, always poised for a long toss or a ready catch. Here was a father determined to fulfill his role counterpoint to his own parents' example. As a child, Dick knew his parents loved him, but they were neither demonstrative in their affections nor quick to express words of praise and affirmation. All their time was spent on work with little left over for play.

Busy with their jobs and chores about the house, Dick's parents expected their children to occupy themselves. He purposed to moderate all that with his four. The neighborhood kids benefited too as Mr. Vigneulle became everybody's best buddy!

One evening as Peg and Dick enjoyed a quiet moment after getting all the kids to bed, the doorbell rang. When Peg opened the door, a four-year-old boy from down the street (who had slipped out of his house unnoticed) looked up.

With pleading eyes, he asked, "Can Mr. Vigneulle come out and play?"

One of Harold Vigneulle's family standards that his son upheld was shared mealtimes. Dick's family usually joined together for their evening meal, but attendance at breakfast was mandatory for everyone. The morning mealtime was the family altar time too, but Dick mercifully reversed his own father's agenda by allowing the kids to eat before Bible reading and prayer began. The breakfast gathering built character as well as faith. The children's chores had to be done—making up beds, taking out trash, or setting the table—and everyone was expected to be punctual. If one of the twins dawdled, their father would not curtail family devotions, even if it meant missing the school bus. The long walk to school would discipline any slacker.

Dick would read the Scriptures, often from the book of Proverbs, and then ask each child for his or her prayer requests for that day. The response might range from supernatural aid for a math test to divine deliverance from a playground bully. The children look back on the family prayer time as the place where they learned that God was concerned about each of them in an individual way, and that they could trust the Heavenly Father with the cares of life, no matter how big or small.

Even with a good job, Dick as well as Peg was careful and deliberate in making the new house uniquely their own. Dick's domain was the yard.

Rick, Mick, Diane, and Tom as youngsters

He loved working out of doors, even as he had as a boy. The couple's familiar weekend routine reserved Friday night for a date night, oftentimes joining friends for dinner out. Sunday would be the Lord's Day, to be devoted to church services and ministries. But in between, Saturday was for chores about the house, often to the children's consternation but their father's delight.

At an early age, the Vigneulle children learned to work, just as their grandfather taught their dad. While Dick and his siblings may have labored out of Depression era necessity, he wanted to temper the privileged lifestyle of his sons and daughter. They were expected to help out at home, and when old enough to take on after-school jobs to earn spending money or to save for some big ticket item. By the time they could print their names, the children each had an individual bank account and a box of church offering envelopes, learning early to practice the family values that prioritized saving and tithing from their incomes. Save for the future, and give to God now.

Dick enjoyed working with the soil, toiling with his hands to dig, mow, or plant. Years down the road, when his banking career was behind him, the one thing he missed most was having Saturdays off so he could work in his yard. He had an artist's eye as he created and then executed his landscape designs. On move-in day, the house sat on an undeveloped lawn, the sod growing helter-skelter in rocky soil. Season after season, like Adam toiling in the garden, Dick managed his Eden with skill and delight. With a sack of flour from Peg's kitchen, he would pour a white trail that outlined an island to plant or the perimeter of a patio to be poured. Eventually trees dotted the once vacant lawns, rows of plants brought order and flowers added color. An expansive patio, with a three-tiered wrought iron fountain, became a showplace worthy of *Southern Living* magazine.

While Dick tackled the homeplace's exterior, Peggy was the family's interior decorator. When the Vigneulles first moved into the Sceptor Lane house, Peggy seemed to have more children than she did furniture. For a number of years the living room sat empty, except for the piano placed against a wall. As guests eyed the empty room, Peg would laugh and call it "our music room!"

Dick was proud of his wife's artistic eye. Years later, when moving into a new office decorated by a professional, he ordered all the furniture to be sent back, and then called in his wife to make the selections for him.

He enjoyed shopping trips for the home with Peg. More than once they would arrive at a furniture store, take alternate routes to survey all the merchandise, and then reunite to point out the one "must have" in the store, only to discover that each had picked the same item. They bought furniture not by the roomful but piece by piece, moderating their spending and preferring to buy one fine piece without compromising quality or the family budget. Some years after settling in, they allowed themselves their biggest splurge to buy an elegant dining room set—table, chairs, and breakfront. It was beautiful and expensive. Peg's decorating skills included a gift for flower arranging and staging a room with pretty accessories.

After the new furniture filled the dining room, with all the family china and silver on display, Peg beamed. The room looked like a movie star ready for the camera's close-up. Dick was proud of the room too.

As he put his arm around his wife, smiling big like a prankster, he declared with the sing-song voice he used to make a humorous pronouncement.

"Just remember, Peg, it's all gonna burn one day!"

The one sentence homily was a reminder for him as well. Indeed, this world is passing away. The only real and sure treasures are those that can be taken to Heaven—family and souls won to Christ, good works done in Jesus' name. Dick witnessed many luxuries paraded across his executive path, as well as families destroyed by excess. He tempered himself, never pining for what he did not have, nor holding too tightly to what he did possess.

Music united the family as well as prayer and work, another reflection of Dick's own upbringing. He enjoyed sitting at the piano, and later an organ, to provide impromptu home concerts or to gather his wife and children in musical worship. The twins and Diane could harmonize beautifully with their dad, and home sessions around the living room piano led to public concerts in area churches and Sunday Schools.

Dick loved sports all his life, and the children shared his interest. A favorite family memory recalls listening to radio broadcasts of the University of Alabama football games, long before collegiate games were shown on television. The kids would listen to the radio in their father's home office, gathered around his desk as Dick sat and recorded every play. For each broadcast, Dick prepared a sheet of paper with neat, ruler-drawn lines to replicate the football field, complete with goal posts and yard lines drawn in. A bold line crossed the center of the paper. Notations for the first half of the game were drawn on the bottom half, and the top half was used to record the second half of the game. As the game unfolded and the announcer called the plays, Dick kept track of each one, drawing straight lines to record runs and dotted lines for passes. On the bottom of the sheet of the paper, he kept a running tally of the score. When the game ended, he filed away the sheet until a whole season of plays and scores filled the folder. Years later, one of the twins recalls seeing a book on Alabama football, including diagrams of games. The pages looked just like the play sheets kept by his father.

The Vigneulle children were not the only family members with toys. From his boyhood, Dick fancied train sets. Throughout his adulthood, he has collected and displayed a model railroad. During one of Harold Vigneulle's visits, ever the mechanical engineer, he built a huge display table in the garage for Dick's setup. To maximize space, he rigged the table to a pulley system so that when not in use, it could be hoisted to ceiling height. Even today, now living in a different location, Dick still has his train set. No longer confined to the garage, it is on year-round display in the ample family room. Family and friends enjoy giving him figures and gadgets for the ever-expanding display. Multiple trains travel yards and yards of track, past villages, over trestles, beside a tree-lined pond circled by miniature skaters and carolers. Longtime friend Jim Scott shares Dick's passion for model trains and often invites him to share an afternoon in his basement, assembling his model set. Jim generously provides engineer caps for both of them.

With savings from their paper routes, the twins bought bicycles to replace the wagons they pulled through the neighborhood. As the boys grew older their paper routes grew larger. But their pleas for motorcycles to speed delivery on longer routes seemed to fall on deaf ears. Their father flatly refused, so it was quite a shock for Peg one afternoon when she heard the unmistakable sound of a motorcycle pulling into the driveway. She looked out the back door, and there stood the biggest Suzuki she had ever seen. The smiling rider was her husband. Soon the twins each had their own motorcycles, and in time Tom added a fourth to the driveway line-up. Peg and Diane were content to ride behind Dick on his bike, and that made for great family sport. The Vigneulle family became the neighborhood's motorcycle gang.

Whether singing or praying, working in the yard, tinkering with toy trains or riding motorcycles, the Sceptor Lane house helped keep the family together. Like a meeting house for church-goers, it was the site and instrument for fellowship and harmony, and for that reason the whole family still treasures their old homeplace.

CHAPTER EIGHT

Man of Faith

*A*nyone who met Dick Vigneulle soon learned about his personal relationship with Jesus Christ and His love for the Lord. His influence as a Christian businessman went far beyond the halls of the City Federal Building. Veteran and start-up ministries alike sought his counsel and recruited him for their cause. Likewise, he aided many charitable events. Dick became widely respected and appreciated as a "Man of Faith" whose heart enveloped the whole city.

There were certain wider ministries that stand out from the rest. These special ministries received a greater, larger share of his resources, and they especially prepared Birmingham's well-respected banker for his future— a higher calling.

THE BIRMINGHAM GOSPEL TABERNACLE

Corporate life required many compromises from executive families, but for the Vigneulles an active church life remained a priority. Dick and Peg were faithful church members at The Birmingham Gospel Tabernacle, Peg's childhood home church. Their church membership was not a mere social exercise or business ploy, nor the token "name on the roll but a hole in the pew" type attachment. Both were regular attendees actively involved in church life. From childhood, Dick and Peggy were raised in homes committed to the local church, a conviction and practice constant in courtship and all their married life. A natural expression of their allegiance to the Lord was loyalty to a church and fellowship with God's people. For their children as well as themselves, church life provided instruction and accountability with a spiritual network that kept them centered.

Soon after their move to Birmingham from New York City, the Vigneulles joined the Tabernacle. Peggy grew up under the Tabernacle's long-term Pastor, Glenn Tingley, a family friend and the minister who married Dick and Peg. Short, stocky, and bespectacled, Pastor Tingley held spiritual stature greater than his height. Always dressed in coat and tie, he was a powerful preacher and developed a respected camaraderie with his congregation. But in personal encounters, he could be very blunt. His requests sounded more like orders.

One day, as he passed Dick in a church hallway, Tingley blurted out, "We need a minister of music, Dick. You can start next Sunday."

"But Brother Tingley, I've never done that."

"You'll learn!" was the pastor's only reply, and with that he walked off.

Song leading came naturally to Dick, having watched his father for years. His college ministries honed his skill. But leading a choir was altogether new.

Dick's natural talent and love for singing opened the door to wider ministry in the church and eventually in the city. For thirteen years he would serve as the Tabernacle's music director, leading congregational singing and the choir.

The rehearsals were demanding and rigorous. One dear lady's ambition exceeded her skill. Whenever she reached for a high note, the result was a piercing, shrill sound that unnerved the singers around her. Dick urged her to find another church ministry. The high standards for faithfulness and excellence served only to fill the choir loft and expand the music ministry. Dick developed soloists and special groups, including his own young children.

His daughter, Diane, recalls, "Our family would sing at home and in the car as we traveled. When Daddy noticed the pleasing blend of our voices, he got excited and started practicing with us. Rick could harmonize, and Mick and I sang melody. At home and church Dad would accompany us on the piano and sing the third part."

Diane, the shy one, was easily coaxed on to the platform out of sheer love for her daddy. The twins, rowdy natural performers, may have even balked a bit at first.

But as their father recalls, "After their first performance ended with rousing applause from the congregation, they were hooked! They loved an audience."

As the choir grew so did its reputation for inspiring concerts. The Tab's new minister of music burst with enthusiasm that dispelled any qualms about his lack of experience. He brought with him a new kind of music.

Musician and songwriter John W. Peterson modernized church music across the country, transforming the sounds of worship. His upbeat music offered a wider menu and new options for musicians and congregations. Dick brought the new sound to the Tabernacle.

"You can only sing *Amazing Grace* the same way so many times!" he explained. "Peterson's new music attracted a young audience while his lyrics moved the hearts of older folks, blending perfectly with the old hymns of the church. The syncopation made a sweet counterpoint to the 1-2-3-4 staid rhythms of the old songs."

His innovations held to high standards of musicianship without succumbing to the abrasive, rock music trends that would follow.

Dick brought a new look as well as a new sound to church concerts, elevating them to major productions. A church member paid for a scrim screen which brought a whole new dimension to Easter and Christmas musicals. The technology was not complex, and even simple by today's hi-tech standards. But in the 1960's it was innovative. The screen was made of light, netting-like material. With a light shining on the front of the screen, it was opaque and provided a standard backdrop for actors and musicians. When lighted from behind, however, the screen became transparent so that actors and images once hidden now appeared to the audience.

For a Christmas production, for instance, a woman portraying Mary the mother of Jesus, sat in a stable setting in front of the screen. Then with a switch of a spotlight, angels suddenly appeared behind the now transparent scrim screen to sing their herald.

Spellbound audiences loved it. The Tabernacle was reportedly the first church in Birmingham to use the device, and the dramatic effect helped draw even larger crowds.

JIMMIE HALE MISSION

One of the wider ministry's Dick felt called to support may have surprised some business associates. It was an inner-city mission. For a man who spent his days dressed in suit and tie, making huge corporate loans in an executive office, it seemed an unlikely choice. But for those who knew his heart, Dick's hands-on involvement with a skid row outreach made perfect sense. His Christian duty and privilege demanded it.

73

Founded in 1944, the Jimmie Hale Mission began as a storefront chapel on Second Avenue North in downtown Birmingham. The Mission's mission was to help men on the street struggling with addictions and homelessness. The ministry's founder and namesake had been a bartender and town drunk before his conversion. He related to their desperate plight, and knew firsthand the difference Christ can make.

Jimmie Hale lived only months after opening the Mission, but his wife, Jessie Hale, continued the work of faith. In time she was aided by Leo Shepura who became co-director, providing on-site and hands-on oversight. "Brother Leo," as everyone called him, became the voice of the Mission, not only preaching to the men but also keeping the ministry before churches and potential volunteers. But when Leo called Dick at his City Federal office, his plea was not just for a chapel speaker.

As Dick put the phone receiver to his ear, Brother Leo's steady, forceful voice came right through.

"Mr. Vigneulle, I need your help down here at the Mission."

It was not unusual for Dick to be asked to sing or give his testimony.

"How can I help you, Brother Leo?"

"Dick, we need you on our Board here at the Jimmie Hale Mission. We need a man with your understanding of finances as well as your standing in the business community. I want you to join our Board, and maybe you could help me recruit some other Christian professionals to join you."

"Well, let me have a little time to pray about it."

When Peg heard about Leo's request, she was a little apprehensive.

"Honey, it's a great opportunity, but my only concern is for your safety. The Mission is not in a safe neighborhood, and it's bound to be scary at night when you have to park and walk in that area. All I ask is that you be careful."

However unsettled Peg may have been, Dick was not.

"Peg, I understand your concern and I appreciate it, but someone has to help. I think the Mission finds it easier to get preachers than lay leaders, and Leo wants help with the business side of the work. I need to try to help."

As he would recall later, "I truly believe the Gospel is for everybody! If I know the Gospel and people need it, then I should take advantage of any opportunity to share Christ."

He went on to explain, "Sometimes God asks you to do something that you do not want to do, or something that is less than pleasant. More than once when I let God take me out of my comfort zone, God deepened my walk and widened my ministry."

Board members were expected to attend monthly Board meetings and to speak at the Mission as well, at least once a quarter. Dick dutifully took his turns as chapel speaker. But in an unlikely twist, the distinguished banker felt intimidated by the audience, not the other way around.

Sometimes the men were hungrier for the meal that followed in the cafeteria than for the Bible manna offered in chapel. Many were hardened to Gospel claims, and so their faces reflected minds enduring a message, not listening to it. Still others were too woozy to care. Dick needed a way to connect with the men.

He found the answer under his own roof at home. Finding the downtown area secure to relieve his wife's concerns, he took the twins and little Diane with him to the Mission. The kids made perfect ambassadors for Christ. The Vigneulle children often sang at their church and for neighborhood Sunday Schools, and so they were naturals for this outreach opportunity. Besides, they loved the outings with their daddy. Likewise, the Vigneulle kids' trips to Jimmie Hale provided unspoken life lessons about privilege and responsibility.

The men of the mission came alive at the sight of the children. Before and after the chapel time, the kids would mingle and greet the men. Happy smiles and little voices built a bridge for their father to his audience and the Gospel message he preached.

One night, as Dick preached, an old white-haired man sat hunched over on the front row, weeping through the whole service. Dick gave the invitation, and as he always did at the Mission, invited men to come forward to kneel at the altar and receive counseling.

> I saw workers quickly move to share with each of the men until everyone was attended except for the old man from the front row. No one was beside him. I saw all the workers were occupied and so I needed to step up. As I moved toward him, the stench was so bad my stomach churned. 'Lord, help me with this one!' I quickly prayed. I opened my Bible and then led him to the Lord. Instantly, the gloom was gone, and he was one happy man. I still remember the change in his countenance when he knew he was forgiven

by God. I reached out my arm to shake his hand, but he brushed it aside as he wrapped his arms around me in a big bear hug! And I was glad to return the hug to a new brother in Christ!

THE BILLY GRAHAM CRUSADE: BIRMINGHAM, 1972

Dick could not say no to his boss, Mr. Mark Hodo. Dick's position and his heart required compliance. A summons to the Chairman of the Board's office often resulted in a new assignment, not always one confined to the operations of City Federal.

When Dick answered such a call in 1972, he entered his boss's office to find a circle of strangers sitting before him. Mr. Hodo's greeting was a simultaneous introduction and commission.

"Gentlemen, this is Dick Vigneulle, my assistant. If ever you cannot reach me, here is the man who will do whatever needs to be done."

And with that statement, Dick "volunteered" for the Billy Graham Crusade to be held that fall in Birmingham. Mr. Hodo accepted the Graham organization's invitation to serve as honorary chairman of the crusade, and in turn recruited Dick to be his hands and feet.

1972 Billy Graham Crusade in Birmingham at Legion Field. Mark Hodo of City Federal was honorary chairman of the Birmingham Crusade and delegated the coordination of the event to Dick.

The event would mark Dr. Graham's first return to Birmingham since his 1964 crusade, which proved to be historic for both modern-day evangelism and the Civil Rights Movement. Just a year before, the whole nation's eye had turned to Birmingham with the death of four black children in the bombing of Sixteenth Street Baptist Church. The city's ensuing upheaval mirrored the strife erupting throughout the South and the entire nation, not just Alabama.

Dr. Billy Graham offered himself and his team for a city-wide crusade. There was only one stipulation: the meetings must be integrated. Crowds gathered from near and far to hear the world-famous evangelist. On Easter Sunday, 1964, Legion Field, site of the crusade, was filled with an audience, the largest integrated gathering in Alabama history at that time.

In 1972, Dr. Graham returned to Birmingham bringing his crusade ministry to advance the inroads of his earlier campaign, still preaching a message of the Gospel and urging racial reconciliation. In addition to the Graham team, a host of '70's era celebrities crossed the platform, including famed Dallas Cowboys coach Tom Landry and much-loved singers Norma Zimmer, of the popular Lawrence Welk television show, as well as former Broadway star-turned Gospel artist Ethel Waters.

Dick loved the crusade work. It harkened back to his father's revival ministry. To see souls saved and to witness an opportunity for racial healing in the city made light work of his nondescript role as "gofer" for Mr. Hodo and Billy Graham. He was privileged to meet members of the Graham team. From his platform seat, each night of the meetings, Dick thrilled to watch the team at work and to observe the great crowds filling the bleachers. Billy Graham's preaching stirred conviction. George Beverly Shea's solos, with his deep, flowing voice, gave one more reminder of Harold Vigneulle. But it was when Cliff Barrows would stand before the Legion Field crowd that Dick's heart really took a spin. With great grace and power Cliff Barrows lifted his arms to direct tens of thousands of voices in hymns of praise. Legion Field became one grand choir loft.

"Man, that's the job I'd love to have!" Dick told his friends.

YOUTH FOR CHRIST

Youth for Christ was one of many ministries spawned out of World

Youth for Christ outreach event in 1968. "For Pete's Sake" – Billy Graham movie premiere at Alabama Theatre, 1000 motorcycles along 3rd Ave. (with mayor's approval!), Free event where over 600 decisions for Christ were made. Dick was Chairman of Youth for Christ.

War II. Committed to youth evangelism and biblical Christianity, YFC grew from youth rallies in England, Canada, and the United States. Its slogan defined its mission and approach to soul-winning: "Anchored to the Rock, Geared to the Times." The Gospel of Jesus Christ never changes. But message and methods should not be confused. An orthodox message need not stifle creative outreach strategies. Modern methods facilitated fruitful, extended outreach to new generations.

In the 1940's and 1950's, the YFC sponsored Saturday night youth rallies. Then in the 1950's and 1960's the ministry began to establish Bible clubs in schools. The clubs became a feeder for the monthly rallies. YFC focused not only on reaching teens with the Gospel but also discipling and training them to share Christ with their classmates. Teen-to-teen evangelism was born.

When the national organization selected Birmingham as its next expansion site, their appointee needed help getting established. When the YFC newcomer called on Mark Hodo, he referred the young caller to Dick Vigneulle.

Dick gladly complied. Soul-winning and young people were great loves of this businessman-evangelist. After Dick helped YFC organize a Board for its Birmingham ministry, he was asked to chair it.

The city was open and responsive to the needs of its young people. Youth for Christ clubs quickly multiplied until over thirty clubs were scattered around Greater Birmingham. Club sizes varied with a dozen or so students in some schools while others reached fifty or more per club. The YFC Board recruited college students, largely from Birmingham's own Southeastern Bible College, to serve as directors of the high school clubs.

The monthly Youth for Christ rallies grew even more quickly, starting with a hundred teens and then skyrocketing to nearly a thousand. To keep in contact with the teens and maintain the ministry's momentum, leaders kept holding the YFC rallies throughout the summer months. Some became "giant rallies" with big name speakers sharing their testimonies for Christ.

For one of the giant rallies, Dick and the YFC Board went out on the limb, hoping for an over the top event. The date was set for Tuesday, April 27, 1965. The Board secured the stadium at the Alabama State Fairgrounds, which had a seating capacity of over ten thousand. A top-notch list of speakers agreed to come, headed by reigning Miss America, Vonda Kay Van Dyke, and sports hero Steve Sloan, quarterback for the University of Alabama's Crimson Tide.

Heralded as the beauty and the hero, the two gave clear testimonies for Christ.

The beauty queen addressed the young people first.

"If I could encourage one of you here to find Christ as your friend I would feel that this would add more meaning to the crown of Miss America."

Steve Sloan told the teens, "You don't inherit Christianity from your parents. Each person must decide for himself. Christ is everything to me and I believe to follow Christ is the only life."

Another popular speaker was Mike Helms, star end on the 1964 Auburn University football team, who challenged the young audience to a life of commitment and service.

"Christ works through your life and gives you the opportunity to serve. I want to serve Christ by serving people."

For months in advance, YFC leaders and staffers had worked hard and prayed even harder. As the big day drew near, the daunting responsibilities weighed heavier on the sponsors and organizers. They wanted to reach teens for Christ, but there were also practical concerns. Would the attendance provide a big enough audience and offering to cover the expensive venture?

Dick made sure plenty of advertising hit the media, including ads purchased in the local newspaper, *The Birmingham News*. Still concerned, he decided to call in a favor and telephoned Vic Hanson, the paper's publisher.

"Vic, I sure hope you're going to help us promote this giant rally!"

Mr. Hanson, nonplused and mild-mannered in his response, said, "Dick, don't worry about it. I have it covered. Everything is going to be fine."

Hanson's assurances fell short. Like a doubting Thomas, Dick persisted.

"I know I'm imposing on you, Vic, but I sure hope you're going to take care of us!"

Dick arrived at the Fairgrounds early that evening. The vast expanse of empty seats and vacant parking lots unsettled him. Once inside he began to climb the steps to the top of the stadium, finally reaching an upper level vantage point with a view that surveyed the whole scene. Just beyond stood the Bessemer Super Highway. Within a short time, to his great relief, the four-lane highway had become stacked with traffic, filled with cars lined up to turn into the Fairgrounds. Dick knew it was going to be a great evening!

The crowd grew as thousands and thousands of people filled the bleachers. Some estimates put the night's attendance at ten thousand. An even more inspiring number was the tally of decisions made for Christ that night. When the invitation was given and the youth were asked to stand if they wanted to receive Christ as Savior, hundreds stood and made their way to the grandstand for counseling.

Only after the rally did someone hand Dick a copy of the evening's "Late Final" edition of *The Birmingham News*. Immediately beneath the paper's masthead were pictures featuring the Youth for Christ guest speakers. On the left was a picture of Coach Bear Bryant with his arm around Steve Sloan. On the right was a picture of Miss America. Between the pictures of the young Christian superstars was the headline: "THE DEVIL HASN'T GOT A CHANCE!"

KESWICK CONVENTION

The circle of Dick's ministry friends was as wide and diverse as his business contacts. When his secretary announced, "Pastor David Jones is on the line for you," he picked up the phone and heard a familiar voice. Jones pastored Grace Bible Church in Center Point, a congregation just outside the city. Heavy-set and with a large frame, Jones had a constitution as strong as his voice.

"Dick, I need some help!"

"What do you want me to do, David?"

"I want you to help me bring KESWICK to Birmingham! Let's meet for lunch and I'll tell you how you can help."

"That's fine, David, but what's a 'KESWICK?'"

Originating in Wales and England, the Keswick Convention was a deeper life ministry organized to sponsor weeklong Bible conferences in churches. The movement found great favor and spread across Great Britain, Canada, and the United States. Despite the city's many churches, Birmingham was hungry for heavy-hitting Bible teaching—the kind that called for personal accountability and response to Christ's Lordship.

Pastor David Jones sought Dick's help in organizing a Board to sponsor Keswick in Birmingham, and in recruiting other city leaders who shared their love for Christ and the orthodox teaching of God's Word.

Keswick conventions became eagerly anticipated annual events for Greater Birmingham. The event lasted five days, Monday through Friday. A variety of denominations provided host churches as the Keswick week located in different parts of the city year after year. Dick would lead the singing and emcee the event, and then Pastor Jones would introduce the guest speakers each night.

The effort brought world renowned pastors and Bible teachers to the city: Ian Thomas, Stephen Olford, Ravi Zacharias, Peter Lord, Dave Burnham, and Stuart Briscoe among them.

Dick recalls, "The people of Birmingham loved Keswick. They did not want to miss one meeting! The deeper life message had not been taught like this in our city."

After Dick became SMI's lay Pastor, his Keswick ministry provided a perk for him and the church. He would invite these heavy-hitter preachers to stay over to preach at SMI on Sundays. Their visits edified the young congregation and gave it a stronger voice in the community. Of all Dick's wider ministries, Keswick was one of the most rewarding for him as a believer and a Pastor.

The meetings went on for years. Keswick helped build the body of Christ in Birmingham, as well as unify it. Likewise shared sponsorship of the convention intertwined segments of the Christian community otherwise strangers to one another.

Dick Vigneulle's community ministries built his faith, not just proved it. As his path of life continued, God's grander plan for him unfolded largely from these city-wide ministries. When Pastor David Jones, Dick's partner in Keswick leadership, learned that some of his Methodist friends wanted to start a church in Hoover, he called with a recommendation.

"You folks need to invite my banker friend, Dick Vigneulle, out to your little church in that insurance building. Ask him to give his testimony. I think the Lord will use him out there!"

CHAPTER NINE

Higher Calling

$\mathcal{A}$ telephone call can change one's life. Dick Vigneulle received just such a phone call in January 1969. When he picked up the receiver, sitting in his City Federal office, he knew the gentleman on the other end was a stranger because the man did not know how to pronounce his name.

"Hello, Mr. VIGGEN-U-WELL!" he said with a smile in his voice.

Mr. Gaston McGavick, as the caller identified himself, quickly moved on to explain the purpose of his call. The matter was pressing, but it was not banking that was on his mind. He needed a preacher, or at least a speaker, to lead a service on an upcoming Sunday.

"I'M A BANKER, NOT A PREACHER!"

A splinter group recently broken from an Over the Mountain Methodist church now met in an insurance building in a Hoover strip mall. A leader in the group, McGavick's duty was to line up a minister. It was short notice, but Dick received many invitations to speak or lead music for churches and various ministry or community groups, so he felt comfortable accepting the invitation to come for just one Sunday to give his testimony.

"I'm a banker, not a preacher, you understand," Dick insisted, "and it's just for one Sunday."

He had recently resigned from his long-held post as Minister of Music at the Gospel Tabernacle. He and Peg wanted time to take their children camping and to travel with their family singing group to various churches, so Dick certainly did not want any long-term commitments tying up his weekends.

On the appointed Sunday, with his family in tow, Dick drove the short distance from his home on Sceptor Lane, down Highway 31, to the Employer's Insurance building in Hoover. Gathered in the open office area were twenty-

Insurance building where "banker" Dick first preached to the 25 eager listeners in January 1969. Located in present-day shopping center with Green Valley Drug – Hoover, Alabama

five people eager to hear the Christian businessman who would be their morning speaker. Few of the people, if any, had ever met Dick, but some may have felt they knew him because of his popular television commercials promoting City Federal.

Whether or not the face was familiar, his ready smile and charismatic personality filled the space and soon put everyone at ease. The group, curious and maybe a bit wary, eagerly anticipated their guest's message. The idea of a banker "preaching" seemed a novelty even in the Bible belt. Dick spoke from his heart and gave a simple, straightforward message titled *What Is A Christian?* He closed the sermon with an invitation to receive Christ as personal Savior, and five people responded.

The crowd, excited yet moved with curiosity, wanted to hear more. Eagerly spoken "thank yous" were quickly followed by pleas for his return. This time they correctly spoke his name.

"Mr. Vigneulle, you must come back next Sunday."

"Please!"

"Sir, we insist!"

The people were gracious, and the Lord's presence unmistaken, so Dick agreed to return for one more Sunday. That following Lord's day, when he again gave the invitation, three more people responded—none other than Mr. McGavick, the man who first invited Dick, and his two teenage children.

Though gratified by the professions of faith, Dick felt relieved that his obligation was over, but again the people urged him to return and continue preaching. Some even suggested that he become their pastor. He was a banker, a churchman, a singer, and a Sunday School teacher, but a preacher? No. Preaching was outside his comfort zone.

Dick protested and excused himself, repeating what would be his familiar refrain for a long time to come, "I'm a banker, not a preacher!"

Finally, he relented with one strict stipulation: "I will preach for you for eight weeks, but when that's up, then I'm finished."

The tiny group's excitement grew. This was wonderful news.

But the men wondered, "Why only eight weeks?"

Dick answered, "Because I only have eight sermons."

They thought he was teasing, but Dick was serious. A few months earlier, the East Lake Alliance Church in Birmingham recruited Dick from the Tabernacle to come and fill their pulpit until the young preacher recently called by the church could relocate to the city. He preached at the Alliance church for eight weeks. It was those eight sermons that filled his homiletics portfolio, and when he repeated those eight for the Hoover group, his supply ended!

By the time the eight weeks ended, most of the people in the group had come to a saving relationship with Jesus Christ. Their religion, for the most part, seemed to be built on tradition, not a born-again experience with the Savior. Dick's calendar deadline came and went, and both he and the tiny congregation ignored it. Challenged by his teaching, the band of mostly new converts began inviting family and friends to come and hear the Gospel. A steady stream of the curious came, heard the Good News, and responded. More and more folks trusted Christ until 50 to 60 excited believers crowded the limited office space.

A Sunday night service was added, and Dick recruited longtime business friends to come and share their testimonies: from the legal profession, Bill Longshore; from the medical field Drs. Bill Buck and Sam Peeples; from the real estate and development arena, Wales Goebel. People marveled to hear strong testimonies of faith from businessmen. Such outspoken faith was expected of preachers, but for professionals to speak out for Christ and tell of lively personal relationships with Jesus fascinated the hearers. As a result even more came to salvation.

The newest converts and even visitors became some of the most zealous promoters. When a young high school student named Susan Kennedy began attending, her father was suspicious. After all, he had never heard of a "banker-preacher." He decided to check out this religious group that won his daughter's following. He and his wife, Vira, attended a service, and Dick followed up with an in-home visit to the Kennedys.

As Dick sat on the fireplace hearth in their living room, he carefully explained the Gospel, sharing verse after verse of Scripture. Glenn bowed his head and prayed to receive Christ that very night. Months later Dick learned that Vira was eavesdropping behind the kitchen door, and as her husband prayed the Sinner's Prayer, she did too! In time, all five of their children also became Christians.

The Kennedys opened their home to host a Thursday night visitation program. Dozens came to pray, divide up into teams, and then go out visiting to share the Gospel. At the end of the visits, everyone would return to share their results and enjoy a meal prepared by Vira. The testimonies were thrilling as family members, friends, church visitors, and even strangers came to Christ—all because someone came and knocked on their door. Some evangelism teams, excited about the salvation decisions resulting from their visits, could not wait to drive back to Glenn and Vira's and so they would call in their reports. These Christians, many of them new believers and some spiritual veterans now revitalized, awakened to the power and responsibility of sharing their faith. Each Thursday night witnessed another celebration of new life. The evangelism meetings in the Kennedy home took on the whoopla of diehard fans at Legion Field celebrating a touchdown!

Another couple won to Christ was a local school principal and his wife, Dick and Peg Lovelady. They too had started attending because their two daughters, Pam and Patty, came home excited about their new church. The family lived on a beautiful piece of property in the country with a lake and an old log house restored and filled with antiques, quilts, and collectibles. Known as "Hallelujah Hill," the Lovelady homestead became a frequent spot for Sunday afternoon church picnics followed by baptismal services in the lake.

Mr. Lovelady approached Dick with a solution to the crowded services in the insurance building. He could secure the use of his school for Sunday services. The rent would only cost about $100 a month. The new site met with popular approval, and so the group moved to Vestavia High School, initially meeting in the school library.

Teams arrived every Saturday night to set up for the church service the following morning. Eager volunteers set to work. First the space would be tidied up, workers busily sweeping and mopping or vacuuming. Then the schoolhouse would be transformed into a church house. Dick gave explicit directions: chairs must be lined up in perfect rows, and tables must be ar-

Dick Lovelady's country homestead with lake, known as "Hallelujah Hill". Used for special Sunday afternoon picnics and baptismal services. Attracted many young adults – 1972

ranged across the back of the room to establish a defined, chapel-like area. His fastidious ways at the bank followed him to church. Lewis Ingram, owner of cabinet and construction businesses, personally built a pulpit for Dick as well as a portable prayer altar for the schoolhouse sanctuary.

As space expanded so too did the crowds. On Sunday mornings, Dick would hide away in the school's band room where big windows looked out on the parking lot. Each week he would pray for more and more cars to fill the spaces.

"Lord, give us 50 cars today!"

Like Abraham wagering with the Lord, each Sunday Dick would up the ante by ten more cars and then twenty. It was a big day when he dared to ask the Lord for one hundred cars, and the Lord provided! As Dick prayed in more cars, ushers set up more chairs. When the library space was maxed out, the services were moved to the larger cafeteria where two hundred could be seated.

Vestavia High School's library accommodated the growing group of believers. Space limitations soon required the church group to move to the cafeteria – early 1970's.

Within a year or so of the Vigneulle family's first visit to the storefront ministry, a church was officially established. On July 5, 1970, sixty-seven charter members organized as a church and called it the "Shades Mountain Methodist Church (Independent)." The new church's name alluded to the founding group's origins, but a year later "Methodist" was dropped and the church was known from then on as "Shades Mountain Independent," giving a truer identity of its creed and people. From its inception, the forming congregation gathered visitors and members from a cross-section of denominations, as well as many unchurched people. By 1970, while still insisting he was a banker not a preacher, Dick relented to some of the old guard's insistence that he be ordained. It was a peacekeeping gesture on his part, and by no means was it to be construed as a change of heart. Whether licensed or ordained, it mattered not to Dick, though this tip of the hat to his clerical role allowed him to conduct weddings and widened his shepherding role when conducting funerals. Even so, his post was temporary and secondary to his City Federal job. He was a professional man, not a preacher-man.

No one was playing church. Shades Mountain Independent was a first-century type gathering of believers, going house to house to evangelize, coming together to worship and celebrate, and continuing in a commitment to care for one another. With few exceptions, there were no traditions to break down, and everyone was pretty much a "newcomer" to the fellowship, so no one felt like an outsider. Because the preacher was a banker, responsibilities needed to be shared and shouldered by the entire fellowship. Everyone had a job to do.

Dick, still resolved to be only a temporary shepherd, kept reminding his would-be flock, "I'm a banker, not a pastor!" Even so, these founding months and early years allowed him a broader discovery of his own spiritual giftedness as an evangelist.

Just as he once teamed up with Brom Cowser when they were BJU students leading revivals, he still continued to volunteer for crusade and rally events. Now he teamed with his longtime friend Wales Goebel who had recently left the business world to serve God full time, founding his own "Wales Goebel Ministry." The believers rallying around Dick affirmed his gift. He won many lost people to the Lord, while awakening Christians to their duty to fulfill the Great Commission. By his example, he trained and motivated his congregation to tell others about Jesus Christ.

This was the era of the Jesus Movement and Jesus Freaks. The wave of evangelism rolling through this emerging church swept over a community of young people who were looking for "the real thing." Young people began to converge on SMI. The kids came from every walk of school life. The British invasion led by the Beatles and the Dave Clark Five swept in cultural changes that shook more traditional groups. But not this church—everyone was welcome to "come as you are" and they did. The collegiate-looking football players and cheerleaders sat with long-haired, disheveled hippies and dropouts.

When Sunday morning came and worshippers gathered in the high school cafeteria's makeshift sanctuary, one half of the room filled with young people, almost outnumbering the adults sitting across the aisle. But neither side was put off by the other. The diversity of the group delighted everyone: the believers wanted to tell newcomers about Jesus and the seekers wanted to hear.

People reached out to their peers at work, in the country club, or around their own neighborhoods. Staid professionals, upright churchgoers, and community do-gooders, along with high school and college-age young people, whether skeptical scholars or shaggy druggies, gathered in a common search to fill the emptiness in their lives. Dick's lack of formality, in manner and title, disarmed them. Many were fueled by curiosity to hear in person this successful downtown banker who preached on weekends.

A group of high school cheerleaders, hearing about Dick Vigneulle's and Wales Goebel's Friday morning prayer meetings, decided to do the same. Alarmed upon hearing the young girls met unchaperoned at Lover's Leap on Shades Crest Road for pre-dawn gatherings, the men secured a safer site in a local church on Green Springs Highway for before-school prayer meetings.

Dick led in song, Wales gave a devotional, students shared testimonies, and then broke into small prayer groups, each led by an adult from Wales Goebel Ministry, including Jean Goebel, Joyce Yancey, and others. News spread to area high schools, and soon over 100 teenage boys and girls met weekly. Dozens came to Christ. Motivated to share their faith at school, teens who attended the prayer gathering wore an orange sticker to school to visually identify and encourage one another. This "orange brigade" of evangelists funneled many other youth to their new church.

Another feeder system fostering SMI's explosive growth consisted of small groups. Many who heard the Gospel on Sunday morning were enlisted in a weeknight Bible study in a church member's home to hear Christ's claims explained in a quiet, private setting.

The Bible held great sway in Southern life and culture. Many folks treated church as part of their family heritage, as if to say, "Why, my grand-daddy and daddy were Presbyterians [or whatever denomination], and I am too." Church for many was a matter of brand loyalty, like a preference for a political party or make of automobile, swayed more by family tradition than thoughtful personal choice. The declarations that good works or church membership do not save shook the expectations and security of many. The Bible studies, as well as Dick's continued evangelistic preaching, brought many to see the light!

TROUBLED TIMES

The young church's experiences were not all happy ones. Even in the early years, Dick and the congregation endured tests and losses. One of the first fiery trials to singe the ministry was a doctrinal dispute lighted by a few of the original founders. A young couple who regularly attended the church asked Dick to dedicate their newborn baby. He welcomed the opportunity, and so a special part of a morning service recognized the little family before the whole congregation. Dick gave a solemn charge to the parents to raise their child in a godly example of their Christian faith, so that when the child reached an age of understanding, the little one's appetite for Christ would be whetted by the parents' example and teaching. The charge extended to the congregation, calling them to live exemplary lives before all the church's children and to partner in ministries to serve and encourage young families.

The mini-service closed with a prayer of dedication for the baby and parents. This beautiful service met with an ugly aftermath.

When morning worship ended, a small posse of some of the founding members circled Dick with a protest. They demanded to know why he had not sprinkled the baby. Dick was blindsided by their vitriolic stand. For one thing, the Vigneulles themselves never practiced infant baptism with their children. It was a non-issue for his family. Furthermore, from its inception, the young church singularly focused on evangelism and the major tenets of the evangelical faith. Secondary doctrines and nuances of denominational practices were not prioritized, as the emerging fellowship built on common ground. Dick was neither a theologian nor, as he still frequently reminded folks, a permanent let alone full-time pastor. He preferred to leave these finer points to the man the church would eventually call as their "real" pastor.

By nature, Dick did not like confrontation, but he would not shy away from it either, especially in matters of evangelism and integrity. Even though a banker by profession, he had the discernment of an evangelist. He explained then and repeatedly through the years, that he had met too many people who mistakenly thought they were going to heaven because of good works and that included religious ones. No one was saved by baptism (at any age), confirmation, charitable giving, or walking a church aisle.

Dick would underscore the Apostle Paul's teaching: "For by grace you have been saved through faith, and that not of yourselves; it is the gift of God, not of works, lest anyone should boast" (Ephesians 2:8-9).

The dissenting group remained adamant. Not wanting to stir conflict, Dick offered his resignation. His intention all along was to serve a limited, part-time role. The work was now on solid footing with scores of new believers, emerging young leaders, and a savings account of ten thousand dollars. Perhaps it was time to leave.

The episode was disappointing. The Vigneulles headed for home. Later that same Sunday night, as Dick and Peg settled in the family room with their children, they heard a commotion in the front yard. They turned on the porch light and opened the front door. Standing in front of them were some fifty church members, many with their children gathered around them. It was a peace march! The dear folks covered the lawn and began raising their voices in a loving appeal.

"You led us to the Lord, so please don't leave us!"

"Come back!"

"We want you to be our pastor!"

Humbled by their appeal, he heeded their cry.

"Bless your hearts! Yes, of course, I'll come back, but only long enough to help you find a *real* pastor."

The protestors could not be reconciled, and they chose to leave, reportedly taking the church's savings with them to start their own new work, one that floundered and dissolved not long afterwards.

The dissenters' departure grieved the young church, but another tragic loss soon struck SMI, one that would require "Banker" Vigneulle to preach his first funeral.

———————

Lew Bagwell never met a stranger, and his many admirers—fellow teenagers and adults alike—knew he was destined for greatness. He reminded some of a young Dick Vigneulle, with his natural leadership abilities and warm personality. But even more, Lew had a radical devotion to Christ. He delighted to tell his fellow teenagers, or anyone else who would listen, about his Savior, Jesus Christ. He organized many of the youth group outings and outreaches. Especially popular were the Sunday night after-church gatherings at Pasquales Pizza Parlor in Hoover.

His parents, Lucille and Lew Bagwell, were distinguished educators and world travelers. Devout Christians and members of Shades Mountain Baptist Church, the Bagwells were glad for their son's joy in attending the new church meeting in the high school. In fact, the parents oftentimes attended SMI's Sunday night services to hear Dick preach.

In the summer of 1971, Mr. and Mrs. Bagwell planned a trip to Peru. Just before their departure for South America, they attended an evening service once more, and afterwards came to Dick with a special request.

"Take good care of our son for us until we get back!"

Giving his assurance, Dick smiled and gave the Bagwells a bon voyage hug.

A few days later, while on an outing with school and church friends, Lew was killed in a scuba diving accident on Lake Martin. Dick had to call the Bagwells in Peru and deliver the news any parent dreads to hear. The family asked Dick to preach the funeral at their church. He had never preached a funeral in his life, and he stumbled through the protocol of such a service.

Barely in the pulpit long enough to acknowledge the crowd, Dick quickly moved to the piano and began to sing—*In Times Like These You Need a Savior.* As he returned to the pulpit in the huge Baptist church, he looked out at a congregation of a thousand mourners. Everyone was still numbed by the loss.

Dick hardly remembers what he said that day, except that he gave the Gospel and invited those who needed to be saved, or who wanted assurance that they were heaven bound, to pray silently with him as he repeated the Sinner's Prayer. As he spoke the "Amen," with heads still bowed, he made a simple request.

"If you prayed that prayer with me just now, look up and catch my eye."

By his recollection, half the crowd looked up. The response unnerved him.

FINALLY. . .A CANDIDATE

By 1973, three years after the church's founding, Dick was still preaching from Shades Mountain Independent Church's pulpit. At times his boss at City Federal, Mark Hodo, became unsettled.

"Dick, those folks keep calling you their pastor!"

Confident he was a banker for life, he dismissed it and urged his boss to do the same. Mr. Hodo's concern seemed credible. No longer a fledgling church, Shades Mountain Independent had purchased land and built its first building. With a sanctuary of their own, the congregation now numbered in the hundreds. SMI, as the church became familiarly known, made attempts at Dick's urging to find a "real pastor."

To help with the pastoral demands, church members welcomed input and partnership. Dr. Sumner Wemp, then President of Southeastern Bible College, became Dick's confidant, encouraging and mentoring him and even filling the pulpit for a season. The church hired its first part-time employee, a college student named Hank Erwin, to be Youth Pastor. Then a church secretary was added to the payroll, Ruth Hobson, SMI's first full-time staff person.

But as fast as Dick's pastoral duties multiplied so too did his City Federal responsibilities. He was expected to assume soon the title of President of the bank. Mr. Hodo appreciated Dick's service to the church, but he quietly contacted church Board members and urged them to relieve Dick and hasten to find a replacement. The demands as the bank's top officer would be too much even for Dick. Besides, there were bank Board members who might balk at a preacher as president of the firm.

With Dick's public insistence and Mr. Hodo's covert prompting, the search for SMI's "real preacher" ratcheted up. To Dick's frustration, literally dozens of eligible ministers came and went. None captured the congregation's confidence, let alone its heart. But as Christmas 1973 approached, the most serious candidate ever considered by the search team was presented to the congregation. The trained young preacher, with seemingly impeccable credentials and winning ways, had been put through rigorous tests. After several positive interviews and small group exchanges, and a very good trial sermon, it seemed that SMI had found its Pastor. Dick was relieved that the shepherd's staff would finally be handed to a "real preacher."

With joyous expectations the vote was taken. While church elders counted the votes, Dick ambled into the sanctuary and sat at the piano, playing hymns as he waited and contemplated a significant change in his future and his would-be replacement's. To his amazement, however, when the count was tallied, the man did not receive the required vote to be offered the call. The church's constitution required a 75% favorable vote, but for this shoe-in candidate the vote was just the opposite—75% rejected his call. This unexpected turn of events stunned Dick. The pressure mounted, yet the search was back to the beginning.

Even so, he kept a commitment to accompany the church youth to an after-Christmas retreat in Gatlinburg, Tennessee, the popular resort community in the Smokies. During that retreat, while alone in his hotel room, Dick cried out to the Lord and wrestled with the predicament he found himself in. The church needed a full-time leader and so too did the bank.

As Dick would later tell the story, it was during this hotel room prayer vigil, and not until then, that God called him to leave the bank and surrender to full-time ministry at SMI.

Months before, as others urged him to leave the bank, Dick sought the advice of ten trusted friends, some in the ministry and some in the business world. He asked each one the same question.

"What do you think? Should I stay at the bank? Or should I go to the church?"

The response was a split decision. Five said he should stay at the bank, and five said he should go to the church. When the answer came, it would have to be God's doing. And that is just what happened in Gatlinburg—Dick heard God's call.

Outsiders might mistake his response for delayed obedience, and even some friends might have thought him blind to the obvious. The issue, however, was the "fullness of time" as the Scriptures often put it. God's timing was at work.

Dick knelt beside his bed, an open Bible before him, as he agonized in prayer and soul-searching. The Lord brought to mind once more David's prayer promise from Psalm 16:11, "Thou wilt show me the path of life." Like a compass guiding a pilgrim lost in the woods, God's Word gave him direction and calmed his spirit.

Dick knew that God's will was not like a piece of merchandise to be taken out of a display case for him to examine and then accept or reject. A clear answer from God first required a yielded heart, no matter what the future held.

Finally, peace came over him, not because He knew God's plan yet but because he was surrendered to whatever God wanted. But if God was calling him to leave the bank and to become SMI's Pastor, the call would be tested. Dick was enmeshed in several complicated business deals that would require a lengthy and ongoing role at the bank. It would be unethical to walk out on them. But SMI needed a Pastor now! And Dick needed resolution too.

"What will it be, Lord?" he cried out.

Nagged by what seemed like common sense, Dick figured that even in an ideal economy and turn of events, it would be miraculous to close out his business commitments in less than a year.

As he later explained, "I just gave God a deadline. Things either had to work out by then or I'd give up the church job."

And so Dick came up with his own Gideon's fleece, and made a pact with the Lord, one outright audacious if it had not been prompted and proven by faith.

"Lord," Dick appealed, "You can work out these business matters in six months because You've got the power. But I can't wait six more months, and neither can the church. If You can do it in six months, Lord—and You can—then You can do it in six weeks! If You truly are calling me to quit my job and become SMI's full-time preacher, then do it within six weeks, and I will know it is You at work. I will follow."

Then as an afterthought, he added, "But Lord, I think it's going to take a miracle!"

The dilemma switched so that now it was God's problem. In his heart of hearts, Dick still did not know if he would be leaving the bank or not, but for sure he now had peace in his heart and was ready for whatever the Lord had in store. Traveling back to Birmingham from the retreat, Dick shared with Peggy his story.

"Peg, I told the Lord to work it all out in six weeks."

Peggy, quite willing to follow her husband wherever the Lord led, simply replied, "Honey, I don't think you've given the Lord enough time."

For the first few days nothing happened. The only change was in Dick's spirit—the pressure was gone.

"Even though I did not know what the Lord had in store for me, I had total peace. As I drove down the interstate to the bank each morning, I would sing loudly to the Lord and talk to Him. 'Lord, You're going to do something, one way or the other. It doesn't matter to me.'"

Despite Dick's praise songs and the church family's prayers, nothing happened—that is until the last week of the deadline. What transpired in a three-day period was miraculous, a harbinger of what the Lord had in store for the man and ministry. God would do the impossible.

On Wednesday of that final week, Dick knew something supernatural was stirring. Unexpected phone calls came in to his bank office. Unsolicited offers were made, and negotiations speedily concluded. Suddenly the complex business deals that could stall or abort his call to ministry were quickly resolved and about to come in place.

Dick had never in his entire banking career ever seen anything like it.

"It was as though, with hands behind my back, the pieces of a jigsaw puzzle on a table before me began to move on their own and lock together in perfect arrangement to form the puzzle picture."

That night after midweek Prayer Meeting, he stayed late in his church office. By the time he got home, Peg had already gone to bed. Dick tossed and turned, and stared at the ceiling. Finally, unable to contain his excitement, he shook his sleeping wife.

"Peg, I believe it's happening!"

Roused from deep sleep, Peg could hardly make sense of what her husband said.

"What's happening, Honey?"

"The miracle!"

By Friday afternoon, the deals were done, the miracle realized. Dick sat alone in his City Federal office, pensive and stunned not just by the happenings but the speed and timeliness of it all. When God moved, He moved quickly.

Cold chills covered his body as he prayed, "Lord, You have done it. I don't know whether to be happy or sad."

He would describe this deadline week as one of the most exciting, miraculous times of his life. For years to come, Dick would point to that Friday, January 11, 1974, as the day God called him to the ministry.

Dick knew what he had to do. God kept His part of the bargain, and now Dick must keep his. There was nothing left to do but take the final, most difficult step and submit his resignation to Mr. Hodo. In fact, he would be submitting two resignations, one as Executive Vice President of City Federal Savings and Loan and the other as President of its subsidiary, Service Corporation of Alabama.

He was about to turn away from a dream job, on the brink of his highest promotion, being named President of what would be Alabama's largest Savings and Loan Association. More troublesome to Dick than leaving a career he loved was disappointing the man who was his long-standing mentor and friend. It weighed heavy on his heart.

After Mr. Hodo heard the news, he said, "Dick, if it was another bank, I would try to talk you out of it. BUT GOD'S CALLING IS HIGHER THAN MINE."

With that, Hodo bowed his head on his desk and sobbed.

At the next weeknight meeting of SMI's Board, Dick confided all the recent happenings in his life. And then he concluded with a long-awaited announcement.

"I am now a candidate to be the full-time Pastor of Shades Mountain Independent Church!"

Hands clapped and tears fell. What the congregation longed for was now about to happen.

Dick continued with a grin, "And if the church doesn't call me, I'm in a heap of trouble because my resignation is already turned in to the bank. My son Rick told me, 'Dad, you're mighty happy for a man who doesn't have a job!'"

Dick wanted to temper the timing of this good news announcement.

"Let's not tell anyone until I can speak to the church family this Sunday morning," Dick suggested.

But one of the Board members, who had slipped out of the room momentarily, returned in time to hear Dick's request.

"It's too late, Dick. I've already called and told my wife!"

The news was out, climaxing a story that became legendary in Birmingham's business and Christian communities.

As the day of his departure from the bank loomed, Dick was troubled only by one thought and that was the possible public misconception that he and Mr. Hodo had had a falling out. Some might construe the report of his call to the church as only window dressing to a private breach of friendship and business partnership. There was nothing he could do. Dick left his reputation with the Lord, and God again intervened.

Pastor Dick elected to City Federal's Board of Directors – 1974

Mr. Hodo came to Dick's office before he left that day with one final request.

"I've just met with the City Federal Board, Dick, and the vote was unanimous. We want to invite you to serve as a member of the bank's Board."

That was it! Such an offer would show to the public the ongoing friendship and trust that existed between him and his former boss. Dick's spirit was free! At forty-three years of age, he was about to begin the biggest job of his life. Like Matthew forsaking the tax collector's table, Dick's surrender to the pastorate would be total and final.

CHAPTER TEN

Barn-Raising on the Mountain

SMI had a building before it had a Pastor. Growing crowds forced the church to search for a permanent site. As gracious as the school authorities had been, even they now urged the church to move on to a more accommodating space. Determined to build their own building, church leaders began looking for a suitable building site. A Hoover businessman donated a tract of land, but church planners, concerned about possible swampy conditions at the site, graciously returned the gift. One location that did catch their interest was a wedge of land at the V-point of Old Tyler Road and Tyler Road.

Their initial inquiries were put off by naysayers who dismissed the site as impossible to acquire. U.S. Steel owned the land, as well as a thirty-acre tract across Tyler Road, and it was not for sale, nor was the corporate giant apt to sell. Prayers for direction became appeals for heaven's intervention. Convinced the Tyler Road island was the perfect place for SMI to begin building, church leaders in a leap of faith submitted a contract, and the church family prayed even harder. Their offer was for $10,000. Weeks and weeks passed with no response. As long as there was no refusal, hope remained alive and so too the prayer meetings. Finally, after SMI's offer was forwarded from one office at U.S. Steel to another, until fourteen committees had taken action, the answer came: offer accepted!

The church family, joyful at the good news, now faced the daunting task of raising money to pay for the land and then a building. On the Sunday night before the Monday morning deadline to pay for the land, there was still a shortfall. The fellowship responded the way churches often do— they prayed and then took up an offering. After ushers counted the offering, they announced the total was $192.76—the exact amount to the penny still needed. Dick wondered if the ushers had added some change to make the amount come out right, but the men assured him nothing had been added or taken away. This miracle offering, the first of many, strengthened the young church's faith. Members were confident that indeed this was the very spot where God intended for them to build a church.

Dick recalls this signal event, "That offering was God's signature that we were in His will. God was clearly saying to all of us, 'Follow me and I will meet your needs.'"

A greater test of the young church's faith came in raising a quarter of a million dollars to build a sanctuary. What financial institution would consider SMI a credible client? The church had only a brief history and no denominational identity, and since Dick was still full time at City Federal, there was not even a full-time pastor. No doubt Dick's business and personal reputation helped, and a few young businessmen in the church were willing to literally put their name on the line.

Leroy Clark was one of them. A transplant from Atlanta to Birmingham, he was a young husband and father when he began attending the services in the insurance building. Dick led him to the Lord, and Leroy committed himself to Dick and the church's mission. He and others put together an ambitious plan to sell bonds. While a reasonable approach to financing, still the plan was daring for so young a congregation. Dick began to sound like Dr. Bob Jones Sr., the founder of his alma mater, as he repeated his own maxims to build the faith of his congregation and to direct SMI's building plans.

He said, "Faith and a plan operate like a railroad track—they go side by side in the same direction!"

In an act of faith, the church approved a bond program, and SMI's members put feet to their prayers by stepping out to buy and sell bonds. With locomotive speed, all the bonds sold in ten days. It was time to build.

BARN-RAISING

Dick secured the services of an architect named Buddy Elliott.

"Dick, what do you want the church building to look like?" he asked, struggling to come up with a design approach.

Dick knew for sure what he did not want.

"Don't plan another red brick colonial with big white pillars! That's the last thing the South needs."

Then almost as an afterthought, Dick threw out an idea, one that would prove to be inspired.

"Buddy, make the building look like a big old barn that says 'Come on in!'"

Dick knew the power of appearance, not only with an employee but also a facility. City Federal taught him that, and after all, the Bible cautions that "man looks on the outward" (I Samuel 16:7c). And so SMI's sanctuary was built, a brick structure with barn-inspired features, such as a gambrel roof clad with cedar-like shingles and entrance porches made of rough-hewn timber.

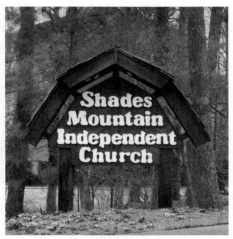

Sign in front of SMI Sanctuary
Photo: Brittany Moore

Instead of stained glass, the towering windows were clear-paned, reaching from floor to ceiling with a country style arch at the top. Flooding the space with warm light, the windows filled most of the side walls, and looked out to wooded vistas. The barn motif became the pattern for all the other buildings to follow, and even for the SMI logo and the gambrel-shaped signs on the property and throughout the community.

SMI's original sanctuary completed 1972. Located between Old Tyler Road and Tyler Road in Hoover, Alabama

Defying the model of most church construction, the end result was a worship center that indeed resembled a barn, a truly beautiful building, restrained yet suited to its suburban neighborhood. Its unexpected design and imposing size demanded attention and got it. The look of the building beguiled folks, arresting their attention as they drove past and disarming them as they walked in. Many eventual members recall first driving past the church and then, intrigued by the look of the structure, decided to visit and check

Original sanctuary with addition of offices and nursery completed in 1976

Annex building for Shades Mountain Christian Schools and
Sunday School classes completed in 1978

out this new church on the mountain. As passers-by glanced through the big windows, stirring their curiosity even more were the huge crowds that continually filled the interior, on Sunday nights as well as Sunday mornings. Even the church's ample parking lots were always full.

"What's this place all about? What's going on in there?" folks pondered or even asked out loud as they drove down Tyler Road.

Shades Mountain Independent Church built the unexpected, and the building itself hinted at the Pastor's and congregation's fresh approach to telling *The Old, Old Story*.

Greater Birmingham seemed to be a worn notch on the Bible belt. The church's name "Independent" spoke of denominational detachment. It was a non-denominational church. Freedom from labels—Baptist, Catholic, Lutheran, Presbyterian, or whatever—removed barriers so that folks with varied

SMI's Sanctuary expansion completed in 1980 (Miracle '80)

SMI's Family Life Center completed in 1988 – location of present-day high school

religious traditions were not put off. One Bible conference speaker, however, once suggested, probably with some humorous intent, that the name be changed to "Shades Mountain *Dependent* Church"—reminding Christ's followers to rely solely on God.

Even though Dick and SMI refused to be earmarked by one church group or a mainline denominational tag, there was no compromise in the fundamentals of orthodox faith. In fact, early on, church leaders developed a statement of faith based on Southeastern Bible College's doctrinal statement. The church's open-door attitude and commitment to majoring on the majors enabled Dick and the ministry to bring many to Christ who were religious but lost, "having a form of godliness but denying its power" (II Timothy 3:5a). Likewise, because the church was brand-free, SMI seemed to have an edge at reaching the "unchurched," those raised without religious instruction or else burned by bad experiences with churches and so-called holy men.

Giving further credibility to SMI's message before skeptics and seekers alike was the Pastor's reputation as a successful businessman. SMI's parish circled the affluent and ambitious. It must have arrested their attention to hear of

103

"Old Fashioned" Day – August 1975.
Community outreach opportunity of SMI

a man who attained what so many sought after, yet who walked away from it all. At least a first hearing was assured with many because of Dick's story.

Another winning effect of the "big old barn that said 'Come on in!'" was its appeal to a wide audience, attractive enough to please affluent visitors yet simple enough not to make uncomfortable the folks of modest means who also attended. Here was a church that looked unlike any other and whose members welcomed everyone. Perhaps because the building did not look like a church, seekers came in more open-minded and relaxed.

The poor in spirit were not intimidated because there were neither steeples nor cathedral arches. The facility's inviting look may have drawn many visitors, but it was the loving welcome they received once inside that kept them. As the church took on some of the trappings of a regular church— now with its own building and established worship times, and even a pastor— the people never lost the first-love excitement of their early days in the insurance building and high school cafeteria.

Visitors and members alike so often repeated a refrain when describing the church that this catchphrase became a by-line in SMI's advertising and part of people's invitations to attend this amazing church—"Come to WHERE THE LOVE IS!"

DR. HAMMOND AND KAY JONES

Not all SMI's neighbors, however, welcomed the church's arrival. No one was more irritated than the medical doctor and his wife who lived right across Old Tyler Road from the "big old barn." Their expensive home, with stately grounds and swimming pool, lost its woodland view when SMI's sanctuary went up. Dr. and Mrs. Hammond Jones built their dream home years before when residing in Hoover meant living in the country. The arrival of church folk across the street interrupted their country idyll and ruined their expectations of solitude in Jefferson County. But then they met the new church's Pastor and got to know folks in the congregation, some who were friends and neighbors. Before long, the Joneses warmed to SMI, as seeming insults and prejudices suddenly dissolved.

Not long after winning their friendship, Dick shared the Gospel and led them both to the Lord. "Doc" and Kay, as their new church family lovingly called them, became dedicated followers of Christ. Kay Jones, a soft-spoken and petite lady, often shared her amazing transformation with believers and unsaved alike. She loved to tell the Good News!

"My husband I were church members. But we went to church for all the wrong reasons. We went to church because it seemed the right thing for folks to do. And we wanted our daughter to have religious training, yet her daddy and I had no understanding of the Bible. You might say church for us was more of a social event than a worship experience."

With a twinkle in her eye and the corner of her mouth tilted in a grin, she would go on to say, "In fact, I think our former church felt more like a country club than a sanctuary. Sad to say, Doc and I were religious but lost! There was no peace in my life. I was afraid of dying too! In fact, whenever I had to get on an airplane, after buckling myself in the seat, first thing I would call the stewardess and order a cocktail! I thank God that accepting Jesus has changed all of that. God gave me peace."

The conversion of this prominent couple, well beyond middle age, opened a new way of living. When Doc had major heart surgery, his new church family rallied around him with unexpected care. The Joneses found not only encouragement but also a calling as a result of SMI folks' compassion. Wanting to give back, they reordered their lives.

Hammond began witnessing and not just practicing medicine in his office. Kay gave up a busy social life to give more time to church work and then, going a step further, joined her husband's office as a receptionist. She did not need a paycheck, but she did want a ministry. Even though trained as a nurse, the good doctor's wife felt compelled by something more than just assisting her husband's staff. Kay realized she could witness to more people by working at the front desk. Hammond's patients became her mission field. Many times, by the time Dr. Jones greeted patients in the examination room, his wife had already introduced them to the Great Physician while in the waiting room.

Dr. and Mrs. Joneses' love for the Lord, as well as their gratitude for the Pastor and church that brought them to Christ, led the couple to take a generous step. They offered their property to the church with a generous financial arrangement for SMI. The agreement allowed the Joneses to live there for the remainder of their lives. With the couple's blessing, even before they moved or went to be with the Lord, their property became an action spot for SMI ministries. The swimming pool was used for baptisms and swimming lessons. Their living room hosted Bible studies and outreaches. The downstairs family room eventually became the singles ministry center. Part of the land became a parking lot while the beautiful lawns hosted many church picnics. Greater than the transformation of the property was the transformation of the property owners—all because they found SMI to be the place "Where the Love Is."

MIRACLE '80

When the church was still a newcomer on Tyler Road and only the worship building completed, the adjacent land on the tiny island, vital to future development, became the property of a developer. To a church member's horror, driving past one morning, a bulldozer was on the land and about to break ground.

The church member stopped his car, got out, and ran up the embankment, shouting to the surprised construction worker.

"You cannot build here! Our church needs this land!"

The uncertain workman stopped his machine and called his boss. Negotiations soon followed. The developer readily agreed to a sale, and seemed relieved to do so.

She confided to church leaders, with an uneasy laugh, "I thought this land was cursed! Every time the workers tried to start, some hindrance would come up. If it wasn't the weather, then a machine would break down. I think your church was meant to have this land!"

SMI's education buildings now stand on the site.

The term "miracles," perhaps subject to sloppy misuse in the modern church, does aptly describe much of what happened in the founding of SMI. Like Old Testament patriarchs retelling wilderness miracles to the younger generation, SMI's Pastor and founding members never forgot and oft re-told what God did in the church's life. The telling became holy inspiration for newcomers to catch the vision and appreciate the fact that they literally walked on holy ground.

SMI miracles were never taken for granted, and for some, came to be expected, if not always by the congregation then by the community. By 1979, SMI's sanctuary could no longer hold all the crowds coming. Two morning services and folding chairs in the aisles could not keep up. It was time to ex-pand the auditorium. The projected cost exceeded one million dollars. Dick and the church Board again launched a bond program. The effort fell flat with less than half a million dollars sold. Interest rates were climbing and so bonds were no longer an attractive investment. Even more stinging was the rebuke of a friend of the ministry. When a church member approached this man about buying a bond, he seemed crestfallen.

The man said, "I cannot believe that SMI—with all the miracles that have taken place there—has to resort to selling bonds."

It was a loving reproach, and after he heard about it, one that Dick took to heart. He went away for a few days to attend a church leadership con-ference and to get some alone-time with the Lord to seek His direction. As a banker, Dick knew what his options were. As a pastor, however, he wondered if God might have some higher plan in store for SMI. With an open Bible and an open heart, SMI's Pastor sought God's will. When Dick returned home, he shared the vision God gave him—a fund-raising plan right out of the Old Testament and carried out by Moses. With the start of a new year and a new era in SMI's continuing miracles, Dick named the new approach to fund-raising "MIRACLE '80."

From the pulpit, across his desk, and over restaurant tables, Dick told the story.

As I read the Bible, asking the Lord to show me how to raise the needed money for His work, I began read-ing in the Old Testament about Moses' plan to gather the materials to construct Israel's first worship center. Because

God's people had not yet reached the Promised Land, they still lived their lives as nomads, so their House of Worship had to be portable. It was a Tabernacle—that is, a tent! It had to be large enough for the worship services, and fine enough to be worthy of God. To pay for it, Moses invited believers to donate not just money but their stuff, to give from the best and excess of their possessions. People responded with open hands, and they gave because of their gratitude for all that God had done for them. And the gifts poured in—jewelry, coins, and other costly goods. The idea caught my imagination. We could do the same today!

In January 1980, Dick began sharing his vision for Miracle '80. An aggressive bond sale was halted. The remaining money needed would be raised from the gifts of God's people.

Dick continued to retell the story of Moses, explaining the plan God gave him to finish paying for the sanctuary expansion. The challenge was simple and open-ended: people who had a burden to give could present whatever the Lord put on their hearts. Ushers distributed offering plates, passing them up and down the pews, and what came back was unlike any offering they had ever received. The offering plates came back heavy-laden not just with cash and checks but also with diamond rings, watches, and even automobile keys. The gifts continued until not only the offerings but also the stories behind the giving became part of the miracle.

Dick led a local medical doctor to Christ, and shortly thereafter he and his wife reconciled after a nasty divorce. Now part of the SMI family, their marriage healed as they grew in faith.

The doctor stopped Dick one day and said, "My wife and I are so grateful to God for what the Lord has done for us through this church that we want to be part of Miracle '80. We have prayed about what we could give. Would the church accept a house?"

The doctor no longer needed the expensive bachelor pad he bought for himself, and so the reconciled couple donated it to the church.

Some folks came with tears and others with smiles and laughter, but all with willing hearts. After every service, more stuff continued to come in— golf clubs, art work, gold jewelry, photography equipment, coin collections, and land deeds. SMI's church house, for a while, became a storehouse. Various nooks and crannies were taken over to hold donated items, including the closet in the Pastor's office. Dick opened it one day, and there was no room to hang his own coat. It was filled with all kinds of furs donated by women of the church—mink, sable, fox, you name it and it was there.

One woman, who came to Christ out of a cult, asked the church to accept the deed to out-of-state land that she and her husband owned. They had planned to build a vacation home on the site one day, but now they wanted SMI to have the lot for Miracle '80.

A quiet young man, a bachelor who thrived in the new believers' classes at SMI, came with his gift—a rare Impressionist drawing.

A couple in the church with two young children had a small collection of silver coins kept in a mason jar. They shared the reason for their sacrificial gift.

"This is really the only savings we have. We keep this glass jar wrapped in a towel and hidden in the back of our linen closet. Whenever we go on vacation, when we get back home, one of the first things we do is check to be sure the jar is still in its safe place. We don't want to be possessed by our possessions. Besides, we want to trust the Lord for our emergency needs. God has told us to give it all to SMI for Miracle '80."

The solid silver coins had a face value of only $150, but in 1980 the silver market spiked. The gift was later valued at around $7,000. This gift took on miraculous proportions, and it happened over and over.

The Associated Press picked up a story about the Alabama church with a creative approach to paying for a new building. Some mocked the Pastor and church when they read the story, but others were inspired. Churches from the East and West wrote to encourage SMI in this faith venture. More importantly, the Lord knew the integrity of the Pastor and cause, and so too did the congregation.

One church member described the whole experience.

"We reached a new level of dedication, excitement, and sacrifice—hilarious giving!"

The Miracle '80 offering built faith as well as a building. God's plan, so contrary to the expected way of doing fund-raising, led to a defining moment for many in the congregation. By 1980, the majority of the church membership only heard the inspiring stories of SMI's beginning from the pioneers who met in the insurance building or school cafeteria. It was before their time. But now they were living participants in the ongoing "Miracle on the Mountain" that was Shades Mountain Independent Church.

Jesus taught His disciples that their hearts would follow their treasure. Because of their sacrificial giving, many SMI families found a renewed love for their church and felt a greater part of its mission to reach the mountain for Jesus Christ—all because they yielded their treasure and their hearts followed.

CHAPTER ELEVEN

Orientation: Ministry 101

*A*fter Dick Vigneulle formally accepted the pastorate of Shades Mountain Independent Church, the first thing he did was leave town.

"I need to learn how to be what I've become," he explained with a grin to the SMI Board.

The church family gladly encouraged him to take a month to travel and visit other ministries.

"EVERYTHING RISES AND FALLS ON LEADERSHIP"

His first stop was Chattanooga, Tennessee to visit Dr. Lee Roberson, Pastor of the famed Highland Park Baptist Church and Founder of Tennessee Temple University. Dr. Roberson, by then a veteran soldier of the cross, had taken a sleepy little Baptist church and built it into a six thousand-member congregation.

The Highland Park church's multifaceted ministries modeled the kind of church Dick envisioned for SMI—from Camp Joy to satellite chapel sites, an inner-city mission and a global mission network, Christian schools with classes for students from kindergarten through college and seminary. Dr. Roberson's radio program called *Gospel Dynamite* was one of the oldest, continuing broadcasts in the South, and the university built a radio station that grew from ten to 100,000 watts.

Dr. Roberson, a handsome man of imposing stature with a full head of wavy white hair, looked like a modern-day prophet, and his voice boomed like one too. His manners were as dignified as his person. He always dressed in his trademark double-breasted navy suit, ready to preach a funeral or conduct a wedding at a moment's notice.

As the secretary ushered Dick into the university president's office, Dr. Roberson rose and extended a welcoming hand. Dick took a seat in front of the huge desk, his back to a wall of windows that looked out on the suburban campus. Both men shared a passion for soul-winning and a preaching emphasis on the second coming of Christ. But this was more than a social call. From this one visit Dick sought a crash orientation to his new vocation from one of the nation's eminent pastors. It was a meeting of Moses and Joshua, a spiritual patriarch commissioning a new generation's leader.

Church members and students alike found Dr. Roberson readily available, but he kept his appointments brief. The inquirer's agenda needed to be short, and his reason for coming stated early on and clearly. Time would be deducted for small talk. The loquacious visitor was apt to meet an abrupt ending, and the rambler would go away disappointed.

The nature of the man and his mega ministry demanded efficiency. Roberson's extensive travels and speaking schedule took him out of town part of every week. But he never missed any of Highland Park's three main church services: Sunday morning and evening and Wednesday night Prayer Meeting. He held his church members to a strict standard of faithful church attendance—"Three to Thrive" was his motto. He held himself to the same standard. As an added pastoral discipline, he also set aside time for sermon preparation and hospital calling. Consequently, his appointment calendar ordered his day, and he kept pace by keeping his meetings brief. Dr. Roberson would listen intently and then respond to his visitors with direct, brief advice. When he stood up, the meeting was over. As the door opened for his guest to exit, the next appointment would enter.

Dick Vigneulle may not have been aware of it at the time, but his visit broke with tradition. Dr. Roberson lavished personal time on him. After Dick gave a quick rehearsal of his call from banker to pastor, Dr. Roberson, no doubt intrigued, atypically swept aside his schedule to spend time with him. He took his visitor from Birmingham on a walking tour of the church and university campus.

Dr. Roberson, in turn, had his own inspiring life story: a humble, Depression era boyhood in Indiana, living in a chicken coop for shelter; his hard-earned education; and early success as a Nashville radio singer. When a vocal coach promised to have him on Broadway, young Roberson refused in order to follow God's call as an evangelist.

As the two men strolled, they paused in front of church and college buildings one after another. Dick's career in real estate gave him an appreciation for his host's business savvy as well as ministry fervor. Each building led to another story. Instead of storybook pictures, here were brick and mortar illustrations of Lee Roberson's ministry. The quaint Phillips Memorial Chapel was the church building housing Highland Park Baptist Church when he arrived in Chattanooga in the 1940's. Beside it now stood the imposing Chauncey-Goode auditorium where thousands now gathered for worship. As the two pastors walked, hundreds of students whisked past them. Roberson's elder statesman status was obvious by his students' hushed but respectful nods and smiles as they greeted their pastor and president.

The campus walk was interrupted by an unexpected reunion. One of Dick's old professors from Bob Jones University, Dr. Fred Afman, now taught at Tennessee Temple. The two met during the walking tour. Dr. Afman was a trusted counselor when Dick left BJU as a college graduate to launch a business career. His beloved professor was in his path once more, now at another significant but midlife change of course. Dr. Afman never forgot one of his students. A tall, lanky man with a laid-back manner, he offered a wide smile as he shook Dick's hand.

"Dick Vigneulle! What are you doing here?"

Dick condensed twenty-five years of his life into a two-minute testimony, giving a quick canvas of post-university life. Greenville to New York City to Birmingham. Salesman to banker to preacher.

Both men wore weathered countenances that traced the years that separated them. But here they were again, teacher and student on a university campus, albeit a different one. After hearing about Dick's call to the pastorate, Afman affirmed his former student. The old prof spoke as if pronouncing a blessing, and Dick listened as if it were a prayer.

"You can do it, Dick. You will make a great pastor. Remember the things old Dr. Bob taught you. And your experience as a businessman will give you insight for building a ministry, and it will give you authority as you evangelize business people. I am proud of you."

The meeting was a God-moment as Dick's past caught up with the present, and his history affirmed his future.

As lunchtime approached, the tour ended and so too Dick's time with

Dr. Roberson. Hearing the story of Highland Park Baptist Church and Tennessee Temple University—from the Pastor and Founder himself—inspired the newly called preacher. Roberson's parting advice was the simple admonition that Lee Roberson constantly repeated to his staff, congregation, and students. It was his personal creed.

"Everything rises and falls on leadership."

"THINGS WON'T HAPPEN IF YOU DON'T HAVE A VISION!"

The following day, Dick and Peg were back in their car, driving closer to the Mason-Dixon Line. The road to their next stop on the tour turned northward to Lynchburg, Virginia, a small city that lies along the Fox River, about one hundred and sixty miles southwest of Washington, D.C. Beautiful countryside led the way, woodlands interspersed with the pastures and barns of gentlemen farmers and horse breeders. The bucolic setting belied the trip's serious mission.

Dr. Jerry Falwell and Dick – circa 1980s

The Vigneulles looked forward to a meeting with Dick's old friend, Jerry Falwell, Founding Pastor of the mega church Thomas Road Baptist. He also founded Liberty University, one of the fastest growing Christian schools in the world, and the college the Vigneulles' twin sons now attended.

Dick's meeting with Dr. Roberson had the tone of a father-son session, but with Falwell it was a meeting of brothers. Jerry Falwell was already familiar with Dick's story and knew about the fledgling church on Shades Mountain. Dick had a grocery list of questions about being a pastor, and he had barely begun his inquiries when Dr. Falwell interrupted with a job offer.

"Dick, I can find a pastor for that little church on the mountain. No problem! Why don't you and Peggy move to Lynchburg so you can join my staff? I need a man like you with your knowledge of banking and business. What do you say?"

Complimented but not tempted, Dick politely declined.

"No, Jerry. I know that God has called me to pastor SMI, and God wants us to reach that mountain for the Lord."

The conversation moved outside. A heavy snowfall blanketed Lynchburg, so the school, like much of the city, was closed, enabling Dr. Falwell to spend the entire day with Dick. Falwell chauffeured his Alabama guest about campus, picking up an extra rider to share in the camaraderie. Sumner Wemp, who had preached often at SMI when he was President of Southeastern Bible College in Birmingham, now was part of Falwell's staff.

Dr. and Mrs. Sumner Wemp (Celeste), Peggy, and Dick. Dr. Wemp, known for his "Well, Glory" statement, preached often in the early 1970's at SMI when he was President of Southeastern Bible College – photo taken early 2000's

"Well, Glory!" Sumner's familiar exclamation rang out in a joyful reunion of old friends.

Dr. Wemp wanted an update on SMI. Like three old soldiers exchanging war stories, the three men, all dedicated soul-winners, swapped stories about folks brought to Christ. Dick counted both Falwell and Wemp as close friends, let alone inspirational heroes. Their fellowship as much as their counsel strengthened his spirit.

The behind-the-wheel tour would be interrupted by frequent stops along Liberty Mountain as Falwell would hop out of his car, his Birmingham friend in tow, and trudge through snow or along scraped but slippery sidewalks. There were buildings to see and people to meet.

While walking through an academic building, Dick made a new friend, Dr. Harold Wilmington, theologian as well as prolific author and now faculty member at Liberty. Even at this first introduction, there was an instant connection. Dick respected Wilmington's scholarship, and from their first meeting, the spark of kindred spirits started a lifelong friendship. For years to come, Dr. Wilmington's Bible knowledge and pastoral insights would be a reliable source for the banker called to preach.

Back outside, continuing the tour, Falwell beamed with saintly pride over his campus and students. Dick saw the same look of satisfaction mixed with anticipation in Lee Roberson's face when they walked across Tennessee Temple's campus a few days before. But he could not help but chuckle at the polar opposites the two men were. Roberson, while a gracious host, was serious-minded and maintained a sort of old-world formality. His students all revered him, and a few perhaps feared him. He was a dignified statesman who never forgot his manners. Falwell, on the other hand, walked among his students as if he were their favorite uncle. He loved fun, and antics marked his style. He was apt to pitch a snowball at a Liberty student or teacher as the men walked the campus. Even more surprising, they threw snowballs back at him!

Levity and high jinx aside, Dr. Falwell was serious about the Lord's work. But his casual style connected him to a younger generation and one closer to his own age. Jerry Falwell was a stalwart fundamentalist in his beliefs, but innovation and daring marked his approach to ministry. Dick admired that.

Jerry Falwell had returned to his hometown of Lynchburg in 1956, right after his graduation from Baptist Bible College in Springfield, Missouri. He started his church from scratch. He and his tiny start-up congregation moved into the old Donald Duck Bottling Company building. Before church workers could paint the walls, layers of cola syrup had to be scraped and scrubbed off. The sprawling campus testified like living stones to what a man of faith could accomplish.

While invading ministry with a larger than life personality, each man held secure in his personal identity, driven by a sense of destiny. They shared a gregarious love for people. Their interchange, so typical of both men, was charged with laughter and humor. But both were serious about ministry, determined to be leaders in their generation, not just observers. Serving God successfully meant making a difference.

As the sun set on the mountain, Dick's visit drew to a close. A whole day's discussion could be summed up with Falwell's parting challenge to SMI's newly called Pastor.

"Dick, things won't happen if you don't have a vision."

In a short time, Dick's tour had brought him before two giants of his era, and both affirmed his call and neither doubted his future.

Both men seemed to say, "The God who called us has called you. We have tried and proved Him, and you can too."

Dick would never forget their advice, their voices still ringing in his ear. Each man's perspective resulted in wise counsel that served as bookends to prop up his spirit as he too would dare to believe God for the impossible. Dr. Roberson's testimony issued a standard for the Pastor not just the congregation that followed him: "Everything rises and falls on leadership." Likewise, Dr. Falwell's warning about vision reinforced the standard by which a man or ministry would be judged victorious or a failure—a judgment meted out by peers and history.

From Virginia, Dick and Peg continued on to Wilmington, Delaware and a family reunion with two of his sisters and their pastor husbands. Existing loving family relationships took on a new dynamic now that Dick was a Pastor and Peggy a Pastor's wife. Here Dick could learn some of the practical, daily aspects of a pastor's life and routine. His family affirmed not only the couple's call to SMI but also their God-given gifts to accomplish what the Lord had in store.

As the tour ended, wrapping up Dick's crammed orientation sessions for the pastorate, it was time to return home. But there was one more lesson for him to learn about a pastor's life.

Dick found the heavenly rapture of the inspired visits dispelled, if only momentarily, by earth's harsh realities. The global oil crisis going on in the early 1970's resulted in gasoline rationing across America. As Dick drove down the highway and night fell, his mind raced faster than his Buick. Memories of the trip crowded with his planning for the future. Dick failed to notice the gas gauge until it was near empty. In the middle of nowhere, he pulled into the first gas station he saw. The dutiful, young station attendant carefully measured out the limited supply that rationing allowed. But it was not enough gasoline to get the Vigneulles home. The hour was late, and Dick was tired, and so he arched his brows and spread his smile into an exaggerated but sincere plea.

"Ple-e-e-ase, young man, won't you go ahead and fill the gas tank so this tired preacher can get home to Alabama?"

The young man smiled, nodded, and continued to pump gas till the tank was full. By the time Dick arrived back in Birmingham, because of the young attendant's concession, he acquired a final road-trip lesson: preachers have trials, and sometimes privileges.

CHAPTER TWELVE

Get on Board!

$\mathcal{D}$ick left City Federal in January 1974, made his tour of churches in February, and then returned to Birmingham in time to be in the pulpit on the first Sunday in March. This was his first sermon as the full-time Pastor of Shades Mountain Independent Church. Not surprisingly he preached a sermon about vision. The service witnessed a prophetic moment as Dick defined his role and how he would lead the church. The title of his message was *GET ON BOARD!*

According to his own description, it was not a sermon so much as a sharing of the latest saga since his bank resignation. He told about his visits to Tennessee, Virginia, and Delaware. He confided to his flock pastoral excitement and holy anticipation about his future and theirs.

GLORY BOUND!

"When I left City Federal a couple of months ago, I left a dream job— one I loved very much. And I could say the same about my boss and the people I worked with. But I knew without any doubt that God was calling me to SMI full time. After I resigned, however, I spent several sleepless nights. You all know I love a challenge, but becoming your Pastor is the biggest job I've ever undertaken. In fact, this is the most sleepless job I've ever had!"

Until now, the audience sat motionless and quiet, intent on hearing every word, but now they nodded and chuckled.

Dick continued, "As I lay there in bed, trying not to wake Peg, I would just pray and cry out to God over and over. And the Lord kept taking my mind back to the same verse. I knew God was speaking to me. His message to me that night is my message to you this morning: WHERE THERE IS NO VISION, THE PEOPLE PERISH."

A favorite gesture in Dick's preaching – A fond memory for many who trusted Christ after his sermons

The text of his message that morning, Proverbs 29:18, would become the lifelong theme of his ministry. His followers still hail Dick Vigneulle as a visionary, whether describing his character or the energy of his sermons. And now, on his inauguration Sunday, the congregation knew vision would chart the course of his pastorate.

As he began his new job, Dick was troubled by the knowledge that many churches and ministries that started well did not finish well. He issued a warning to the congregation.

"Folks, those churches started out on fire! They were serious about winning the lost and sending out missionaries and building schools. But then something happened, and those ministries began to fade. They became watered down. They became anemic. And finally those ministries became buried in the dust of obscurity and mediocrity."

The congregation again grew still. His voice was familiar, but there was a new urgency in their Pastor's spirit. Dick wanted to inoculate his people against compromise and failure with a shot of vision.

"SMI folks, hear me now! Do you know what happened to those poor churches and preachers? They lost their vision! Don't let that happen here. God has called us to reach this mountain for Jesus Christ! And if we can reach the mountain—and we can—then we can reach the world too! Amen?"

His excitement bordered on agitation. Then as his rhetoric calmed, Dick began to tell a story, an illustration he picked up from Sumner Wemp.

Folks, remember this. The church is like a passenger train. On board is an engineer, along with conductors, stewards, and waiters—all with different jobs to keep the train running and on track, as well as to care for and protect the passengers. Filling the train cars are travelers who have boarded too—all kinds of people with varied histories and appearances. These passengers are busy doing all sorts of things—reading books and newspapers, watching passing scenery outside the window, eating in the dining car, conversing with friends, or getting acquainted with strangers. But they all have one thing in common: they are all going in the same direction! And they have a shared destination! Folks, that's a picture of the church, or at least the way the church should be. We are united in Christ, and we all have a job to do. And together we are all glory bound!

Dick's burden was not just for a church united, but one united by a shared vision.

"Beloved, precious friends, I don't believe God called me out of one of the best jobs in the business world that a man could have to come and sit on my hands. Let's believe God for great things. This church is God's lighthouse on the mountain."

When preaching, Dick used few notes. His outlines were not complicated and often written out in his own hand. Dick was never still on the sanctuary platform. His pulpit became his launch pad. And like a satellite he orbited the stage. On a few occasions he would saunter over to the piano, slide onto the bench and begin to play, never veering from his message. Seamlessly his sermon moved from sentences to songs. To his own accompaniment, he would sing out hymns, serenading listeners. On other occasions, such as today, he walked to the platform edge

Sometimes Dick would sing at the piano during his preaching. Tenth anniversary of his becoming pastor of SMI – 1984

and down a step or two closer to his audience as if to confide a secret.

"From our corner here at the intersection of Old Tyler Road and Tyler Road, we can touch the world! Someone said, 'If you aim at nothing you're bound to hit it.' God has given me big plans, folks. You may be thinking, 'Come on, Dick, get your head out of the clouds—you're just dreaming! This is ridiculous!' But I would remind you, WE SERVE A BIG GOD! I challenge this congregation today to catch the vision. Let God's vision for this place and for you stir your souls! Let God's vision for SMI thrill your imagination! Let it grip your heart!"

SMI was about to begin a new journey. The excitement in the sanctuary that morning was like the thrill of travelers in a great train terminal about to embark on the trip of a lifetime. Jesus was the Engineer. And like a train conductor making a final boarding call, lest any stragglers be left behind, Dick cried out to his people.

"Come on SMI, GET ON BOARD! Men, women, and young people who are called of God—GET ON BOARD! All of you—GET ON BOARD!"

The congregation shuffled not with restlessness but anticipation. The Holy Spirit moved on hearts as Dick continued to preach, issuing a serious warning.

Past successes, his own and SMI's, were no guarantee of future successes.

"Too many churches get sidetracked! They get off on some minor issue. And before you know it, they are going nowhere! Have you ever seen a train car disconnected and off on the side of the train yard? There may even be workers bustling with activity inside that car, but they are going nowhere! Uncoupled from the train and separated from the engineer, a sidetracked car is not moving. It is standing still."

SMI's preacher grew more passionate, his voice rising with fervor. He preached his first sermon as Pastor as if it were his last.

"Folks, there can be no standing still in the lives of Christians or the work of the church. God has given us a vision to accomplish. We must not become sidetracked by doctrinal squabbles or people conflict or small-mindedness. We are one in the Lord! There are lost souls to be won to Christ! This church must be an outreach center to the world! We have a ministry to build, and God has called you to be a part of it. If we forget or become idle, the vision and its potential will die and so too will our people."

Excitement continued to build in the sanctuary, as church members smiled and nodded to affirm one another in agreement with their Pastor's message.

"There's a job for everyone in this church. And the train is pulling out of the station today—are you on board? I can't do what God has called me to do without you."

Then he repeated the call.

"All aboard for a church with a vision! No detours! No sidetracking! No griping or complaining! Let's all get on board! Let's reach this mountain for Jesus Christ!"

Yet again Dick repeated the call.

"Let's get on board and reach this mountain for Jesus Christ! And let our vision here at SMI go beyond this mountain we stand on today until we have reached the world! The whistle is blowing! The train is moving! Last call! ALL ABOARD!"

MAN OF VISION

The church and community loved and esteemed Dick Vigneulle for many reasons. First, his larger than life personality, irresistibly welcoming, embraced anyone and everyone. Second, his business savvy, probably inherited from his father before it was refined by university training and later his banking career, brought clarity and order to anything he led. Another of his charms was his music. From college days on, he found music as a means to minister as well as rally a following. He won admirers with his music skills, whether playing the piano or singing a hymn.

One follower suggested, "He was a musician first and a preacher second."

Melodies and keyboards did more than convey his message. Music became Dick's shepherd's staff, a tool to call and guide his flock.

Another point of admiration was his zeal and fruitfulness as a soul-winner, making him the poster boy for the spiritual gift of evangelism. Countless friends, co-workers, and later SMI church members became believers because of Dick's personal witness. God had used him to bring them to Christ, and so their gratitude engendered loyalty to him. And when he said the Gospel can change lives, they knew it was true from personal experience.

But there was a crowning jewel that folks treasured in Dick as a Pastor: he was a visionary. His capacity for vision strung together all his other gifts like pearls on a string. Dick was a visionary in business and in ministry. Whether they served on the church Board or listened from a pew, church members thrill to recall Dick's vision—for the church at large and for their individual lives too. As he led SMI, even from its earliest days as a lay Pastor, Dick created a stir by setting goals and dreaming dreams.

His vision was a gift separate from and beyond leadership skills. His training and offices prompted him to think long range and lay out plans. This defined leadership, and he required the same of his employees, whether at the bank or the church.

But Dick's power as a visionary, to his followers' thinking, was something more. There was a difference between being a good leader and a great visionary, like the difference between a vocation and a calling, or a natural talent and a spiritual gift. Goals came from men, but vision was imparted by God. A vision, in Dick Vigneulle's vernacular, was a supercharged ministry goal so beyond human expectation that it required more than daring from believers. It required faith. Vision for him was a goal so unlike-

Original sanctuary filled to capacity

ly or impossible that only God could make it happen. And God would make it happen IF His people believed and took action.

Not only could SMI's Pastor shape a vision, he also could impart it to his followers. Not all leaders are imaginative, and only the truly great ones can light a visionary fire in others.

When Dick would share his vision for the congregation, SMI listeners were no longer sitting on a pew in a Southern church. They were pilgrims at the foot of Mount Sinai ready to receive a message from on High. Passive Christianity became energized by a new-found zeal for God and the church's mission. Dick's vision became everyone's vision, and the result was a collective partnership, transforming their faith into a lively experience that made God real and their lives purposeful.

Jimmy Haley, Dick's brother-in-law and Assistant Pastor for many years, knew him behind the scenes and on the platform, as a banker and later as a Pastor. When asked what Dick was like as he shifted from business executive to full-time Pastor, Jimmy answered quickly with a straightforward observation. There was no change.

"He was still Dick. He had a charisma. You could not know him and not love him."

Dick's sanctified imagination allowed him, at times, to see the future so clearly that he could describe it with the detail and authority of a historian recounting the past. And when he spoke, he did so with the passion of a father and the courage of a Moses. One could trust his "father," and who would want to be left behind by Moses? Consequently, his followers rallied and caught the vision.

Misguided hero-worship could not be tolerated. Dick's aim was to transfer loyalty and confidence in an earthly leader, the pastor, to the Lord Himself. His higher goal was to build faith not just church buildings. He echoed Paul's admonition, "Be ye followers of me, even as I also am of Christ" (I Corinthians 11:1/KJV).

His dreams for the SMI ministry, fired by his sure conviction they were God-given, called the church to faith and action. In fact, one of his popular maxims, repeated in private and proclaimed boldly over and over from the pulpit, reminded believers that vision requires a proactive faith.

"You cannot operate in faith unless you step out in faith."

And step out he did! Action marks the difference between a dreamer and a visionary. The former only has big ideas, but the latter acts on them and brings them to reality. Vision for this Gospel General did not end at a table mapping out strategies but rather culminated in a battle cry and charge to victory.

Whatever the task the Lord put on Dick's heart, he first tested it with long periods of prayer. Then he shared with the church Board. By the time the congregation heard, the plan was not something that SMI might do but rather what the church must do!

Sometimes following the Lord meant taking small steps and other times big ones.

A needed building for the expansion of Shades Mountain Christian Schools and Sunday School classes - 1977

Early on, soon after agreeing to remain with the small group meeting in the Hoover insurance building, he challenged the crowd of forty or fifty folks to double their size.

"Folks, start inviting your neighbors! Tell them you know this crazy banker who has a message they must hear. Let's start knocking on some doors! We need to be inviting strangers too!"

The challenge came in spring, and those believers caught the vision. By the fall church attendance doubled. Five years later, Dick stood before a congregation numbering five hundred. And more would follow. People had caught the vision!

Another example of Dick's engineering a vision to reality came in the early summer of 1974, just a few months after coming to SMI full time. During a Sunday night installation service for new church Board members, he called out ministry after ministry that the community needed and SMI could provide—

Dick and Dr. Bruce Peters (Principal and Administrator of SMCS and Director of Christian Education) – circa late 1970's

A typical classroom scene at SMCS

provide, that is, if the congregation had vision. Believers must have faith to believe and courage to put their faith in action. Near the top of Dick's list of new ministries that night was a Christian school to provide young people with a Christ-centered education without sacrificing academic excellence. The church caught the vision and stepped out quickly. That fall Shades Mountain Christian Schools opened its doors.

Dick served a community of largely educated, independent thinking people. This was not a crowd easily swayed. Many were used to leading not following, and their professional mindset accompanied them to church.

Typical of human nature, these movers and shakers might have expected to make things happen by human effort not faith and prayer. If God was regarded at all, they hoped the Lord would accelerate their efforts and sanction their opinions. But SMI did not function that way. Christian faith transformed the way SMI folks did business in the marketplace and in the Lord's house.

These people embraced Dick's vision not because they were pushovers, but because, as one member related, "We got excited because we knew it was not just our Pastor's vision, it was God's vision."

———————————

What made Dick Vigneulle credible to his congregation and his power as a visionary so effective?

First, according to the testimony of church folks, his Christian character sterilized any effort from suspicion of his motives and authority. Plans for the future emerged from prayer meetings not just Board meetings. As a result, people were convinced in their hearts not just their minds. The dreams for SMI aimed to uplift the Savior not the preacher, to reach the lost and hurting, not magnify the man behind the pulpit.

Further, people knew Dick was not a silly man, chasing windmills like Don Quixote. Business success proved he had common sense. And his willingness to leave the bank to be SMI's Pastor, at great financial sacrifice and personal risk, roused loyalty from followers. Dick practiced what he preached. And so the congregation believed his vision and joined him in sacrifices and life adjustments necessary to accomplish the mission. People were captured by his example and so did not hold back from following him.

Also compelling was his proven track record. God honored his faith time and again as the "impossible" became reality. Unsaved friends and relatives, hardened to the Gospel, came to Christ. Land deemed unaffordable had become part of SMI's campus. Nothing was off limits, in the will of God.

In addition, Dick was a powerful communicator. The vision became the church's, in part, because he communicated with authority what God required. He was not tentative in demeanor or speech. And he was enthusiastic.

Once God impressed his heart with what needed to be done, he never wavered in belief or pursuit. For a man who knew how to get things done, when his visionary expectations required long periods of waiting, he was not put off and rarely discouraged.

His testimony was constant in public and in private: God honors faith! That faith must be built on God's promises, not earthly appearances: "Now faith is the substance of things hoped for, the evidence of things not seen" (Hebrews 11:1).

Dick repeatedly challenged his flock by saying, "Reality will not be a surprise when you have a vision. Believe God for the impossible!"

His daughter, Diane, remembers growing up and watching her father as a man of unwavering vision and confident faith.

"Daddy and Mother taught me faith as a child not just by what they said but also by the way they lived. When Dad trusted God for something, he never doubted. He was never down in public or at home."

"Roundup Sunday" – Dick initiated an outreach to "roundup" guests to visit SMI – 1980

SMI's vision ventures were not the schemes of capitalists or the calculations of committees, but rather the Spirit-led faith walk of God's people. And their Pastor, Christ's under-shepherd, would clear the path and lead them. The impossible served to include and prove God—without Him it would never happen! Even more exciting, through the testimony of the congregation, God's reputation spreads as a prayer-answering, faith-honoring

Heavenly Father.

A leader must be far-sighted, anticipating needs or foreseeing opportunities even before the crowd does. An ineffectual leader may fail to foresee needs or to set goals. Equally essential, effective leaders must be more than good planners. They must be able to enlist a following. Cooperation cannot be presumed or demanded.

Another more subtle shortcoming lurks. There's a wise saying that the difference between a leader and a martyr is six blocks! The point is, if a would-be leader gets too far ahead of his people, they will turn on him. When a leader fails to create and impart a vision, followers feel abandoned and at risk. Then the leader has run too far ahead of his followers. The breach renders management ineffective. The fearful or short-sighted will not heed his call. Even more costly, such a leader hazards a revolt and overthrow initiated by the very people expected to follow and execute the plan. The would-be champion ends up a victim, a "martyr."

The Lord gave Dick the wisdom and grace to avoid such pitfalls. When he needed to plant the seeds of a vision or quicken the congregation's resolve for a dream yet to be fulfilled, he would utilize a skill familiar to any parent. He would tell a story. Following the example of Jesus, the Master Teacher, SMI's Pastor had a knack for telling living parables. That is, he would recount the episodes of a Bible hero or a miraculous episode from the life of the church. Sometimes these stories were the heart of his sermon, and other times he seemed to interrupt himself to retell them.

For example, he would retell the story of the land offering that came in to the very penny. Or he would call to the platform Glenn Kennedy, one of SMI's venerable pioneers, and relive the night he sat in Glenn's living room and led him to Christ.

No one seemed to tire of hearing their favorites. Veteran members enjoyed reliving their past, and new ones appreciated hearing about their spiritual heritage. The result was more than nostalgia. It fortified courage and energized ambition. "Do it again, Lord!" the congregation seemed to say. And so a vision or dream began.

One church leader, a converted career military man, recalled, "Dick had a unique gift. He was a super storyteller. He could give a mental picture of his vision and communicate so you wanted to be part of it. He could make the unreal seem real. He could involve a person even when they didn't want to do something. That's leadership."

God gave SMI's Pastor big dreams, as sweeping as the vistas from atop Shades Mountain. The congregation never knew when he would pop a new one on them. But they were ready. By the time he finished one of his stories, the unattainable seemed already accomplished.

30 ACRES MIRACLE

Perhaps the ultimate example of Dick Vigneulle's prophetic leadership was his dream to purchase the thirty acres across Tyler Road. The land, now site of Shades Mountain Independent's Family Life Center and high school, was then owned by a corporate giant, United States Steel. Their executives insisted the land was not for sale and never would be sold. Even if a "For Sale" sign sat on the land, the price tag would be huge because of the prime location. On top of that, a gigantic communication tower on the land was a prized asset, pushing the site's value even higher. Ownership seemed impossible not just improbable.

So when Dick began to interrupt his own sermons and point out the huge sanctuary windows to the thirty acres across Tyler Road and declare, "God is going to give us that land!"—well, people believed him. Such was the power of his vision. He described buildings and ministries that would one day stand there, and even if folks could not see the buildings with the naked eye, the faithful believed it would happen with the eye of faith.

One staff member told visitors, "Our Pastor looks at a field, and where we see trees, he sees buildings!"

Dick was never capricious. The church would soon be landlocked on the ten-acre island it filled at the split between the two Tyler Roads. The future of SMI required that never-to-be-sold tract of land. While the history of the church was filled with impossibilities that became realities, the hope of the thirty acres acquisition tested the congregation's vision and loyalty. They wanted to believe, and many did right from the start. But for others, well, earthly obstacles seemed unmovable.

Dick charted his preaching and ministry planning by God's promises, not men's limitations, including his own. An expert real estate developer himself, he knew the critical importance of this real estate acquisition for the ministry. It made good business sense. On the other hand, his business experience told him that for all practical sense, it was absurd to hope U.S. Steel would ever sell the land. But now he was not a banker, he was a Pastor. And this was God's work on the mountain. Bring in the miracle factor and anything is possible in God's will.

The thirty acres became SMI's "Promised Land," and none wanted to be naysayers doomed to wilderness wandering for unbelief. "Thirty acres" no longer numbered land size—it was the name of SMI's biggest vision.

Years passed as time tested the vision. Dick made annual pilgrimages to the U.S. Steel offices in nearby Fairfield, Alabama to meet with the officer in charge of the company's surface properties for the state.

"Sir, our church needs that land. Our congregation is ready! What do you say?"

The U.S. Steel executive shared the Pastor's Christian faith and respected the church's need. But there was nothing he could do.

"Dick, believe me when I say that I've tried. There is nothing I can do. As I have told you before, our company is not in the habit of selling its land. Management feels that property across from your church might be needed down the road. Sorry, Dick. I have to say it again—the thirty acres are not for sale."

Dick would not be put off, neither would his expectations wane. Nor would his spirit sour. He was as persistent as Moses before Pharaoh, pleading for God's people. But in this case, at least, the relationship was cordial not cantankerous. Dick's many repeat visits over six years fostered a friendship as well as kept the dream alive.

Just as Dick never wavered, neither would he allow SMI folks to abandon the dream. He kept the vision alive. To do that he drew on his powers as a raconteur, preaching a story from the life of one of the Bible's greatest generals—Joshua. The account would be repeated so many times that SMI families came to cherish the story as their own.

The sermon, etched in the congregation's heart, came from the Old Testament book of Joshua, chapter four. Moses had died and his captain and successor, Joshua, now led God's people. An earlier generation, under Moses, failed to possess land that God had set aside for them. Defeated by default, they lacked faith to believe it was possible to take ownership. Unbelief dissolved any courage. Lack of faith and failed vision led to outright disobedience to God. The result was loss and confusion, until that wayward generation perished, wandering in a wilderness.

But now a new generation, standing on the shoulders of their ancestors, led by Joshua, determines not to repeat their parents' failure.

As Dick explained the historical context of his sermon text, the SMI congregation quickly caught the parallel.

"Folks, God has given SMI some promised land too! Look out the window across the road. You see those thirty acres? God is going to give it to us. Are you going to believe Him for it? Or are you going to hold back? Are you thinking, 'Preacher, it's never going to happen! We've been told *no* too many times!' Beloved, where's your faith? Believe the vision! Don't let go of God's promises!"

More often than he repeated the O.T. text for a sermon or illustration, Dick would repeat the exercise. Interrupting an order of service or his own preaching, totally out of context to the business at hand, he would raise his voice and bellow out a repeat command.

"Hey, folks, look out those windows to the thirty acres! God's gonna give us that land! Do you believe it! Folks, keep praying. It's gonna happen! Remember, we serve a Big God!"

When Joshua led his followers into the Promised Land, God repeated the miracle of parting the waters. Just as the Red Sea parted for Moses, now the Jordan River parted for Joshua's generation. They were about to step from the wilderness into the land of plenty.

Dick pointed out that as the priests and people crossed over the dry river bed, at Joshua's command, a representative for each of Israel's twelve tribes picked up a stone and carried it to the other side. Once there, Joshua ordered an altar to be built from those special rocks.

Dick called them "memorial stones." God Himself, not just Joshua, wanted the people to remember the miracle they had witnessed. And the altar they built from those memorial stones would stand as an "Ebenezer"— a perpetual reminder of God's power and blessing on behalf of His people. Generations to come would pass that holy pillar, and puzzle as to its significance. Then seizing a teachable moment, their elders would recall the day of miracle, explaining when it was built and why. The memory stones served as an altar of praise to God and a teaching tool for future generations.

One evening, as Dick retold the story of Joshua and the memory stones, he moved the service outside to the thirty acres. The whole congregation followed.

"Folks, tonight we are going to walk these thirty acres and claim this land for the Lord! I want you to break up into small groups, and as you walk, stop from time to time and pray."

This faith walk was not a spur of the moment idea. Days earlier Dick had instructed the maintenance staff to clear a trail through the brush. He wanted a clear, safe path because this walk would be open to everyone—children and elderly included. The preacher and his flock were not guilty of holy trespassing. U.S. Steel had given permission for the church to access the land, and even to use a portion of it for a much needed parking lot.

Before SMI's pilgrims invaded their promised land, their Joshua gave one more command.

"SMI, as you walk these thirty acres tonight, I want you to pick up a stone and bring it back here to the parking lot. When we finish the walk, we're all gonna gather around and each one of you can put your own memory stone on the pile. We're gonna raise up our own Ebenezer right here on Shades Mountain."

And that is exactly what the SMI congregation did. They walked the land. They prayed. They gathered stones. When the service closed, a huge circle of prayer warriors surrounded a rock pile that to them was more precious than gold.

Looking back years later, Dick recalled the event as one of the most important in the church's life to that point.

"I wanted to build the people's faith. We needed a practical expression to demonstrate our faith. And that rock pile was no gimmick. Joshua intended his Ebenezer to be a reminder for future generations, and that's what I intended too. I figured we could take those rocks and build them into a fence or something when God did finally give us the land."

Not just months but years passed, and the thirty acres remained the property of a corporate giant. No matter. The preacher and his followers still believed. And ministry life continued. There was a mountain to reach for Christ.

In 1980, while attending a conference in Washington, D.C. Dick heard his name called out over a public address system.

"Telephone call for Dick Vigneulle. Telephone call for Dick Vigneulle."

Fearing a calamity at home or an emergency at the church, he rushed to find a telephone. He made his way through a crowd to the conference registration desk and picked up a receiver. The voice was familiar yet not one he could quickly identify.

"Hello, is this Dick Vigneulle?"

"Yes, it is."

"Hey, Dick! This is the officer from U.S. Steel down here in Alabama. Remember me? You have visited my office many times but I never had good news for you."

Dick's heart skipped as he tried to steady his voice.

"Sir, I hope you've got some good news for me today."

"I sure do! Dick, if you can be in my office back here in Alabama at 10:00 tomorrow morning to sign a contract, the thirty acres is SMI's!"

"Sir, you realize that I'm up in the nation's capital, but if I have to sprout wings and fly, I'll be there!"

Dick kept his promise, though he used the wings of an airline to do it. He arrived early at the executive's office, accompanied by two men from the church: Leroy Clark, Chairman of the SMI Board, and Greg Beers, Chairman of SMI's Development Committee.

None of the SMI folks would deny God's hand in this land deal. But just the same, why did United States Steel change its mind? That morning they found the answer. According to the story passed down, a newly installed national executive had initiated a policy for the company to sell off any properties not specifically tied to their steel operations. When the Alabama office received its orders, a phone call quickly went through to Pastor Vigneulle.

The contract was signed, on the condition of the church congregation's approval. The price was $10,000 an acre. For a total of $300,000 the land was theirs—land worth ten times that amount in today's economy.

Dick recalls, "I felt as light as a feather. And as hard as it would be, I asked the men to keep the news a secret until Sunday. Then we could announce the good news to the whole church family at once."

The secret held.

As the saints gathered to worship at Shades Mountain Independent Church that Sunday, Dick was antsy as he held back the announcement for a few more minutes. The million dollar sanctuary expansion was underway.

Huge sheets of heavy plastic closed off the new construction area so the original sanctuary could still be used for services. With the platform temporarily dismantled, the pulpit sat on the main floor for the time being. Carpeting was gone so worshipers walked on exposed plywood, making clickety-clack racket whenever they took a step. It was a strange setting for so grand an announcement as Dick was about to make.

During the service that Sunday morning, Dick stepped aside from his pulpit and once more pointed out the windows to the land across the street.

"Hey, folks, look out there at the thirty acres! How many of you believe God is going to give it to us? Come on, folks, how many? Raise your hands as a show of faith. How many of you truly believe it?"

He repeated the challenge his church family heard so many times before. Their preacher was testing their faith once more. But when he repeated the question a second and third time, he seemed to be teasing them. And with each repeat of the question, more and more hands went up till nearly everyone had their hands in the air.

Dick was always animated in the pulpit, like a hyperactive child. Over-the-top enthusiasm was his norm. But on this day, the congregation slowly recognized a heightened excitement in their Pastor. Dick Vigneulle did not walk across the sanctuary floor, he seemed to hop.

"Folks, hold on to your hats! Look what I have in my hand!"

And with that, Dick waved the signed contract with U.S. Steel.

"The land is ours! Praise the Lord! The land is ours! God did it! He gave us the thirty acres!"

The SMI sanctuary that morning made New York City's Times Square on New Year's Eve look like a graveyard. Even sedate church members whooped and hollered. Shouts of "Amen!" and "Praise the Lord!" went up as tears fell down.

The jubilant crowd turned to offer each other celebratory handshakes and hugs. As

Sanctuary expansion construction for "Miracle '80" when purchase of 30 acres announced – 1980

135

they shuffled and stomped their feet, construction dust flew up into the air. While the happy commotion played out, the heavy sheets of plastic popped and snapped. Ten minutes passed before the crowd regained its composure and the preacher could continue. Ordinarily a man who did not like to be kept waiting, Dick did not mind the wait one bit!

If ever the congregation was "All on Board" it was that Sunday morning. And as never before, the folks of SMI were convinced that God's hand was on their Pastor. He was a man of vision—God's vision—and they would follow.

———————————————

There are two ironic postscripts to the "miracle of the thirty acres."

Only days after U.S. Steel began its sale of its extraneous properties, company executives halted proceedings. In a sudden reversal, headquarters issued a directive that property be leased, not sold. The only exception would be those properties already under contract. With its signed agreement, SMI had the little window of opportunity needed. Their deal already struck, the sale held. SMI saw God's hand in the fateful twist of circumstances. As a church historian later wrote, "That's not a coincidence; that's a miracle!"

There was another twist of events, this one a sentimental disappointment. After SMI purchased the thirty acres, the parking lot already on the site was expanded and repaved. The workers saw the pile of stones—the "Memorial Stones" altar from the historic prayer walk—and thought it was just rubble. The monument was knocked down and paved over. Disappointed at the discovery, Dick decided the loss was providential. The best monument for believers would be made of grateful hearts and unfailing memory. Stones and mortar would not be needed after all.

CHAPTER THIRTEEN

Light on the Mountain

A fond tradition for the SMI family, one established soon after Dick's arrival, was the presentation of a giant birthday cake at the church's anniversary celebration every July. Dick adapted the cake idea from Dr. Glenn Tingley, his Pastor at The Birmingham Gospel Tabernacle. Measured in feet not inches, the giant confection was actually dozens of standard size sheet cakes carefully interlaced and stacked by volunteer bakers who worked like brick masons, except they used icing for the mortar. The cake, always in the shape of a cross, would be wheeled out before the congregation, beautifully but simply iced.

Sandy Wheeler, one of the first volunteer cooks, recalls one little boy's excitement when he saw the giant cake: "Wow! I'd like to see the oven that came out of!"

As the number of SMI's converts grew so too did the size of the cake. Dorothy Chapman, who worked on the birthday cake in later years of Dick's pastorate, remembers baking fifty or more cakes to form the giant cross. One year the church's air conditioning was accidentally turned off. In the morning Dorothy discovered her creation melting and the top layer sliding off the base. In a nick of time quick hands and extra icing put the cake back to perfection!

True to tradition, at the height of the Birthday Sunday festivity, Dick would make a request of the congregation, one repeated year after year and always anticipated by the worshippers.

"Folks, all of you who came to Christ through the outreach of Shades Mountain Independent Church, please come forward! Whether it was in one of the worship services, or through one of the ministries like Shades Mountain Christian Schools, or the testimony of a SMI'er knocking on your door that resulted in you accepting Christ as your Savior, I want you to come up on the platform with me right now."

Birthday Sunday cake – annual celebration of SMI's founding in July 1970 – any person who received Christ through SMI or a ministry of SMI placed a lighted candle in the cake.

Standing in eager testimony, people got to their feet and moved to the platform, forming long parallel lines on each side of the cake. Young and old, individuals as well as couples and even entire families, people kept coming until the crowd surrounding the cake outnumbered the SMI members remaining in their seats.

"Here's what I want you to do," Dick would continue. "Take one of the birthday candles handed you by an usher, then light your candle and put it on the birthday cake. Your candle and its light are a testimony of your new birth, your new life in Christ!"

Some moved solemnly and others bounced with jubilation. Parents guided their children's hands, and some couples moved hand in hand. Folks inched along. The platform crowd swelled and then diminished as each person, task completed, returned to his or her place in the congregation. But the burning candles remained, a cluster of tiny flames now shining like one huge beacon.

Again the Pastor spoke.

"Each of those candles is a life, someone reached with the Gospel through SMI. Praise the Lord! And there is something else—don't miss it! Just as these people lighted a candle and placed it in the cake one at a time, that's a reminder how we are going to reach our world for Christ—one person at a time. And let me tell you, just as each man, woman, and young person put that candle on the cake for himself or herself, so you have to decide for yourself—what will you do with Jesus?"

Then Dick would call for the ushers to dim the lights.

"Folks, look what happens when the room becomes dark—the candles just burn brighter! Even one candle by itself casts out darkness, but look how bright the light is when the candles burn together! We are living in a dark world, damaged by sin and filled with people who need the Light of Christ. So remember, SMI, you are here to tell someone else. God wants you to be His LIGHT ON THE MOUNTAIN!

TESTIMONY of GREG & EVELYN BEERS

To kick off a bus ministry, Dick and his staff organized a door-to-door campaign to canvass the neighborhoods surrounding the church. Working its way down O'neal Drive in Hoover, one of the teams reached the home of Greg and Evelyn Beers. Evelyn recalls the Sunday afternoon when she answered the knock on her front door.

"Standing there were two smiling teenagers from Shades Mountain Independent Church. They came to invite our children to Sunday School. Our three girls were not happy in the church we were attending, so our visitors caught my attention. But rather than send our girls with strangers, Greg and I decided to take our children ourselves."

Greg and Evelyn and their three blonde daughters, all with professional model good looks, presented the picture of the perfect American family. But behind closed doors, their marriage held only by a thread. Behind their smiles was a wife suffering deep depression and a husband stifling anger and disappointment.

Washington, D.C. natives, Greg and Evelyn were raised devout Roman Catholics, and Greg was educated in parochial schools. His career path started with the CIA and later shifted to sales and manufacturing. After stints in the Midwest, they moved to Birmingham in 1970. He had accepted a position with a small material handling automation company located in Hoover. The Beers were desperate, however, for more than career success. Greg's description of those days is grim.

"We should have been living the American dream, but instead our lives were a nightmare. Our marriage was falling apart. And I take full responsibility for our marriage failing. I had slowly become a cynical agnostic as well as a

workaholic. I was in a career that was faltering, our finances were in shambles, and I was running with an ungodly crowd of drinkers and gamblers."

Greg was on the road a lot. Weekends he reserved for his own pursuits, preferring to spend hours at the country club and on the golf course, either socializing with buddies or pursuing business contacts.

Evelyn, sinking deeper and deeper into depression, sequestered herself in her bedroom. She did not want her daughters to see Mommy crying all the time.

"Since life seemed to be spinning out of control, I sought professional help, but continued on a downward spiral. After hearing that I would require years of therapy, which we could not afford, I left the therapist's office feeling utterly hopeless."

With seemingly nowhere to turn, Evelyn decided to retreat to her home to sequester herself in her bedroom.

"I drove home feeling more desperate by the minute. At home, I immediately went to our bedroom, grabbed Greg's childhood Bible and fell to my knees. I cried out to God, 'If You're there, please help me!' I randomly opened the Bible to Jeremiah, chapter thirty-three. I read these words, 'If you seek me with all of your heart, you will find me.' These words jumped off of the page as if they were speaking directly to me. Through tear-filled eyes, I prayed, 'Dear God, I am seeking you with every fiber of my being. Please help me to find You.' And He did just that."

Years later, looking back on that life-changing moment, Evelyn says, "My salvation experience was simple and private, but the God Who created the universe had spoken to me. With no Christian friends in my life at that time and so shut off from people all together, I kept to my quest for God. The Word became alive, and I began to get better. My conversion was like the Apostle Paul's, unexpected and followed by three years of discipleship alone with the Lord—Paul in the Arabian desert and me in my bedroom."

Greg was the first to notice Evelyn's transformation. His religious heritage left him unfamiliar with terms like **saved** or **born again**, but he could not deny a remarkable change in his wife. Serenity displaced her fears. In place of the tears and isolation were smiles and hugs. At first, he was relieved that her depression was gone, but soon the "new Evelyn" made him uncomfortable, putting a new kind of strain on their relationship.

"My reaction was that this may be the straw that broke the camel's back. With everything in my life seemingly pointless, to make matters worse I was now married to a Jesus freak. My wife's dependence on Christ and her sudden *interest in the Bible made our marriage even worse for a few months."*

Evelyn's growing faith renewed her love for her husband. She showed it in ways Greg could not ignore.

"Slowly and begrudgingly I noticed Evelyn had a new-found love for me and a willingness to meet me on my grounds, no matter how selfish I was."

Greg softened both to his wife and her growing spiritual pursuits. In small doses, he began to open up to her and talk about faith matters. He even agreed to accompany her to Bible studies, but what he heard there contradicted his religious upbringing. He took offense, and began to argue with himself not just with Evelyn.

"It made no sense to me that God, Whoever He was, would forgive my sins and promise me eternal life simply by my committing my life to Him. As a former Catholic, I felt it ridiculous that God was not interested in my good works. Even though I knew I had no good works, my thoughts were that at some point in my life, I would get busy and cover that base just in case there was in fact a God."

Friends invited the Beers to attend a Pat Boone concert. Greg enjoyed the music, and the entertainer's testimony moved him.

"My eyes were opened finally to the fact that I had failed in my marriage, failed as a father, failed in business. As a last resort I turned my life over to Christ that night. The changes were immediate and dramatic. I stopped drinking, stopped hanging with a crowd that was unhealthy for me, and God opened the doors for me to start a new business."

Now both Greg and Evelyn were eager churchgoers and Bible readers. They returned to the church of their childhood but found the services unfulfilling. The liturgy was beautiful, but they wanted intensive Bible preaching. As lifelong Catholics, if only nominal ones, they found it difficult to break with tradition. Where should they go?

Then the SMI evangelism team knocked at their door.

The Beers often drove past SMI church. Especially on Sunday nights when she typically went to the grocery store, Evelyn would pass the church on Tyler Road and marvel at all the cars filling parking lots. Even more moving were the large crowds of people walking in. What was drawing them? Some nights when the service was underway, she could hear the music of their praise songs drifting outside. Glancing inside the building, she noticed that the congregation looked happy and excited to be in church.

So with little hesitation, after the evangelism team's invitation, the Beers *family decided to give SMI a try. To ease their transition, the family decided to start with the Sunday night services. But their initial visit was unsettling, like a Yankee eating grits for the first time.*

For Evelyn, by then a faithful listener to Christian radio, the service was like a dream come true. Now she could be a part of what she could only listen to on the radio at home. The music, happy praise choruses, and the fellowship of believers, so welcoming and accepting, made her feel right at home.

For Greg, it was a different matter. Steeped in formal religious services, starting with his boyhood parochial schooling and chapel masses, Greg was startled and taken aback.

"Everything seemed upside down. My first impression was a puzzled curiosity. Why were these people so noisy and having so much fun in church? At any minute, I fully expected the ushers to start handing out bags of popcorn."

Any misgivings were short-lived. The entire Beers family, parents and children, was won over. The people were welcoming to the point that the newcomers felt at home in a church they had never attended before that night. The music, so startling at first, appealed to them. Praise choruses and hymns were sung out in lively melodies, not just by the choir but the whole congregation and the Pastor too. Every word Dick preached seemed directed just to them. When he gave an invitation at the end of the service—another Protestant practice that intrigued them—the Beers got excited when people started going forward to accept Christ.

Dick and Peggy Vigneulle made follow-up visits to their home, and soon Greg and Evelyn made SMI their church home.

"Dick and Peggy befriended us," Evelyn recalls. "I was stunned that the Pastor of this huge, dynamic church could even remember our names. We couldn't wait to be at church—Sunday morning, Sunday night, and Wednesday night—all to hear Dick's preaching and teaching. It was life changing for us."

At Dick's behest, the couple attended the New Believers' classes where their spiritual growth quickened. Admittedly a novice in faith matters, Greg embraced his new-found personal relationship with Jesus Christ.

"We were being taught from the Bible by Dick Vigneulle, and he kept reminding us that Scripture is God's Word, written and preserved for us. Dick's preaching made the Bible approachable and relevant to our lives. I found my life changing week by week as I listened to Dick talk about the saving grace of Christ and the Lord's promises to heal broken marriages, to heal broken hearts, to rebuild relationships with our kids, to give us peace in our lives. Good gracious, I

142

was truly a baby beginning to learn to walk!"

Greg and Evelyn's three daughters soon accepted Christ after attending SMI youth events. The Beers family's faith changed their view of each other as well as God, perhaps for Greg most of all.

"My love for Evelyn grew more than I could ever imagine. I realized that she was not simply my partner whom I picked out of a crowd, but rather she was a gift from God to me, someone who could help me become the person that God wanted me to be. This unbelievable journey for me was underway, and I had found a person in my Pastor who was teaching me how to rebuild my life. God gave me a new life, a new start."

Evangelism was Dick's spiritual gift. Evangelism was SMI's core mission. The life of one enhanced the other, setting direction and maintaining accountability for the man and his ministry.

Dick's driving passion for sharing the Gospel made his gift for evangelism obvious, but further proof was his effectiveness in winning people to the Lord. When Dick Vigneulle went fishing for men, he rarely came home without results. Positive results confirmed his giftedness. He led countless numbers of people to accept Jesus as personal Savior.

Naturally and easily, Dick could bring everyday encounters back to life's most urgent question: *What will you do with Jesus?* Whether in personal evangelism or public evangelism, with small groups or large, Dick kept telling the story of Christ. As a result, his example inspired other Christians to witness. By word and deed his life became a constant reminder, affirming the willing and prodding the slackers. His personal example gave him the authority to coax folks into speaking up for the Lord. If his followers would not seize an opportunity to share their faith, then their Pastor would create one.

Greg Beers recalls, "As a new Christian I was not quick to witness publicly for the Lord as I should have, and Dick knew it. Many times when the two of us met at a restaurant for lunch, I would run into old friends and sometimes even my employees and suppliers. When I would introduce my Pastor to them, Dick would put his arm on my shoulder, smile real big and say, 'Greg, have you told this man what Jesus Christ has done in your life?' Back then I got embarrassed, but today I'm grateful."

Dr. Bob Jones Sr., Dick's university president and one of his favorite college chapel speakers, repeatedly prodded his students to be effective

Dick was a fisher of men's souls more than a fisherman! Dick and Peggy with 250 lb. shark he caught in Boca Raton, FL in 1970. (This is a "business" trip?)

witnesses for Christ by being intentional ones. Evangelism means more than just spewing a message. Dick never forgot one of Dr. Bob's proverbs to guide "fishers of men":

"When you throw the net out, you need to bring it back in to gather the fish."

Dick threw out the net often. Furthermore, when he shared his faith, he expected results. Heeding Dr. Bob's instruction, he never failed to gather the net. After sharing the Good News, Dick would then ask for a decision.

"Will you receive Jesus Christ as your Savior and Lord?"

Whether as a college student or banker or Pastor, he never waned in his dedication to evangelism. Dick's love for the Lord and the strength of his biblical conviction that people need to be saved compelled him to share his faith. In fact, it was every Christian's duty to tell others. All Christians have a call on their lives to share the Gospel, just as the Lord commanded: "Go therefore and make disciples of all the nations" (Matthew 28:19a).

Dick's obedience to Christ's Great Commission as well as his intentional style of personal evangelism was shaped, in part, by two personal life experiences.

First, he never forgot his own unsettling teenage experience when he went forward after an altar call at a Christian camp. Because of the unclear counseling he received, he left confused about how to get saved and without any assurance that he truly was a Christian.

Consequently, Dick purposed to present the Gospel in a clear way so that any adult or child could understand. And he always concluded with a moment of decision for the lost person to make a *yes* or *no* decision to receive Christ. Friends, customers, and church visitors typically never left his presence without a clear understanding of how to be saved and a direct offer to pray and accept Christ if they had never done so.

A second influence further shaping his evangelistic zeal was living in the deep South. Life in the nation's Bible belt brought Dick widespread contact with people who were religious but lost. Southerners might be well-versed in religion but clueless about a personal relationship with Jesus. Many lost church members confused infant baptism or confirmation or walking a church aisle for a personal, saving relationship with Jesus Christ. Dick Vigneulle made it clear that religion and its rituals save no one. Neither did an emotional experience or good works and good intentions mean someone was converted, even if their names were written on a church membership roll.

To thwart this misdirected religious zeal, he challenged the notion that salvation was a moral achievement. Dick often used the Apostle Paul's term for salvation—calling it God's *gift*. "For by grace you have been saved through faith, and that not of yourselves; it is the gift of God, not of works, lest anyone should boast" (Ephesians 2:8-9).

TESTIMONY of GLENDA MASSENGALE

Glenda Massengale was a lost church member, and Dick Vigneulle was her Pastor. The longer she sat under his evangelistic preaching, the more unsettled she became about her spiritual state.

The root of Glenda's problem was not a lack of religion but rather too much. From childhood she was a Sunday School girl. She grew up learning Bible verses and singing Sunday School songs. "Jesus Love Me" and "The B-I-B-L-E, Yes That's the Book for Me." She knew them well. Her loving parents were devoted Christians and active members in a little Baptist church near their home in West End, so for Glenda going to church became as routine as brushing her teeth or going to school. And she loved it all.

"My mother played the piano for the service and sat on the front pew. Since there was no nursery or childcare in those days, I sat with my daddy during the church service. I recall one Sunday, while we waited for the service to start, turning through the pages of the hymnal. Daddy used this as a teachable moment. He stopped me and pointed to a word in one of the hymn titles that was unfamiliar to me. 'Cancelled.' 'Glenda, when you accept Jesus as your personal Savior, God will cancel or do away with your sin. I'm praying for you to be saved when you reach an age of understanding.'"

When Glenda was ten years old, a revival preacher came to her church, and her family did not miss a night of the weeklong services. On the last evening of the revival, the preacher warned about hell, the eternal destiny of all those

145

who are not saved. Already under conviction, Glenda fidgeted in her pew. Then the invitation song began—"O Why Not Tonight?" One stanza led to another and then another.

"I continued to stand there, shaking as I held on to the pew. When I put my hands to my face, my cheeks were hot to my own touch. Each time the congregation sang yet another stanza of 'O Why Not Tonight?' I would dawdle, telling myself 'If they sing one more stanza, then I'll go forward.' Finally, I broke away from the pew and headed down the aisle, stepping quickly as if to make up for my delay."

The Pastor greeted the young girl with a smile and handshake. Without further word, he instructed the child to sit down and fill out a card.

Glenda recalls, "The pastor congratulated me and then announced to the congregation that I had joined the church. 'Is that all there is?' I thought to myself. My so-called Christian life began with uncertainties, not security. I walked back down the church aisle to where my parents stood, my heart filling with doubts about what becoming a Christian was all about. How could I be sure I was going to Heaven?"

She stepped out an earnest seeker and returned to her pew a confused one. Too shy to speak up, Glenda kept her doubts and confusion to herself. Always the "good girl" at home and school, still she knew that something was wrong. Glenda stifled her uncertainties so long that spiritual doubts became constant companions she learned to live with.

After entering high school, she dated a good-looking schoolmate, Tom Massengale, who had a reputation for good manners and a Christian faith. Glenda admired his love for God. Tom had accepted Christ as his personal Savior as a boy. Because Glenda and her family were members of the same Baptist church his family attended, Tom assumed Glenda was a Christian too. Their dating life included going to church and youth group activities. As teenagers they both met Dick Vigneulle for the first time when they started attending Youth for Christ rallies where Dick led singing and emceed the gatherings. Tom enjoyed his Christian faith, but Glenda felt tortured by hers. She managed to stifle her doubts and persisted in the mechanics of a pretend Christian life.

"When I was in college, I continued to attend church services some-where faithfully. And I always prayed before a test or exam. I had become a super-achiever, maybe because of my younger brother. He was born when I was six years old, and he was mentally and physically retarded. My parents and I

146

loved him and cared for him, but I often wondered why he was handicapped and not me. I felt that I had to compensate for his disabilities, as if there was something to prove to myself or to make up for to my parents. Looking back, it is sad that I trusted the Lord for a test grade but not my eternal future."

After college, Tom and Glenda married. In time, God blessed them with three daughters. Glenda loved being a wife and mother. Church continued to be a central part of their lives. They became members of Shades Mountain Independent Church after visiting and seeing how real and meaningful Christ was in the lives of the members, especially the Pastor. Her church friends were precious. But without any assurance of her salvation, she became increasingly unsettled.

She confided to a few friends her secret, "I'm not sure that I'm really saved."

Her friends' responses all matched, as if they spoke in unison.

"Glenda, of course you're a Christian. You have a godly family. You love God, and church has always been a part of your life. The devil is just throwing these doubts your way to discourage you. Forget about it!"

Pastor Vigneulle began preaching a series on the Book of Revelation. His confidence about going to heaven made Glenda's doubts churn and increase.

"He was excited about Heaven, and I was scared. To make matters worse, a few nights later I dreamed about the rapture. In the dream, Jesus extended His hand out to receive my husband and children up to Heaven, but not me. As they went up to be with the Lord, I was left behind. When I woke up, it all seemed so real that I reached over to my husband lying beside me to make sure he was still there!"

But the doubts persisted, nagging her soul, leaving her spiritually confused. Soul torment led to damaged emotions and physical stress. Tom, ever the devoted husband, tried to assure her, sharing Scripture verses and tracts, hoping to calm his wife's turmoil.

The three Massengale daughters, Kristin, Kelly, and Beth, each came to faith in Christ.

Kristin, the eldest, while still a preschooler would repeat, "There are two perfect people in the world—God and Mommy!"

Glenda assured her that only God is perfect. Just the same her little girl's confidence in her mother was all the more unnerving.

"How can I let my girls down?"

One evening after listening to Glenda read a Bible story, little Kristin unmasked her mother's charade with a simple question.

"Mommy, are you a Christian?"

Glenda did not want to lie to her daughter and managed to dodge the inquiry. But the showdown with her own child was the final straw. Something had to be done, and so once more she turned to her husband for help.

His own resources spent, Tom decided to look elsewhere for help.

"Honey, I think we need to meet with the Pastor."

The Massengales made the appointment and at the same time clued Dick in to the reason for their visit. Tom accompanied his wife to the church. When they arrived at SMI, Dick was standing in the foyer waiting for them.

"Glenda, bless your heart! You want to get this matter settled, don't you?"

Tears already welling in her eyes, she could only nod yes.

"Let's go back to my office and talk there."

Glenda remembers the day as well as her wedding day and the birthdays of her girls.

"It was April 11, 1979. I was thirty years old. I poured out my heart to Pastor Vigneulle, all my childhood religious training and experiences as well as all my doubts continuing into adulthood. He listened quietly, without putting me down. He was the first person I talked to who did not try to convince me that I was indeed a Christian."

After listening to Glenda, Dick looked her in the eye and spoke gently.

"Glenda, if you were the only sinner ever to live, Jesus would have died on the cross just for you."

"No one ever told me that before. Suddenly I had hope. I knew I had come to the right place."

Dick continued, "Glenda, only God knows what was in your heart when you walked that church aisle as a girl. But since you have so many doubts, so many persisting doubts, and no assurance, would you like to pray with me to receive Christ as your personal Savior? Would you like to get saved today?"

"I sure would," Glenda answered.

It was that simple. Years of doubt ended in ten minutes.

"I trusted Jesus that day to forgive me for all of my sins, to come into my heart, and to be my Savior. The peace and assurance that I had longed to have for so many years was finally mine."

Follow-up started immediately. Right after Glenda's prayer, Pastor

Vigneulle began reviewing Bible verses, turning page after page to promise after promise giving assurance of God's forgiveness. Before Tom and Glenda left his office, Dick prayed for them once more. Then he signed them up for his New Believers' Sunday School class where added instruction would equip them both in their spiritual journey—a shared journey!

Now years later, Glenda continues to rejoice in the assurance of her salvation that has never left her. Her heart overflows with joy and gratefulness.

"God led a businessman, to become a Pastor, to start a church, to lead me to Christ!"

Jesus saves—she is sure He does.

Years earlier when Dick Vigneulle accepted the original SMI group's invitation to come to the Hoover insurance building and speak, his very first message was an evangelistic one: *What Is a Christian?* Years later as the church's lay Pastor and then as SMI's full-time preacher, Dick never veered from the emphasis of his first Sunday sermon.

What kept Dick going and on target was not only his love for people but also his love for the Bible. He respected the Bible as God's Word and as the Lord's plan book for life. The more he read the Bible the stronger grew his resolve to be a soul-winner, and to make soul-winners out of every member of SMI. How could a pastor read the Bible and do otherwise?

One of Dick's classic messages, *The Ministry of a True Church*, raised a standard to rally everyone who claimed membership at SMI. Aimed to shape their doctrinal beliefs, his sermon outlined three convictions that formed a progression that would transform how Christians lived.

First, love for God should lead to love for God's Word, a commitment proven by reading and studying the Bible. Second, Bible study then informs and empowers the Christian to do God's will. Even a new Christian can quickly recognize that God's Word calls believers to tell others—at home and abroad. Finally, that obedience mandates personal involvement to evangelism and missions.

How could an honest Christian do otherwise? A born-again believer's gratitude for God's forgiveness should compel a willingness to tell others about Jesus Christ. To Dick it was obvious and inescapable. In fact, he often repeated a compact personal statement of faith.

"Folks, God said it! I believe it! And that settles it!"

Their Pastor's strong convictions and pulpit commands quickened SMI members' understanding of their church's mission and the reason God planted it on the mountain. Church membership was not for a cultural experience or social gathering. Neither a country club nor a lodge, SMI was a mission station. Members must be participants not observers. The Gospel message must be shared, and Shades Mountain was their mission field. Dick and the church had a job to do. He held out a warning and a promise.

"Folks, to accomplish this, it won't just happen. It's warfare—a battle! It will cost us something, but the rewards will be fantastic!"

Not everyone agreed with Dick's plan to bring more people into the church. After SMI's attendance reached about four hundred, one member pulled the Pastor aside in the church foyer. Grabbing Dick's arm, he issued a complaint.

"Dick, the church is just right as it is right now. Let's not grow any bigger. There's a real good spirit in the church. If SMI gets any bigger, we'll lose the closeness we all feel."

Neither put off nor put out with the man's misguided objection, Dick gave a calm but firm answer.

"Friend, if we keep evangelism—reaching out to others and bringing them to Christ and into the church—as our first priority then there will always be a good spirit here and warm fellowship. But if we mistake fellowship as our first priority, and quit soul-winning, then not only will we not grow, but we'll also lose the fellowship."

TESTIMONY of BOB FLANDERS

As a boy, Bob Flanders attended church at his parents' insistence. Rather than excite him about God, the services turned him off to any interest in religion. Church was boring. It was like sitting through a dull movie, only with hard seats not cushioned ones. The rituals held no meaning, and the sermons failed to grab his attention.

By the time he reached middle school age, Bob had grown too big in stature for his parents to drag him to church. Wearied by their son's continual complaints and his constant bucking of their authority, his parents no longer made him attend. By Bob's teen years, his parents dropped out of church too.

But in high school a churchgoing girl caught his eye, and he followed her to church.

"She was a nice girl—nicer than me! I wanted to clean up my act—you know, clean up my language and stop doing things I should not do. Despite my intentions to turn over a new leaf, I dropped out of church again after several months. Even a cute girl could not hold my attention in church. The services meant nothing to me. Even worse, nothing changed in my life—inside or out. Good intentions got me nowhere."

After high school, Bob joined the Marines. After boot camp he was deployed to Viet Nam. Wartime military training and combat-life experiences hardened his heart even more to thoughts of God and goodness.

But one man changed all that. Bob met a born-again soldier whose life and conversation were marked by a prevailing goodness that even the Viet Cong could not tear down. A model soldier, he obviously reported to a higher power than the Pentagon or the White House. This believer in a uniform changed at least one other soldier's thinking.

"For the first time in my life, I thought, 'I have met a real Christian,'" Bob recalls. "His name was Daniel McCarthy Thornton. I wanted what he had—a peace that even war could not drive away. I could see in his face that he had a peace in his soul that I did not have. Even the most disagreeable people or situations could not throw him off course. I wanted to ask him about his faith, but kept putting it off. Then I was injured and shipped off to a hospital. I never saw him again, but I never forgot him."

By the time Bob was discharged and returned to the States, he came home with one striking change in his heart.

"I knew that I needed God! But I was still turned off to the idea of church because of my experiences as a kid. And I did not know anyone who was a Christian. When I heard there was a Bible college in Birmingham, I decided that was the place for me. Maybe in that school I could learn how to know God."

Shortly after coming to Birmingham, Bob heard about a Christian night club called "One Way." He went one night to hear Christian entertainer Pat Boone in concert. Still a newcomer with few friends, he drove solo out to the club. Once inside, he surveyed the crowd and then spied an empty seat at one of the tables. He sat down and introduced himself to a pretty girl sitting beside him. Her name was Suzi. She came with a girlfriend. Delighted to discover she was not someone else's date, Bob continued to banter with this smiling Southern girl. By evening's end they were mistaken as a couple by one of

Suzi's old girlfriends. She invited them both to come to her new church—Shades Mountain Independent.

"Bob and Suzi, you guys would love SMI. There is no church building—we meet in a school. And there is no pastor. A banker does the preaching."

Ordinarily put off by the idea of going to church, Bob's interest was piqued by the girl's description of SMI.

"I thought to myself, 'No building? No pastor? That's as non-church as you can get! I want to try that place!'"

Suzi agreed, and together they attended SMI.

On the first Sunday the couple attended, Dick was not preaching. Sumner Wemp filled the pulpit. Then serving as President of Southeastern Bible College, Dr. Wemp agreed to help the young church by assisting Dick with pulpit duties. When the service ended, the crowd did not immediately leave and take off for the parking lot as Bob expected. The people lingered. They seemed to care for one another and tarried to talk and visit. Folks could be seen praying with one another, some holding hands and others standing shoulder to shoulder in small circles. A few huddled in little impromptu care groups. Most stirring of all was the sound of piano playing. Dick had gone to the piano and begun playing hymns. People listened at first and then started singing. Voices swelled until Bob felt as though he was in the midst of a hootenanny—a Christian hootenanny!

"When I finally walked out of the building," Bob recalls, "I looked up in the sky and said to myself, 'If you want to find God, He is here.' It was awesome. I sensed in those SMI folks exactly what I had seen in that Christian soldier in Viet Nam. I knew I had come to the right place to find God!"

After weeks of sitting under Dick and Sumner's evangelistic preaching, Bob got saved.

"Dick gave the Gospel in every sermon and always closed the service with an invitation. I knew what I needed to do. One verse kept pounding conviction into my heart. It was II Corinthians 5:17 [KJV], 'Therefore, if any man be in Christ, he is a new creature: old things are passed away; behold, all things are become new.'" That's what I longed for—to be a new man! Alone in my apartment one Saturday, I fell to my knees and cried out to God. 'If You are real, God, and can take away my past and make me a new person, I give You my life.' That was the day I found the Lord!"

Bob postponed his plans to enroll in Bible college, preferring to get grounded in faith at SMI.

"I filled up notebook after notebook with sermon notes, soaking up the Word of God."

Suzi and Bob married less than a year after their first meeting at One Way. Her upbringing, polar opposite to Bob's, was in a loving, Christian home. Her pastor led her to Christ as a young girl. But after attending SMI with Bob, she began to grow in her faith with an increasing appetite for God's Word.

Soon after his conversion, Bob volunteered as a driver for SMI's bus ministry. He and Harold White, the ministry leader, would spend Saturdays visiting apartment complexes and neighborhoods, knocking on doors, and inviting families to church. If parents were uninterested in going to church but open to letting their sons and daughters attend, Bob and Harold arranged to return on Sunday morning to pick up the children in the church bus.

One Saturday, while visiting the Maison DeVille apartments in Homewood, the two churchmen, now familiar and popular figures with the kids on their route, found themselves surrounded by boys and girls. A crowd grew even before Harold could knock on all the doors on their list.

"Bob, you stay here in the yard and play with the kids while I go round up the rest," Harold directed.

Bob gladly complied. As the children clamored for his attention, stepping on his shoes and jumping to reach his shoulders, Bob loved every minute. It was quite a change of venue for the Viet Nam vet, and even he took notice. The man of war now looked more like Captain Kangaroo.

"My heart was full of love for those kids, and suddenly it hit me. What a change had taken place in my life! My heartfelt love for children, so real and compelling, showed me most of all that Christ had truly changed my life. I knew for sure at that moment that I was a saved man. God had transformed me from a hardened loner to a kid hugger! The Gospel made me a new man."

The change led to a call. Bob and Suzi surrendered their lives to full-time Christian service as missionaries, serving many years in Japan and then later on the staff of World Reach Inc., the Birmingham-based missions organization founded by SMI. In 2008 the Flanders started a new work called SPEAR International Ministries (Strategic Partnerships for Encouragement, Accountability, and Resources).

Not everyone who prayed with Dick proved to be a shining trophy of grace. When people did not follow through on their private confession of faith or else fell away from the Lord and walking with His people, Dick would be crestfallen. Perhaps their profession of faith was not genuine. Perhaps they yielded to the lure of the world.

He took solace knowing that the Apostle Paul experienced similar setbacks in his day. So distressed by one promising disciple who washed out, Paul exposed him by name and laid out the cause of his fall: "for Demas has forsaken me, having loved this present world, and has departed..." (II Timothy 4:10a).

Admitting disappointment, Dick would confront such dilemmas with a bit of self-reproach and his own assessment of the failure.

"I'm afraid they were *my* converts and not the Lord's."

But the washouts did not deter Dick's call. In fact, disappointments only strengthened his resolve to keep on telling folks about Jesus. His church family loved him for his faithfulness, and Christian leaders praised him for it—some despite initial misgivings about the banker-turned-pastor.

Dr. Sumner Wemp is one of the greatest evangelists of the modern-day church. As a pastor and educator, as well as prolific author, he has been a strong voice and conscience of New Testament evangelism.

Sumner and Dick, as well as their wives, cherish a long-standing friendship, dating back to Dick's first arrival in Birmingham. Dr. Wemp was then a pastor, and Dick dropped into his office one day trying to sell his Memory-O-Matic system.

"I didn't buy the system, but I sure admired the likeable salesman's drive," he recalls.

Sumner Wemp witnessed firsthand Dick's rise to the heights of the banking industry and admired his unblemished integrity as a Christian businessman. When Dick started preaching at SMI, Dr. Wemp became Dick's mentor in ministry. He often preached at SMI too, so he knew the banker and the church well.

In 1974, when Dick visited Jerry Falwell right after accepting the full-time pastorate, Dr. Wemp was serving on the staff of Liberty University as Vice President of Spiritual Affairs. He remembers Dick's visit with him and Dr. Falwell and Dick's eagerness to get a crash course in pastoral ministry.

"Jerry knew that Dick had been a big businessman and was concerned that Dick might get sidetracked as a pastor with the administration chores of a large church. Too many preachers are CEO's running a business

154

and not winning souls. Falwell told Dick, 'Whatever you do, keep going after souls. Don't get bogged down in the crazy things of church life and leave off soul-winning.'"

The warning was clear. Dick understood that building a church required long-term commitment to a rigorous outreach plan, visiting homes and knocking on doors, street after street, one neighborhood after another. Fruitfulness in soul-winning would result in a growing congregation and a bigger salvation army to conquer Shades Mountain for Christ. He pledged to keep evangelism the top priority in his private life and ministry.

Later in the visit, when Sumner and Dick were alone, Dr. Wemp reinforced Falwell's advice with the power of the Lynchburg Pastor's example. By then Thomas Road Baptist Church was already a mega church. But it was not always so. Jerry Falwell had come back to his hometown right after his graduation from Bible college.

Dr. Wemp spoke matter-of-factly about the key to Falwell's success.

> When Jerry started his church in Lynchburg, he visited one hundred homes a day, five days a week for one whole year. And on Saturdays, he would telephone folks he had visited that week who had no church home. Jerry would beg them to come to Thomas Road the next morning for church. Dick, you've got to keep that kind of passion. I know you've got it! I've watched you as a businessman and a preacher. Glory! You're consumed with reaching people. Keep it up, Brother. That's the problem with too many preachers—they are not *consumed* with being fishers of men.

Dick dedicated himself to a rigorous schedule of home visits and evangelistic appointments, not just in his pastoral office but in public places like restaurants and workplaces and homes. He would go where the people were and not just wait for them to come to him. Besides, getting away from the office helped avert the distractions resulting from the "tyranny of the urgent."

Peggy often accompanied her husband on evangelistic calls, and together they made a charming, winsome witness for Christ and SMI.

Sumner Wemp's words of affirmation were not glib compliments. He knew that if Dick kept his focus on evangelism, his pastorate would succeed.

Giving him added confidence in SMI's Pastor were his memories of Dick as a prayer warrior.

Wemp recalls, "There were times back in my Birmingham days, when I would be alone with Dick Vigneulle, praying with him before he went out to preach, behind a curtain or a stack of chairs when we were meeting in the school, and Dick would agonize in prayer. He would cry out to me as he paced before the Lord, 'Oh Sumner, we've got to see people saved! We've got to see lives touched and changed!'"

Dick was the same throughout the week.

"When I would meet Dick for lunch," Wemp continued, "his conversation matched his prayers. You can tell a lot about a preacher by what they talk about. Dick would talk about people—folks he had just led to the Lord or folks he was planning to visit. People. That's what mattered to him."

SMI archives include a Sunday bulletin from August 30, 1970 that included an announcement about Thursday night visitation. It reads like an invitation and a command and certainly underscores the Pastor's and the church's serious commitment to evangelism.

> *Want to share your faith? Go visiting with us at 7:00 p.m. It is a solemn responsibility to have in one's possession a reprieve for men under condemnation and then not deliver it.*

From the church's outset, when folks visited SMI, Dick felt they deserved a return visit. Oftentimes he was the one to make it. His publicized business life, as well as the subsequent media spotlight on his call to ministry, gave him an edge when he knocked on someone's door. People knew who he was, and almost anyone would give him a welcome. Dick's celebrity made it easier oftentimes for folks from SMI to win a hearing, at least one time any way.

The church's heritage, as well as Dick's most enduring legacy, would be preserved in the lives of individuals and families changed and rescued. As a result of Pastor Vigneulle's obedience to the call to "Reach the Mountain" and the congregation that collaborated with his vision, SMI shined as God's light on the Mountain.

In time every house on the mountain received a visit from someone at SMI. Most Over the Mountain families knew someone who became a Christian because of the soul-winners from SMI. To advance Christ's king-

LIGHT ON THE MOUNTAIN

dom, the church made its message known, relying on both standard and innovative strategies.

An effective source of advance work was the printed word. The church blanketed the community with a Christian newspaper, *The Shades Mountain Independent Messenger*, which included inspirational articles as well as promotional ads for SMI's special events. Each issue featured one of Dick's sermons. The paper prepared many hearts for a visit from a SMI soulwinner. And sometimes, the paper did its own work.

Bob and Genny Rollings, who would spend decades as hardworking volunteers at Shades Mountain Independent, first heard about the church through *The Messenger*. Long-standing members in a mainline church, the couple began praying about a new church for their family—one closer to their Hoover home and with a youth ministry for their teenage son. But leaving a denomination where their roots went deep became difficult. Where did they belong? Then one day Genny picked up a copy of the SMI newspaper. She loved everything she read, and the church's doctrine matched what she and Bob believed.

Delighted at the prospects of a new church home, and with a confident new identity, Genny called out to her husband, "Honey, we're *Independents!*"

Because Dick's evangelizing knew no bounds, no house was too grand or small. Nor was any venue off limits for seizing an opportunity to share the Gospel. Sunday sermons, prayer breakfasts, church visitation, and the like were expected territory for a pastor to spread the Good News. But Dick went beyond the norm and utilized the unexpected situations, at least for some, such as funerals.

Dick presided at funerals the way an evangelist preaches a revival. Even in that most sedate, sad situation of life, Dick presented the claims of Christ. His charisma, undergirded by the strength of his convictions, enabled him to talk about Jesus and appeal for a decision without offense.

After sharing a eulogy filled with honorable and often humorous recollections, Dick would move on to reading Scripture and sharing words of consolation. Then came the great moment. He closed every funeral with a simple but straightforward presentation of the Gospel, followed by an invitation to receive Christ as personal Savior. The invitation, quietly and clearly spoken, was discreet but immediate.

"If you want to receive the Lord, with heads still bowed in prayer and no one looking up, in the quietness of your heart, pray this prayer along with me."

And with that Dick would repeat the Sinner's Prayer.

Following the same pattern he used in sanctuary services, Dick invited those who prayed to receive Christ to look up and catch his eye or to see him privately afterward.

The mourners rarely took umbrage, and many were saved not just comforted. The undertaker's cemetery canopy became an evangelist's tent when SMI's Pastor presided at a funeral. Countless people came to Christ over the graves of loved ones. Some who resisted at first later made public professions, crediting Dick's funeral sermon for planting the Gospel seed.

The sacrosanct might flinch, but Dick unapologetically refused to hold back.

"A casket makes folks face their own mortality. I wanted people to know there is hope beyond the grave through faith in Christ. A gravestone does not have to mark the end! For a child of God it's just the beginning!"

TESTIMONY of DANIEL A. MOORE

A renown sports artist, Daniel A. More is celebrated for his photo-realism style paintings that capture dramatic moments in athletic competition. But in the early 1970's he was a lad mourning the death of a boyhood pal, Lew Bagwell.

Danny and Lew were classmates at Bluff Park Elementary School and played on football and baseball teams together. As students at Berry High School, Danny remembers Lew as a stand-out in every way, winning the admiration of students and faculty alike because of his engaging personality and natural leadership ability. A born-again Christian, as the teenager grew in stature, so too did his love for his Savior. He became a winning witness for Christ at school. Everyone loved him too much to be put off by his zeal for Jesus, including Danny.

*In the book "**Crimson & White and Other Colors: The Artwork of Daniel A. Moore**," a collection of his prints along with commentary and a biography written by his journalist brother, David Frazier Moore, Danny pays tribute to his friend.*

"Young people, including myself, wanted to know the innermost 'What' or 'Who' that enabled Lew to always wear a smile, to always offer a handshake with such genuine warmth.... I had a deep respect for Lew's stand for Christ.

He was very outspoken about his faith and spread the Good News about Jesus wherever he went."

When Lew died in a scuba diving accident at Lake Martin, the whole Over the Mountain community, as well as Lew's school, was stricken by the loss. Lew seemed not only too young to die but too good.

The day after Lew's shocking death, an impromptu memorial service gathered some seventy-five students in the school library. A few days later the funeral was held at Shades Mountain Baptist Church where the Bagwell family were members. Danny attended both services. On both occasions Dick Vigneulle's strong voice spoke out in tribute to the life of the godly teen. Lew had become a welcomed part of the SMI faith community and a valued co-worker in reaching and ministering to his peers. Dick felt the blow of the young man's passing as if a member of his own family had died. But true to form, the banker-preacher seized the occasion to preach Jesus.

At the close of both services, the school memorial and later the funeral, Dick gave an invitation to his hearers to receive Christ. On both occasions dozens got saved. But Danny was not one of them.

As never before, Danny heard and understood the Gospel. The Holy Spirit crushed him with conviction, yet he resisted.

"My mind overruled my heart by convincing me that I did not need any help. I reasoned that if I could just tread water a little longer, get my life straightened out, then I could surely save myself."

Weeks later, whether out of nostalgia for a friend forever absent from his life or from persistent conviction and yearning for peace with God, Danny began attending Shades Mountain Independent Church. The fact that the church met at his high school made the decision easier, but even so he opted to attend the evening services, not the morning ones. Every service ended with Dick issuing a call to salvation. As the crowd sang an invitation hymn, Dick invited folks to come down the aisle to learn more about Christ.

Danny recalls, "For me, being basically shy, a big part of the battle was the fear of walking down the aisle in front of everyone. Of course, this was only my mind jabbing at me, trying to rationalize what was happening."

Service after service, conviction grew stronger and stronger in Danny's heart, but still he put off making a decision. Then, after several weeks of attending, during an invitation, Dick said something that gave Danny the help he needed.

"You can be saved right where you are. Walking an aisle never saved

anyone. *If it is your heart's desire, you can be saved where you are sitting simply by asking Jesus to come into your heart and to forgive you of all your sins. Just receive Him as your Savior by faith."*

Danny could wait no longer, nor did he want to.

"I had felt all along that an aisle should have nothing to do with salvation, and Dick confirmed that for me. So, at the age of seventeen, I received Jesus Christ as my Savior."

Danny became a faithful part of the SMI church family. Preaching and discipleship classes grounded him in his faith and gave him the courage to share Jesus with others.

"My mind continued to be renewed and transformed during those initial years of what is an ongoing maturing process. Many more bouts between my heart and mind would occur, but I found that by having Jesus in my heart, I could win over sin and the struggles of life. The victories came as I allowed God's Word to fill my mind."

Already a budding artist, Danny found Christ transformed not just his life but his art too. The Lord strengthened his talent. As his skills at his easel improved, Danny awakened to the Lord's purposes for him.

"I was coming to the realization that I was the brush and God was the artist. My life was His canvas. Upon every part of the canvas that I allowed Him to paint, He created beauty. The areas that I still insisted on painting quickly became muddied colors. I know that everything good in my life was painted there by God."

Just as Dick would not limit evangelism to church services, neither would he accept soul-winning as a solo venture restricted to the pastor. Promoting Dr. Bob Sr.'s admonition to "draw the net," Dick purposed not to be the only fisherman at SMI. He expected the church family to be personal soul-winners, and recruited capable staff members to join church Board leaders in providing training and strategies to reach the Mountain and the world. The Pastor, laity, and staff members worked as one big team to spread the Gospel.

Many of the most courageous soul-winners in the church got saved after someone from SMI visited their home or office. Thousands came to Christ and even more heard the claims of Christ. The Good News was proclaimed from sermons, conference messages, concerts, media outreach, and door-to-door contacts.

For example, a popular outreach strategy merged Dick Vigneulle's two great ministry loves: music and evangelism. Through the years, many talented men and women served in SMI's choir and orchestra. The church became known for top-notch musical productions, but these events—some held off-site in area hotels or even the Civic Center—were intentional evangelistic outreaches. Work began months in advance. The concerts met high standards of technical and musical excellence, but the aim was for more than a cultural experience. Dick, the choir, and crew wanted to see lives changed by the Christ of Christmas!

As the years of Dick's pastorate unfolded, amidst all the change inevitable to ministry and life itself, evangelism remained the heart of every sermon and the unmovable cornerstone of church life. True to his example from the very first Sunday Dick preached before an SMI crowd, he continued to influence by example. Personal soul-winning remained a constant in his life, every year, every day. He did not have to be in a pulpit to talk about Christ. He talked about Jesus everywhere.

TESTIMONY of HIRAM GILBERT

Hiram Gilbert was John Wayne without the cowboy boots and horse. One of Birmingham's noted builders of prestigious executive homes, he wore construction boots and rode a jeep, unless he was atop a bulldozer on a job site. A man's man, Hiram had a handshake as firm as his opinions. Tall with rugged good looks, his head crowned with a thatch of salt-and-pepper hair, he obviously worked with his hands and back. His eyes were piercing like a drill bit. When it came to his work ethic, his standard was as straight as a plumb line.

By his family's account, Hiram raised himself and paid his own way from the time he was nine years old. It is no wonder he had the mental and physical toughness of the self-made and self-reliant. He spoke in a strong voice with a wisp of an accent that told his North Florida/South Alabama roots. He worked hard, and on the rare occasions he took time off, he played hard. At home he could be the gracious Southern host, but on the job site Hiram was intense, even fierce. He rewarded his crew for hard work and loyalty, but they had to meet a high performance standard to earn it. Hiram's name was his bond, and his name was only as good as his crew's craftsmanship, so it had to be perfect. A fault in a poured foundation or handmade cabinets misaligned in the installation could bring down his wrath. His speech was salty, and his anger like a summer storm poured out intensely but dissipated quickly.

Never trained as an architect or engineer, Hiram was self-taught. Friends and foes in his trade, let alone countless Gilbert-built homeowners, more than admired Hiram—they revered him. His homes were works of art, not just fetes of brick and mortar. While he could adapt his architectural styles to suit his clients' preferences, whether a time-honored traditional or rustic contemporary, there was one concession he never made. Hiram refused to compromise on craftsmanship.

As his son Greg recalls, "Dad knew things that even he did not know how he knew them. He had an ability to place a house on a lot that enhanced the look of both. A builder can have great lots and excellent plans, but if the house is not situated as it should be, it can be a mess. Dad always brought out the best in the lot and the house plans. He could take a dog of a site, one no one else wanted to build on, and make the quirks in the land work to the benefit of the job. His houses looked like they just grew out of the land."

Hiram's golden reputation as a builder reached Peggy Vigneulle's ear. From the early years of their marriage, Peg and Dick enjoyed visiting new construction sites and touring model homes. Dick's banking and real estate career held a vested interest in such pursuits, but actually it was a fun hobby of sorts for the Vigneulles. On top of that, they were considering building a new home for themselves. When Peggy visited a friend who had just moved into a Gilbert-built house, she knew she had found just the builder for their dream home.

"Honey, take some time to stop by and visit that builder named Hiram Gilbert. His work is gorgeous!"

Driving down Highway 31 one afternoon on his lunch break, Dick saw the sign "Gilbert Construction" and made a quick turn into the parking lot. He entered the office but none of the workers were in sight, except for a young man sitting behind a desk. It was Hiram's son and business partner, Greg.

"Howdy, young man! Is this Hiram Gilbert's office?"

"Yes, it is," Greg answered. "I'm his son. My dad's on the phone right now talking to a client."

"My name is Dick Vigneulle, and I've come by to meet your father. I'm interested in maybe having him build a house for me."

"What do you do, Sir?"

"I'm a preacher."

By Greg's surprised countenance, Dick felt the Gilberts had never had a preacher for a client before, nor necessarily wanted one.

After a few pleasantries, Greg excused himself to fetch his father. Still standing in the outer office, Dick could hear the exchange between father and son.

"Dad, there's a preacher out here and he wants to meet you."

"What?" Hiram exclaimed, as if a hammer had dropped on his toe. "Now why would I want to meet with a preacher?"

Business was business, and after all, the clergyman was waiting. Hiram stepped out and pasted a smile on his face as he offered his hand in greeting.

"Are you that preacher up on Tyler Road?"

"Yes, I am, Hiram. Shades Mountain Independent Church."

"I know it well because I've built a lot of homes around there."

Hiram arranged to take Dick on a tour of his homes, some still under construction and others finished and occupied by grateful owners eager to give tours. The more time the two men spent together, the more they warmed to each other as mutually respectful friends. For all their outward differences in appearance, they were alike as hardworking men with strong convictions and a gift for gab. Dick's winning ways won a new friend, and in turn he won a hearing for the Gospel of Jesus Christ.

"Hiram, where do you go to church?"

"Well, my wife, Betty, and I are Methodists, but we don't go to church much. She doesn't like crowds, and frankly Sunday can be a workday when you're in real estate. It's a good day for showing houses. If I'm not doing that, then I prefer to stay home and be with my family."

"Listen," Dick answered, "I want you to come to SMI and see if you and Betty might not like it as a church for you and your family. You probably already know half the people in the congregation."

Hiram thought a moment before answering. He never made promises lightheartedly, and when he did make one, he would be sure to keep it.

"Well, what time does the service begin?"

Dick told him, and Hiram promised to be there.

True to his word, Hiram entered the sanctuary the next Sunday just as the service began. He slid into the very last pew. Dick noticed his arrival. When he finished his sermon and gave an invitation, Dick repeated the Sinner's Prayer, inviting those who wanted to receive Christ as Savior to pray along with him, silently where they sat.

After saying "Amen," Dick added his standard request.

"With everyone still keeping their heads bowed, if you prayed to receive Christ with me this morning, I want you to look up and catch my eye. With that you're telling me, 'Preacher, I prayed with you just now to receive Christ.'"

Hiram was the first one to look up and catch the preacher's eye. When the service ended, instead of shooting to the parking lot, Hiram walked down the aisle toward the pulpit to greet Dick.

"Buddy, I'm glad to see you," Dick said. "You prayed with me this morning, didn't you?"

"I sure did."

"Did you mean it, Hiram?" Dick probed further.

"I sure did, but I want to talk to you."

For a good while the two men, now brothers in Christ, sat in a pew as Dick reviewed Bible verses to ground Hiram in his new-found faith. Likewise, Hiram had questions. How could he reach his family—they needed the Lord too. In addition to his wife, Betty, and married son Greg, Hiram had two teenage boys at home. Dick offered simple advice.

"Hiram, here's what I want you to do. Start praying right now for your wife and sons to come to Christ. Then I want you to bring them all with you to church next Sunday morning."

That is exactly what he did. The next Sunday morning Hiram arrived, early this time, with his family in tow. Walking right past the back rows, Hiram marched his family right up the aisle to the front pew. When they heard the Gospel, he wanted them in the firing line!

At the end of the service, the Gilbert boys trusted Christ. Betty had given her heart to the Lord as a little girl, but long ago drifted from her childhood faith. That morning she rededicated her life to Christ.

Dick and Peggy Vigneulle prayed with the Gilberts for their oldest son, Greg, to come to the Lord. About a month after the family began attending SMI, Betty looked up one morning as the service began and spotted Greg coming through the door—all dressed up and carrying a Bible under his arm. He prayed to receive the Lord that morning. Greg's wife, Kathy, got saved months later at the SMI Easter concert. Hiram and Betty's family circle was complete.

When Hiram gave his life to Christ, his work crew noticed the change in their boss the very next day. He did not cuss anymore.

Rarely ever a social drinker, Hiram purposed never to touch liquor again. There was a stash of wine stored in his basement, left over from his son's wedding. With Betty's help, he carried it to the lake in front of their home and poured it all out, bottle after bottle.

The burden he had felt for his family to come to the Lord now extended to his employees. Hiram started praying publicly at the office. He started a Bible study in the workplace too. He already had the stature and daring of the Apostle Peter, and now he took on the Apostle's zeal for reaching the lost. Every occasion became a soul-winning opportunity.

Betty recalls, "A few months after we gave our hearts to the Lord, Hiram's mother died. At her funeral he stood up and gave his testimony. Then just like Dick Vigneulle would do at church, Hiram gave an invitation. Many of his relatives got saved."

The Gilberts received an invitation to their high school reunion. The person in charge of entertainment invited graduates to participate in the program by sharing stories. Hiram wrote back accepting the offer on the condition that he could share his testimony.

"We never heard back," Betty remembered. "But we decided to attend anyway. Hundreds of alumni filled the banquet room. Quite unexpectedly, the emcee announced to the crowd, 'Now we are going to hear from Hiram Gilbert.' Hiram and I looked at each other in surprise. But Hiram jumped to his feet and headed for the platform. He took the microphone and told all our old classmates, 'You all knew me back when, and I want to tell you how I am now.' People got saved that night, including one of his old football buddies who was dying of cancer."

During church services, as Dick would preach, one of the loudest and most frequent cheerleaders in the congregation was Hiram Gilbert. He would bellow out a happy "AMEN" that was unmistakably his.

On weekly visitation nights, Hiram would be one of the first to arrive. He led a number of his workmen to Christ and took a special interest in the men struggling with alcohol addiction. He often visited the hospital rooms of men he knew from the building industry. Not all his old friends welcomed the new Hiram.

"He got thrown out of many hospital rooms," Betty chuckles, "but it never fazed him. He'd just smile and say, 'At least I told him.'"

When Hiram died unexpectedly of a heart attack in 1996, he had long established a testimony as a man of faith. His son Greg, once trying to find the words to describe his father's faith and love, faltered and paused to find the words. Then he settled on a simple but honorable tribute.

"It was real. My father's faith in Christ was real."

Who knows better than a son?

A writer from ETERNITY magazine interviewed Dick for a feature that appeared in the magazine's October 1981 issue (page 21). The article described SMI's Pastor as pleased but not surprised by the church's phenomenal growth.

Dick was not bragging, just celebrating. He remained confident that increase resulted from the congregation's continuing focus on the present, with an eye to the future. Never one to look back, Dick explained to the journalist his determination to keep alive the church's first and preeminent vision to partner in evangelism.

"The vision in the eyes and minds of the early SMI family must be carried on or we perish. If we forget or become idle, the dream and its potential will die and so too will our people—not just physically but spiritually. There is no standing still in the lives of Christians or the church."

Echoing a rousing reminder that Christians are "saved to serve," Dick spoke up for the duty of all believers to fulfill the Great Commission. Everyone in SMI must be on a mission. The result would be a church excited and growing.

As a Pastor, he did not want his congregation to forget its heritage. But memories were not a destination. Instead, memories should fuel the journey to the future. There was not just a community but a world to win for Christ.

"Record Sunday" – attendance over 1,000 broke record – everyone stood to form shape of a cross – circa early 1980's

166

CHAPTER FOURTEEN

World Reach

"*A* church without missions is a church without a mission," Dick Vigneulle proclaimed to his young congregation. "If we don't do anything else here at SMI, we're going to do missions!"

From his earliest days filling SMI's pulpit, even while meeting in the insurance building, Dick preached the Great Commission, Jesus' call to take the Gospel to the whole world (Matthew 28:19-20). While preaching to "Reach the Mountain," Dick was strategizing to "Reach the World."

One early-on church member recalls, "Dick's emphasis on missions was intentional, deliberate. He wanted missions to be the thrust of the church, not something that happened accidentally. He kept the heart of the people outward focused not inward, so their energies were funneled not just in building facilities but in building the kingdom of God—overseas as well as at home! To do that, Dick surrounded himself with men and movements that would turn the heart of the people to missions."

One church member, who eventually followed Dick Vigneulle's path and left the business world for the ministry, dedicated his life to missions. With his enduring and passionate appeals to reach the world for Christ, Dick's preaching turned his heart. Describing his Pastor's influence, he points to visionary leadership.

"One of Dick's best ministry skills was communication. He had the capacity not only to develop a vision for missions but also to communicate the vision. But it didn't end there. He took his vision two steps further. Through his rousing energy and preaching, he helped his hearers to own his vision and execute it!"

More than just a resource center for missionary needs, SMI became a sending station. Scores of church members surrendered to missions. Many young people left home for Bible colleges, or switched majors once in school in order to follow God's call to the foreign field. Even more laymen and women abandoned lucrative careers at home and went to the mission field. Dick's influence went beyond laity too.

One former pastor who surrendered to missionary service later in his ministry, in great measure due to Dick's influence, told him, "If it weren't for you, I could be retired by now!"

FAITH PROMISE

Early in the young church's history, one of the first people Dick turned to was his old college buddy, Brom Cowser. A missionary veteran after years of service with The Evangelical Alliance Mission (TEAM) in Curacao, South America, Brom received an invitation to visit Shades Mountain Independent Church in 1970. Dick wanted Brom to explain a faith-based approach to missions giving called "FAITH PROMISE."

The Pastor's holy aspirations were huge, though the gathering was humble. Still without their own building, the church held the weeknight gathering in Vira and Glenn Kennedy's home, site of SMI's weekly evangelistic meetings. A crowd of thirty members, too large for the living room, assembled in the basement to hear their missionary guest.

No one was more excited than the speaker. A missionary himself, Brom knew firsthand the critical importance of prayer and financial support on the home front. He was hopeful because he knew that Dick and Peggy shared a heritage and lifestyle committed to evangelism and missions. No doubt the fledgling church the Vigneulles now served would be molded by their example.

Prompted by more than his foreign field needs, Brom taught an approach to stewardship influenced by his study of the life and writings of Oswald J. Smith, Pastor of Toronto's famed People's Church, and A. B. Simpson, the Founder of the Christian Missionary Alliance, TEAM's sponsoring denomination. Both men led a movement dedicated to sending and supporting missionaries. In addition to the preaching of Smith and Simpson, Brom learned from the preaching of Paul, especially the Apostle's description of sacrificial giving in II Corinthians, chapters eight and nine.

Brom explained to his basement congregation, "Folks, FAITH PROMISE is a promise between you and the Lord that you will trust Him to supply a certain amount of money beyond the regular amount of money you give your local church with your tithes and offerings. This promise is for one year—between now and next year's missions conference."

The missionary repeated his emphasis that the commitment was for one year and that it was a private promise. Equally important was the faith factor. The amount settled on should come out of prayer and faith, not based on refiguring family finances, as if to calculate "We can afford this amount." Nor was the money to come from a reduction of regular church giving. This would be a gift beyond their normal means.

There was another important distinction to Brom's challenge.

"Friends, I am not talking about a pledge. FAITH PROMISE is not a pledge! A pledge is between you and the church, but FAITH PROMISE is just between you and the Lord. That means no one else will know what you promised, so no one will criticize if you do not reach your goal and no one will be hounding you for your commitment. It's just between you and God. Likewise, because FAITH PROMISE is anonymous, no one gains brownie points because their gift might be larger than another's."

Dick followed up his friend's sermon with a call to action, even as ushers handed out FAITH PROMISE cards.

Folks, here's your chance to believe God! I challenge each one of you to step out and believe God's promise that if you sow generously, you will reap in the same way. I believe that if you give away with a clear conscience and heart, God will give back to you in the same way. God is no man's debt-or. It may not be in material things that God gives back, and I'm sure glad that it's not just in this life that God rewards faithful stewardship. But believe me, folks, I've learned that when I shovel out to God, He shovels back with blessings. And God's shovel is bigger than mine!

The banker-preacher followed the principles of good economics, but there were times when he put aside the rules of the marketplace. Faith can defy common sense, and true love gives. One of the missionaries supported by SMI saluted the church and its Pastor.

"Dick was not jealous of his local ministry. He led his people in giving away great sums for God's work in other places."

As the SMI folks looked over their faith promise cards, their Pastor underscored the privacy and purpose of FAITH PROMISE.

"As Brom said, this is just between you and the Lord. Notice there is no place for you to put your name on this card. But here's what I want you to do. After you pray about it and the Lord lays on your heart an amount for you to trust Him for, then I want you to write in that amount and turn in the card. The church Board will tally the FAITH PROMISE amounts and that total will go to support missionaries on the field. And every penny you give will go to missions! The church will not hold out even a nickel for postage!"

By evening's end the cards were collected and tallied. Dick announced the total to the eager crowd.

"Folks, we've got it! Here it is! SMI's very first FAITH PROMISE is $3,000!"

Dick regularly signed loans and contracts at City Federal with a lot more zeros in the figure than that one, but none pleased him more.

Eager to keep commitments, people became creative in finding ways to give to FAITH PROMISE, including children in the church. The kids in one family sold donuts. One lady scoured garage sales and thrift stores and then cleaned and restored items to sell in her own yard sale—giving all the proceeds to missions. By the year's end the young congregation exceeded their first goal, giving $5,000.

The next year SMI held its first Missions Conference. The theme was "His Last Command, Our First Priority." It was time to step out in faith once more with a new FAITH PROMISE. They tallied a FAITH PROMISE of $12,000. By year's end the actual amount received reached $16,000.

FAITH PROMISE became a two-for-one blessing! The project served to build believers' faith as well as raise money for God's work overseas. One former Board member recalls his first step of faith.

"I did not have much faith for my first FAITH PROMISE, but I felt impressed that the Lord wanted me to commit $1,000. Not long afterwards, a friend hired me to wire his cabin at the lake. Word spread and others asked me too. I earned nearly $8,000 that year for FAITH PROMISE. The lesson came home loud and clear—you can't outdo the Lord!"

By 1998, Dick's twenty-fifth anniversary as Pastor, SMI's FAITH PROMISE topped $600,000.

MISSIONS ON DISPLAY

A stranger could walk into Shades Mountain Independent Church's building on Tyler Road and immediately know this was a missions-minded church—without ever attending a service or hearing Dick Vigneulle preach. Missionary displays adorned all the major hallways. The pictures told the story. Beautiful solid wood wainscoting lined all the corridors of the church. Above it hung custom-made display boards, installed at eye level.

This special display area, framed with wood molding and divided into individual panels, featured different missionaries supported by SMI. Every missionary family had a dedicated space, and they represented just about every mainstream evangelical mission organization. The name of the missionary and the sponsoring mission board headlined each display panel, along with the name of the country served. Each space also featured a photo of the missionary family and their latest prayer letter.

Steven Taylor, a recently converted college student in the early 1980's, came to SMI every time the doors were open, quite a change for the ex-rebel and partygoer. His mother had put him on SMI's prayer list, and after her repeated appeals, he relented and went to church. On his second visit, Steven prayed to receive Christ and responded when Pastor Vigneulle said, "If you prayed with me, look up and catch my eye."

On Sunday nights he came early just so he could walk the hallways and read the missionary letters before the evening service began. What he read and the world mission maps he traced stirred his sanctified imagination with dreams of international ministry. Today, a veteran missionary with a family of his own, Steven serves in Japan with TEAM. Looking back, he credits those displays with planting the seeds of a missionary call.

When you first become a Christian, those early influences and relationships can affect you so deeply, and remain special forever. SMI was where I came to faith in 1982. And it was a very strong missionary influence. The halls of SMI are filled with newsletters and pictures of missionaries they support...hundreds of them. Way back then, I felt God was calling me to step beyond Birmingham. When I would come early every Sunday evening, and spend time walking the halls and reading those missionary newsletters, I would dream about the day when, maybe, my picture would be up there.

MISSIONS COMMITTEE

The Missions Committee at Shades Mountain Independent Church modeled the standards and spirit guiding all the church committees. For selection to serve on any committee, it was not enough to be a professing Christian and member of the church. Selection was restricted to those men and women already proven and active volunteers. The simply curious or faint-hearted need not apply.

Church members serving on the Missions Committee made serious commitments of their time, talents, and resources. The Missions Committee functioned all year with monthly meetings where they prayed, planned mission events, and maintained communications with the SMI-supported missionaries on the field. With neither fleeting attention nor casual involvement tolerated, these hard-core workers ministered with a warrior's spirit.

Jim Scott, converted through SMI's outreach, had traveled the world as a career military officer. As a new believer, he quickly gravitated to evangelism and missions service opportunities. Later in life he became a missionary. He remembers the hard work and devotion expected of the Missions Committee.

Members demonstrated a serious interest in missions and service projects long before joining the committee. Each member was assigned a geographic area of the globe and given responsibility for the missionaries in that part of the world. It was their duty to pray for their missionaries, to write to them and get their specific prayer requests. At the committee meetings, each person gave a report on his or her missionary group and then the entire committee would address the needs with prayer and action. It's no wonder those meetings went on for hours. And we loved every minute of it!

Another duty of the Missions Committee was to interview candidates wanting to go to the mission field or veterans back home on furlough and needing added support. Just as committee members held each other to a high standard, they expected the same from those workers seeking to become part of the missionary family supported by SMI. A change in geography would not affect a change in spirituality. To gain SMI's support, therefore, would-be missionaries had to demonstrate an existing spiritual dynamic, as well as a sense of purpose and planning for on-field ministry.

Jim Scott recalls, "The Missions Committee would interview the candidates. They would ask if the missionaries were active in a local church, if they were represented by a mission board, if their commitment was long term or short term. Members would also ask what the candidates thought their mission field service would be and how they expected to accomplish their goals. There were financial questions too—how much money was needed to get to the field and how much support would be needed to sustain their ministry once on the field."

In an era predating the internet and e-mailing, letters passed in the mail, offering a ministry of encouragement as well as addressing material requests. Missions Committee participation meant more than administrative exercises. Personal involvement made SMI committee members, as well as the staff and congregation, feel an attachment and accountability for the missionaries and their needs, whether big or small.

In the early years, when a missionary confided a need for a washing machine, the Missions Committee discovered their funds were exhausted. Not to be put off, before the meeting ended, they took up an offering among themselves and collected enough to buy a washer.

Another missionary, a single woman with many years experience in the Far East, made a passing comment about coffee being a luxury. None of the committee members could imagine starting his or her day without a cup of coffee, so why should this choice servant of the Lord? Not until she returned to the field did she learn that an extra stipend had been added to her support from SMI—the extra bit was designated specifically for her to purchase coffee!

When an on-field missionary wrote home expressing discouragement and spiritual exhaustion, the group faced the question "Who ministers to the missionary? Who spiritually feeds God's servants as they serve others?" This concern helped expand SMI's cassette tape ministry. Dick's sermons were already recorded and distributed to nursery workers and children's church volunteers who missed out on the worship services in order to carry on their work. It was an easy and practical step to expand tape duplications and begin regular mailings to God's workers in far away places. The missionaries appreciated the tapes. Singing by the congregation and the choir and Dick's messages fed their souls. As the missionaries listened to the tapes, whether under a tin roof or inside a concrete bunker or a tiny, spare apartment far from Alabama, they could feel connected to a church and share in a worship service back home. They were not alone. They were not forgotten.

MISSIONS CONFERENCES

To keep global evangelism a priority, Dick incorporated missions into the church's calendar as well as its budget. The SMI Missions Committee oversaw both. The church welcomed missionary guests throughout the year. But the Missions Conference, usually held in the fall, created a premiere event to orient new church members and stir the veterans to keep alive the vision to reach the world.

The next best thing to taking folks to the mission field, the Conference brought the mission field to Hoover. A dozen or so missionaries were invited to the annual event and housed in the homes of church members, a hospitality ministry that resulted in many enlightening mealtime exchanges and lifelong friendships for the host families. These global workers for Christ represented an array of mission boards. The Conference gave a platform for new appointees to raise support and for those already supported to report on their overseas activity. Audiences thrilled to hear how God was working in the personal lives of the missionaries as well as in the countries they represented.

A variety of events filled the Missions Conference week, affording the missionaries varied formats to tell their stories. In addition to the Men's Prayer Breakfast, the Women's Luncheon, countless school visits, and panel discussions, the missionaries also spoke nightly. Each conference night began with mini-sessions. Each missionary was assigned a classroom to set up a display and hold these nightly seminars. Conference attendees could attend two a night, every night before everyone convened in the sanctuary for the keynote address by the conference's main speaker.

Becky Reitenour Carter, today a veteran missionary serving in Africa with her husband, Chip, points to her teenage experiences at SMI's Missions Conferences as the beginning of God's call to her life's work.

174

My call to missions is absolutely linked to my years at SMI. Because Dick was so missions-minded, he made sure that his congregation was exposed to missions on a regular basis. Visiting missionaries regularly shared the pulpit with him, and reports of missions work from all over were incorporated into church services. I remember attending annual missions conferences as a teenager and, in the process of getting to know many missionaries our church supported, realizing missionaries AREN'T super-saints, just ordinary Christians called to live cross-culturally. I directly link the ease of my transition into considering missions myself to my regular exposure to missionaries from all over the globe.

The conferences afforded opportunities for missionaries to provide a face behind the cause of missions. Hearing their individual stories—about their ministry calls, their on-field struggles, their ministry victories—made their visits personable, even life changing for their listeners.

Becky Carter remembers just such an encounter.

"Of particular value during those missions conferences were the many opportunities I had to sit in small groups or one-on-one with missionaries, and hear their heart for missions. I could ask questions and dialogue with them about the need as well as the tremendous privilege to serve God cross-culturally. I remember Susan McCollum, a medical doctor serving in Pakistan, being amongst those who inspired me to think, 'Hey, maybe God could actually use ME on the mission field!'"

A special feature of the Missions Conference weeks was the roster of world-renowned preachers who served as keynote speakers. SMI was blessed to host some of the late twentieth century's finest missionary spokesmen: Stephen Olford, Ravi Zacharias, Major Ian Thomas, and others.

One speaker shared a special tie with Pastor Vigneulle—Dr. Billy Kim, a classmate from Dick's school days in South Carolina. Now Pastor Emeritus of a twenty thousand-member congregation in his native Korea, and an acclaimed world missions leader, Dr. Kim first responded to the Great Commission challenge as a college student. A welcomed guest speaker at SMI, he remembered Dick Vigneulle's influence as a college classmate.

"Even as a young man, Dick was a leader among his peers and a passionate soul-winner."

Years later when he reconnected with Pastor Vigneulle, Dr. Kim witnessed the same drive in the banker-turned-pastor. Nothing had changed.

"Dick always kept a wider vision to reach the world. I appreciated his perpetual challenge—his undying vision—to 'step out and reach out!'"

Dr. Kim's international ministry often found him comforting pastors frustrated and feeling ineffective despite their high calling and good intentions.

He observed, "Too often Christian leaders become distracted by the daily operations of their ministry, becoming administrators not soul-winners. They are reduced to being managers not leaders. Soon the preacher's vision is lost and his followers become discouraged. As a result, evangelism becomes a casualty."

But Billy Kim detected none of that at SMI. Dick remained focused on evangelism, at home and abroad. Furthermore, Kim cautioned that for many preachers in their generation there were added distractions. Preoccupied by concern for their reputations before rugged traditionalists, they became guardians of convention and watchdogs for compromise. As a result, they lost the larger view.

Dick, however, stayed on target. He kept a higher goal. Proof came with the church's explosive growth and expanding global mission's mindset.

Under Pastor Vigneulle's direction, SMI created in-house learning opportunities for students and ministers in training, including numerous missionary candidates. The Summer Missionary staff, made up of a select group of college students home for the summer, offered short-term ministry jobs.

Dick with Dr. Billy Kim (attended BJU with Dick; now Pastor Emeritus of a 20,000-member congregation in Korea) during the 1977 Annual Missions Conference when $254,000 was pledged for Faith Promise.

Later the program expanded to one-year internships for college or seminary graduates preparing for full-time vocational ministry, whether at home or overseas. Each intern would be assigned to one of the staff pastors

176

for mentoring and in-the-trenches training. The interns could be included in staff meetings and retreats. They also gained an inner-circle access to the Pastor for valued one-on-one discipleship. Many of these young ministers came to faith at SMI, and for them Dick Vigneulle was a spiritual superhero.

One of these young stand-outs was Rob Brannon, whom Pastor Vigneulle led to Christ out of Mormonism. After several years of overseas ministry, Rob felt God's call to stateside missions in the state of Utah. He credits his home Pastor and SMI's intern program with equipping him with confidence as well as skills for ministry service.

"Pastor Vigneulle has an amazing ability to not only lead people but also to identify leaders and to train them up in the ways of the Lord. He is outgoing, and a born leader. I was shy and a reluctant leader to say the least. But his labors invested in me proved successful in setting me apart for the ministry of the Gospel in ways I never dreamed possible."

One of the memorable moments in Rob's intern training came in a private moment with his Pastor.

One day in the late 1980's Pastor Vigneulle took me and Keith Moore on a ministry assignment. We were his two missionary-to-be church interns at the time. As we arrived back at the church parking lot, Pastor Vigneulle finished sharing some off-the-cuff exhortations with us from his vast treasure trove of wisdom in the ministry. He grinned at both of us as he spoke with his characteristic winning smile, "Guys, make sure that you always pick FAT people as your leaders in ministry!" He paused for dramatic effect and then laughed when he saw the confused looks on our faces, as we wondered what he meant by choosing fat people for ministry. He then went on to explain the biblical principles of leadership based on II Timothy 2:2, "And the things that you have heard from me among many witnesses, commit these to faithful men who will be able to reach others also." Bringing home his point, he said, "Fellas, choose leaders who are Faithful, Available, and Teachable." From that day forward, I have looked for F.A.T. people to train as leaders in my ministry both in the USA and overseas.

LIGHTHOUSE

A man in Africa needed a pastor, and he found one in Dick Vigneulle.

John Kirema, a policeman in Kenya found a tract and read it. Convicted by what he read, he prayed to receive Christ. John was eager to tell his countrymen about Jesus and figured the tract that brought him to Christ could be used to lead others. But he had no money, no contacts. Where could he find help? Then he noticed on the back of his tract an address with the name of the publisher—Cornerstone Publishing, Birmingham, Alabama, USA. The Kenyan convert decided to write to America and ask for help.

For years Jim Dewberry, of Dewberry Engraving, and his friend Charles Snook, another Christian layman, had been printing tracts and sending them around the world. They named their ministry "Cornerstone." When mail arrived from Africa with news of John Kirema's conversion and appeal, the two men were thrilled. They generously began supplying tracts for John's ministry.

For several years Jim and Charles kept John Kirema supplied with Gospel literature and the Lord blessed John's outreach efforts. A Kenyan evangelist joined his team to help with preaching and discipleship. As their ministry grew so too did their need for financial and administrative support. Their ministry multiplying beyond the ken of businessmen, Kirema and his team needed a pastor not just a printer. Jim Dewberry had an idea—he called his friend Dick Vigneulle.

Shortly after his telephone exchange with Dewberry, Dick called Jim Haley into his office. As SMI's Assistant Pastor, Jim worked closely with the church's Missions Committee. He shared Dick's passion for evangelism at home and abroad and thrilled to hear the story of John Kirema. Dick elaborated on this exciting prospect.

"Jimmy, this is an open door! The folks at Cornerstone Printing know our heart for missions and thought this was an opportunity right for us. They're giving this ministry to us! But we need to learn more about John and his work over there—first-hand learning at that. Are you ready to pack your bags?"

Within a few days SMI's Assistant Pastor was in Africa. Jim Haley and John Kirema made an instant connection. Jim was excited about the ministry's opportunities, and brought back to SMI a positive report about the native Kenyan and his outreach to his countrymen. But John preferred field work over office routines. He was an evangelist, not an office manager. Jimmy also readily saw that John existed on meager resources. The Kenyan evangelist deserved more personal support and so too did his growing ministry.

Inspired by the Assistant Pastor's positive report, Dick and the Missions Committee and the church Board welcomed John Kirema to SMI's missionary family. Financial as well as prayer support soon followed, along with help in organizing a staff and ministry in Kenya.

SMI included the Kenya operations under the banner of its newly formed ministry called LIGHTHOUSE, a growing in-house umbrella organization for SMI's missions activity. Church leaders long envisioned a missionary-sending organization, especially to aid the dozens of SMI church members volunteering to serve the Lord on the mission field. A group of men met regularly on Wednesday nights, along with their Pastor, to pray for God's guidance in creating just such an agency, men including Jim Scott, Hiram Gilbert, Grady Fox, and Pat Kelly.

In time SMI took a step of faith and formatted LIGHTHOUSE as a separate entity to become, hopefully, SMI's own mission board. The church and its Missions Committee designated funds for its operation and to support its missionaries. When John Kirema and his Kenya ministries came aboard, LIGHTHOUSE already supported a missionary in Honduras.

Shortly after its start, LIGHTHOUSE hit an impasse in raising support for its missionaries. Other churches responded slowly or not at all. The mission agency seemed too closely identified with SMI. Furthermore, a multi-faceted international ministry required specialized administration. For LIGHTHOUSE to thrive and grow, SMI would have to "give it away." Dick and the church had no problem with letting go. They saw the looming transition as a growth opportunity. The vision was succeeding not receding.

LIGHTHOUSE was about to birth a whole new ministry, but first Pastor Vigneulle needed to find a leader to take the helm, one capable of leading a global missions enterprise.

Ultimately, Dick Vigneulle and SMI did not have to look far for a leader—he came from their own ranks. Tim Prewitt, a congenial and hardworking church member, began attending SMI shortly after the church moved into its Tyler Road building. His path to faith carried him far from home and back again.

TIM PREWITT & MRS. ADDIE PREWITT

After graduation from Samford University in 1964, followed by service in the United States Coast Guard, Tim Prewitt began a corporate climb with Sears, a retail giant, taking assignments in Florida and Virginia. A family tragedy brought him back to Birmingham briefly in March 1967. His father, John Prewitt, was killed in a plane crash. Flying to Toledo, Ohio, the elder Mr. Prewitt was headed to his company's headquarters to receive an award from the president of Owings Illinois Glass Company for outstanding salesman of the year. As the family recounts the ill-fated flight, at 15,000 feet the commuter turbo-prop plane encountered a snow storm. The pilot radioed his intent to go to a higher elevation to get over cloud cover. Moments later the engine failed, sending the plane into a tailspin. No one survived.

Tim traveled back to Birmingham from Titusville, Florida to attend the funeral and to comfort his mother, Addie Prewitt. Tim found solace in his family's Christian faith. Both his parents were believers and faithful church members who raised their children in church.

Following the burial service, family and friends gathered at Tim's parents' home, including Wales Goebel, a longtime family friend. He participated in the service and dropped by the house afterwards with more than just consolation on his mind. Tim recalls the afternoon well.

"Wales came to encourage my mother as well as my older brother and younger sister and me. Ever the evangelist, he wanted to be sure that we all had the hope of heaven in our hearts. One by one, Wales looked us in the eye and repeated the same question to each one of us in the room: 'Do you know Christ as your personal Savior? If you died tonight would you go to heaven?' I answered him just as directly, 'Yes, Wales, I'm a Christian.' With that he moved on to the others who answered just as I did."

A few days later Tim was back in Florida. Late on a Sunday night the phone rang. Tim answered. He recognized the voice immediately and began exchanging a few pleasantries. He remembers that long-ago phone call so well that to this day he can recite it almost line by line.

"After some chit-chat, the caller asked how I was doing and then went on to explain the reason for the call."

"Tim, the reason I'm calling is that I want to be sure you understand what it means to be a Christian. If you died tonight and you stood before the gates of heaven and God asked you what right do you have to come into His kingdom, what would you say?"

Tim remembers his answer.

"I shot back to the caller with a litany of things—my Christian home, my Bible reading, saying my prayers. The caller listened patiently, then after twenty minutes of my rambling, the voice on the other end asked me a direct question."

"Tim, have you ever made a personal commitment to Christ? You must recognize you were born a sinner and apart from Christ you cannot save yourself. It is by Christ and Christ alone that He will save you—but you must acknowledge and confess your sin and invite Christ into your life. Have you made that commitment?"

Tim was twenty-five years old, and he had run out of excuses.

"I don't think I ever have."

The caller continued, "Tim is there any reason why you would not like to receive Christ as your personal Savior at this very moment?"

"No. I'm ready."

After Tim prayed to receive Christ, the caller went on to explain what his decision meant and to encourage him in his new spiritual life. To her dying day, Tim remained grateful for the caller's concern for his soul.

"The caller," Tim explains, "was my mother. She wanted to be sure I had what she had. On the heels of our father's death, the Holy Spirit impressed her to call each one of her children and be sure we truly knew the Lord. Her other children were in Birmingham so she made a personal visit to my brother and sister for a face-to-face, loving confrontation. Because of the geographic distance separating us, my mother telephoned me. Mother told me later that after leading me to Christ, she hung up the phone and prayed out loud, 'God, if You can use me to win one to the Lord, even my own son, then You can use me to win others.'"

Addie Prewitt became known to her family and friends as the "Telephone Evangelist." For the rest of her life, she dedicated two evenings a week to telephone evangelism—Tuesday and Thursday nights, 7:00 – 9:00. Later she added a third night—Mondays. She started with the "A's" and worked her way through the phone book, confining her calls to residences and only after mealtimes. A kind and mild-mannered person, she followed a simple, straightforward format.

"My name is Addie Prewitt. I wonder if you would be kind enough to give me two minutes? I am taking a religious survey."

She never promoted denominations or a particular church. With five simple questions, Addie began her telephone survey by asking "Do you attend church?" Her final question was "Who is Jesus Christ?"

Often completed in less than two minutes, the survey garnered mixed responses. Sometimes the person vehemently objected, and on occasion some even cursed her. Always kind and even-tempered, she followed the familiar maxim that honey draws better than vinegar. She never lost her cool and simply moved down the phone book list and called the next number.

For those who affirmed faith in Jesus, she offered her phone number, repeated her name, and closed by saying, "If I can ever help you in the future, please call me." If her contact gave an uncertain or unbiblical answer, Addie would repeat the person's name and ask permission to continue. If the prospect declined, she thanked him and repeated her name, number, and offer to be available in the future.

If the person was open and gave the go-ahead to continue, Addie explained in simple terms the plan of salvation. If the person prayed with her to receive Christ, she again asked permission—this time to send by mail follow-up material to help them grow in the Lord. There was always one more offer repeated every time someone got saved over the telephone: "Is there anyone else in your home tonight that needs to hear the Gospel?"

One night after a lady prayed to receive Christ, when Addie made the offer to speak to others, the woman grew excited but uncertain. Then she began to whisper.

"Oh, Mrs. Prewitt, my husband needs the Lord too, but I'm afraid to mention it to him. Why don't you call right back—I'm going to hide in the bathroom and he will have to pick up the phone. Then you can talk to him."

Addie agreed. She called back and about fifteen minutes later the man prayed to accept Jesus as his personal Savior. Addie again made her standard offer.

"Sir, is there anyone else in your home who needs to hear the Gospel?"

The man responded quickly, "Well, he doesn't live here, but my brother needs to get saved too. If I give you his telephone number, will you call him too?"

Mrs. Prewitt kept her word. She called and later that night the man's brother was converted. He too offered a loved one's name to call. By evening's end, Addie Prewitt had led five members of the same family to Christ.

Many encouraged Addie in her outreach ministry, including Dick Vigneulle. To help this determined widow carry out her work, Shades Mountain Independent Church supplied literature and tracts to follow up her converts. She kept meticulous records, using a number code written in the margin of the phone book. The number one meant the person received Christ. Another number indicated a lost person who rejected the Gospel. Yet another number by the name meant the person was already a believer. Another code meant follow-up literature was sent.

She carried on this work for over twenty years, until her death on June 11, 2000 (Carol Prewitt's birthday). At her funeral, Mrs. Prewitt's children spread open several big telephone books, all ink stained and marked—the tools of her home missions ministry. The family followed their mother's strict instructions for her farewell service. While still on her sickbed, as Tim leaned over, Addie grabbed his shirt and pulled him closer for a nose-to-nose exchange.

"Now remember that when I die, I will go directly into the presence of Jesus, so my funeral is to be a celebration service—do you understand me?! I want Wales Goebel and Dick Vigneulle to co-lead the service, but Tim, I want YOU to preach the sermon. I want you to share the grace of God."

Before her passing, in her last days, though confined to a wheelchair, Addie remained very alert and mentally sharp. She regaled her family with stories from her telephone evangelism mission.

"THIS IS WHAT GOD DID!" she exclaimed, and then looking to Tim, she glowed, "Son, can you imagine that He used me? Can you imagine! And, Tim, you were the first one to receive Christ."

Recalling his mother's unfading excitement, Tim gratefully acknowledges, "I cannot tell you how indebted I am to Mom. She carried out a great mission. She was obedient to the greatest call of all—evangelism. Yet she never left her home, never needed a passport or visa. She could go where otherwise no one could go because, as she explained to us, people who would not answer the door would answer the telephone."

By 1972, Tim and Carol Prewitt had moved seven times, adjusting time and again to the family turmoil of corporate advancement and relocation. But with the death of their second child, Kimberly, they were ready to come back home to Birmingham permanently. Tim took a position in his father-in-law's business, Nuncies, one of Birmingham's oldest and most respected music stores. The couple enjoyed reconnecting with family and old friends. They joined Shades Mountain Independent Church, one recommended by Wales Goebel. He got active with The Gideons International, the Bible distribution ministry led by lay professionals. At home, at work, at church—the Prewitts felt their lives coming together in a wonderful way. Tim and Carol and their children Timmy and Christie looked like the happy family on the cover of a Sunday School quarterly, and they truly were happy.

"I was having the time of my life," Tim remembers.

One of their interests was foreign missions, a family passion stoked by their Pastor, Dick Vigneulle.

"Reaching the world was our church's core task, and fulfilling that goal required intentional, deliberate effort. Dick kept the congregation outward focused. To do so Dick surrounded himself with men and movements that would turn the heart of the people at SMI to missions. He called these veterans in world evangelism 'God's elite.'"

For many years, Tim and Carol supported five missionaries in particular by contributing to their support and praying daily for them. One of those was Bruce Woodman, Founding Director of South American Crusades. In the mid-1970's, while a guest in the Prewitt home, Rev. Woodman began talking to Tim about his life's direction and challenged him to think about becoming a missionary.

"Even before Bruce's arrival, I sensed that God was doing something in my life, stirring my heart for some kind of change, but I didn't know what it was. When Bruce challenged me to consider the ministry, the upheaval began to make sense."

Tim confided in his Pastor.

"I cannot explain to you what is happening in my life right now because I don't understand it myself. But there's an urging of God stirring in my heart. I think maybe God wants me to leave the business world and go into full-time ministry."

Dick was elated. Tim's testimony resonated with his life experience. His own call to leave City Federal still fresh in his mind, Dick could address

Tim's heart concerns with hands-on perspective. He spoke with authority about life in the business world and life in the ministry, and especially about the call of God that had led him from one to the other. His suggestion was straightforward.

"Tim, let's pray about this."

Dick became both an advocate and a coach as Tim pondered the call of God.

"Every time I came to church, Sunday and Wednesday, as soon as Dick saw me, he'd grab my arm and say, 'Come on Tim! Let's go back to my office and pray!' We prayed for weeks and weeks, months and months. I kept begging God to make it clear—what did He want me to do? I was consumed with concern that I not disappoint God."

The idea of turning his back on his life's career weighed heavily. Just when his children and wife thought they were settled and life hummed along beautifully, Tim was about to turn everything upside down. The children loved their friends and school. Carol finally had her dream house and only recently purchased her prized possessions—plantation shutters for the windows. How would they respond? What would Carol say?

Tim finally broke the news to Carol. After a lengthy explanation, recounting Bruce Woodman's challenge and Pastor Vigneulle's prayerful counsel, Tim said to his wife, "I believe God is calling us out of the business world into full-time ministry."

Carol's response was blunt and bottom line.

"Tim Prewitt! I don't want to leave my plantation shutters!"

With that she packed up suitcases for her and the children, loaded them into her car, and drove off to North Carolina where she could stay with an aunt.

"I left him," Carol recounts, laughing at herself. "It was too much to process. I needed space and perspective. I think I was both angry and confused. Tim's idea of a call came out of the blue, even though we were both active in local church ministries. We had moved so many times already in our lives, and now when we were finally back home and settled in with family, we're going to leave again? Our return came after so much prayer effort, why would it change? Worst of all for me, my dad was still unsaved, and I thought God was going to use Tim and me to bring him to the Lord."

Tim prayed earnestly: "God, if this is of You, then call Carol too."

A few days later, Carol returned home calmer but still unsettled.

"I told the Lord, 'I am going to follow Tim because You are calling him. My responsibility is to follow my husband. I know You're working in Tim's life. But Lord, if this is NOT of You, please reveal it to Tim so we do not misread Your call.'"

Tim and Carol found common ground through their Pastor's counsel as well as in their prayer life. Dick thrilled at the prospect of another SMI family going to the mission field. He knew Tim and Carol would make a terrific team. Their faithfulness to the Lord's work at home assured they would be effective workers on the field too. Furthermore, professionals such as Tim Prewitt could bring business excellence to the Lord's work, a standard ever important to Dick.

Tim remembers his Pastor's advice.

"Tim, aim for personal excellence. Be the best! Don't settle for average, don't be typical—be different!"

Recognizing the Prewitts' need for guidance, Pastor Vigneulle gave them advice for finding the will of God.

"Knowing and understanding God's will for your life," Dick explained to the couple, "is not some vague, mystical, 'out there' experience. It is real. God's will ultimately rules by peace in your heart as you yield to Him. Here are five basic steps to follow.

First, PRAY and ask God to speak to your heart about this issue—to speak to both of you intentionally, specifically.

Second, READ GOD'S WORD, but even before you open your Bible, ask God to direct you to passages that will address this call of God in your life. Some of the passages may be familiar, others not. Don't open your Bible randomly but with respect for God's direction.

Next, SEEK GODLY COUNSEL. Search out two or three other believers who you know walk with God. Ask them to covenant with you before God to meet with you regularly for prayer and accountability, for advice and encouragement.

Fourth, WATCH THE CIRCUMSTANCES in your life as God opens doors that were closed, and closes doors that were open.

Finally, as I said at the beginning, wait for the PEACE OF GOD that passes all understanding. Then you will know that God is doing what you cannot do."

186

The process was not overnight. For eighteen months Tim and Carol continued to follow the five steps. As he recalls that season in their lives, Tim credits his wife's reluctance with bringing a wonderful balance to their life. They continued to pray, persistently and always together. God's Spirit moved, and Tim's call to ministry proved unquenchable. Looking back, they realize the seeking process was part of the equipping process for the job waiting for them on the mission field.

As the news spread of Tim's plans to leave his business career for the mission field, church friends rallied around the couple. Despite their supporters' good cheer, Carol continued to balk.

Friends would hug her and say, "You're excited, aren't you!"

And she would always answer honestly, "NO!"

Her reluctant spirit persisted, but Carol's love for the Lord and for her husband prevailed. She consented to step out in faith and follow Tim's call to the mission field. Obedience to God's will, however, did not mean she had to like it!

They accepted the invitation from their old friend, Bruce Woodman, to join the staff of South American Crusades (SAC), a radio ministry serving Central and South America and headquartered in Boca Raton, Florida. As Executive Director of SAC, Bruce carved out a new position for Tim as Director for Special Services. Tim's job would be to promote the mission and its work, traveling and preaching in churches and conferences, to enlist more workers and raise support. In time he would help coordinate overseas evangelistic crusades in key areas that rallied listeners to Bruce Woodman's preaching and other SAC programming. The crusades reached lost nationals as well as helped solidify faithful radio listeners. The meetings also served to disciple new believers who were given Gospel literature and directed to evangelical local churches.

As the couple began visiting different congregations to raise support, more than once, as they approached a new church, Tim would look at Carol as they pulled into the parking lot and say, "You're NOT going to give your testimony today, are you?"

Despite his wife's misgivings, Tim grew more and more excited by the prospects of the international ministry awaiting him, though he faced the daunting tasks of raising financial support and breaking the news to Carol's family.

The SMI congregation and Tim's family enthusiastically rallied around the Prewitts, but Carol's unsaved father, not surprisingly, did not. In fact, when Tim broke the news, Mr. Nuncie disowned him.

He curtly added, "I don't care what you do with your life, but I want my daughter and her children in my home!"

Tim was concerned that his call to ministry not become a stumbling block to his father-in-law's getting saved. Even though it was difficult to speak to Carol's Dad, Tim needed to make one more appeal. Caught in an awkward situation, Tim still needed his job at the music store while he raised support to go to the mission field. It was in January 1977 that Tim made his plea to keep his job in the music store till their departure date.

"Pop, I don't expect you to understand what is going on in my life because I don't understand it all either. But Sir, with your permission I would like to stay on here at the store until we leave for the mission field in September."

Mr. Nuncie snapped back, "Why are you telling me NOW?"

"Well, Pop, I need time to finish raising support and to sell our house."

Silence separated the two men for a moment, and then the old man spoke.

"You're right. I don't understand it! But yea, you can stay."

Sadly, there was no mistaking it—the relationship between the two was strained if not broken.

Tim recalls, "For months it was like 'stone-city' at Nuncies Music Store. When I arrived at work, he never acknowledged me, and by the time we closed the store at the end of the day, he had not spoken one word to me. It continued that way day in and day out, week after week."

Increasingly distraught, emotionally and spiritually, Tim continued to pray.

"God, I don't understand this conflict in my family. I want unity not disunity. I know, Heavenly Father, that you are not the Author of confusion. Give me grace and strength and stamina. Lord, only You can do what needs to be done in Mr. Nuncie's heart. I have tried to be a godly example before him in my business integrity and especially in my care of his daughter. I want the blessing of my in-laws."

Tim and Carol both purposed to move forward and follow God's call to the mission field. Tim was following the Lord, and Carol was following her husband. A Bible promise strengthened their faith and orchestrated their pre-field efforts: "He who calls you is faithful, who also will do it" (I Thessalonians 5:24).

"We needed to see God's handprint in our lives," Tim explains. "I was not asking God to let me walk by sight but to strengthen my faith. We put out some fleeces not to test God's will but to know it. Carol and I had witnessed God doing miraculous things in our Pastor's life and in the ministry of our church—like getting the property from U.S. Steel. We were trusting God to do it again, making our call clear, complete, and concise."

Dick Vigneulle often retold the story of his own call to leave City Federal and become a Pastor. A miraculous turn of events in his business and personal life climaxed the call.

"It was as if my hands were tied behind my back, and before me was a jigsaw puzzle. All of a sudden the puzzle pieces began moving on their own, coming together to form a clear picture."

Tim and Carol began to witness their own puzzle pieces coming together.

For one thing, their home went up for sale in the midst of a weak real estate market. Competition was fierce. In their own Birmingham neighborhood, sixteen other houses had "For Sale" signs in the front yard. Their well-intentioned real estate agent suggested selling the house for less than its value to gain an immediate sale. But the Prewitts were moving to a high-rent district in Boca Raton, site of the mission headquarters, so they needed to get top dollar from the sale. Tim and Carol held tight to God's promises and continued to pray. In just a few days, the house sold—at the asking price.

In addition, churches and families quickly responded with promises of prayer and monetary support. Within nine months, the Prewitts reached their financial goal. One hundred percent of their support was committed and coming in. It was time to pack and leave for the field.

As their departure date drew closer, Mr. Nuncie, Carol's father, softened.

"I walked into the music store one morning," Tim recalls, "and after months of silence, Pop spoke to me, starting with a simple 'Good Morning.' God softened his heart, and my father-in-law drew closer to me and loved on me as he had never done before."

God's work in confirming Tim and Carol's call to the mission field continued even after their arrival. Tim began traveling and speaking for the South American Crusades at home and overseas. Carol supported the mission work too and worked actively in their local church in Florida. About a year after their move to Florida, the Prewitts got a phone call from Carol's family. It was good news—Gospel "Good News!" Mr. Nuncie had been saved. A Christian salesman stopped by the music store and seized a lull in customers to share the *Four Spiritual Laws* tract, and Pop Nuncie prayed with him to receive Christ as his personal Savior.

After joining the South American Crusades staff, Carol continued to be like Jonah, an obliging but reluctant servant. Carol felt she loved the Lord. But life on the mission field was a begrudging surrender. Her heart remained back home in Alabama. She resented the place God called her to. To her credit, long before the moving van pulled out of Birmingham, Carol had begun to pray, asking God to change her heart.

Then one Sunday, after two years in Florida, while Tim was away, Carol attended church as she always did. It was an ordinary Sunday in that no special program or emphasis ordered the day. She cannot even recall the preacher's text and sermon from that life-altering service. When the invitation was given, Carol went forward and knelt at the altar.

> I fell down before the Lord and cried and cried. I was shaking and so emotional that some folks thought I was just getting saved! As I poured out my heart to the Lord, He was speaking to me that morning about serving Him. My husband's call finally became mine. I was no longer just a missionary's wife. I too was called of God. The Lord lifted my burden, and immediately a love flowed over me for the people God called us to serve on the field, the very people I had resented for so long. I used to confide to my friends, 'If it's do or die between me and these people, it's gonna be me first!' But no more! These precious people would come first. I would be last!

WORLD REACH

By the time the Prewitts reached their four-year anniversary as missionaries, their shared zeal for serving the Lord had only increased. They loved the South American Crusades staff and the fields reached by SAC's radio broadcasts. Tim had chalked up hundreds of thousands of flying miles,

190

but even more significant was his growing vision for missionary service. His personal Bible study led to a growing burden for church planting ministry, along with a conviction to be part of a local church-centered mission.

Was God calling them to something new?

After much pillow talk and prayer, Tim and Carol agreed to call home and seek the counsel of the Pastor who walked them through their call to South America. Tim dialed Dick Vigneulle's office number.

After an update on their SAC ministry and family events, Tim unloaded his burden. In great detail he shared his vision for a new kind of ministry for himself and Carol.

"Dick, what do you think?"

"Tim, you don't mean it?" Dick Vigneulle exclaimed, with no hint of censure or disappointment.

In fact, he was excited at the news and the timing of Tim's phone call.

"Buddy, you're an answer to my prayers! Let me tell you, Tim, what I've been asking the Lord for."

Dick went on to explain LIGHTHOUSE's expansion and SMI's decision to recruit someone to take the helm, transitioning LIGHTHOUSE into an independent, full-fledged mission board.

A few days later Tim was on a plane to Birmingham. He met with Pastor Vigneulle and missions leaders from the church, including Jim Scott. Tim repeated his vision for missions and learned more about the open doors at SMI.

Shortly afterwards, Tim resigned his position with South American

Dick and Tim Prewitt at World Reach headquarters in Birmingham, AL – March 2009

Crusades and brought his family back to Birmingham. In 1982 LIGHTHOUSE became WORLD REACH, led by its newly appointed General Director, Timothy Q. Prewitt. Governed by its own board, the ministry would be independent of Shades Mountain Independent Church. In recognition of its heritage, however, three board positions would be filled by SMI church members. Dick agreed to serve as Chairman of the World Reach Board. Bill Longshore and Wales Goebel, Dick's old friends since City Federal days, joined forces, along with others, to encourage Tim and help with legal and financial planning. WORLD REACH was incorporated in the state of Alabama as a nonprofit organization—an evangelical, nondenominational Christian missionary organization.

WORLD REACH leaders adopted a clear, pointed purpose statement: "Our purpose is to fulfill the great commission of Jesus Christ." They further clarified the mission's strategy: "WORLD REACH carries out its purpose in close cooperation with local churches through evangelism, discipleship, training national leaders, church planting, and physical relief efforts."

In effect, Tim became a pastor to the world, carrying out the vision Dick Vigneulle preached from his first days as a Pastor. As others came to him for counsel and direction about a life in missions, Tim found himself time and again re-creating the role Dick played in his and Carol's life.

One of those influenced by Tim Prewitt and WORLD REACH was Becky Reitenour Carter. Following college graduation, she had returned to her home church, joining the faculty of Shades Mountain Christian Schools. After years of sitting under Pastor Vigneulle's preaching and attending countless SMI missions conferences, first as a teen in the youth group and now as a staff member, Becky grew more and more fascinated with the idea of serving God overseas. Rift Valley Academy, a mission school in Kenya, Africa captured her heart.

> I was excited that God might be calling me to serve in this way, but I wasn't absolutely SURE of "THE CALL!" I guess I was looking for a lightning bolt with a note attached that read "Go to Rift Valley Academy!" Then a friend of mine challenged me, "Becky, why don't you stop asking God SHOULD I go, and start asking Him COULD I go?" That was the kick in the seat of the pants I needed to get me started in the right direction. I took a month-long trip to Kenya with

WORLD REACH and visited the Academy. I started the application process with Africa Inland Mission, and fervently prayed all along that if God DID NOT want me to go that He would slam the door in my face. Not only did God open the doors, but at times it felt like He picked me up and THREW me through some of the doors He opened!

Today WORLD REACH serves in twelve countries on three continents. With an ever expanding team of staff and volunteers, WORLD REACH continues to identify itself as a ministry "committed to upholding the highest standards of integrity in message, finances, relationships, and moral standards."

An important part of WORLD REACH's unfolding ministry began in the early 1990's when the mission began founding Bible institutes. Most of their work is in rural, primitive areas. Pastors and Christian workers desperately needed training, but their poverty and remote locations hindered them from traveling to big cities. Most of the pastors were bi-vocational and could not leave their jobs. Their families as well as their churches needed them at home. When pastors did relocate to cities for jobs and training, too often the lure of electricity and fast-food restaurants made them reluctant to go back to their villages.

Dick and Tim presented a plan to take the school to the people. WORLD REACH began its MOBILE BIBLE INSTITUTE ministry. They followed the Apostle Paul's biblical direction to train the proven faithful who modeled servant leadership (II Timothy 2:2). The institutes provide over two years of instruction, using college level curriculum. Pastors, aspiring pastors, and Christian workers are given biblical, theological, and practical teaching within their national cultural setting.

Since the institute ministry's inception, WORLD REACH has graduated over four thousand Christian workers. Today there are now ten Bible institutes in six countries with four hundred students enrolled.

Perhaps more than any other ministry Dick Vigneulle has helped launch, none fulfills his vision more than WORLD REACH BIBLE INSTITUTES. Tim recalls Dick's tribute. While presiding at a Board meeting for WORLD REACH, Dick opened with a testimony of praise.

"Men, the Mobile Bible Institute is the greatest ministry that I have ever witnessed in all of my life because of the far-reaching effects it has on the communities and countries it serves."

With WORLD REACH, Dick's great love for reaching the lost found its most satisfying fulfillment. SMI, the church on an Alabama mountain, was doing its part to reach the world.

CHAPTER FIFTEEN

"Everything Rises and Falls on Leadership"

*D*ick Vigneulle approached ministry with a businessman's mindset. The offices and staff of Shades Mountain Independent Church functioned in a corporate environment: long-range planning and goal setting, budget projections and financial reviews, standards for office management, staff reports, and mandatory dress codes for employees—including all pastors in shirts and ties. Moving from a banker's office to a pastor's study, Dick brought with him a marketplace savvy for doing God's work, a sensibility beyond the ken of most novice ministers.

One of Dick's former SMI staffers, beginning his first pastoral ministry, recalls his experience and first impressions.

> When I was in seminary, whenever an alumnus returned on campus, those of us still in the classroom swarmed that graduate to ask "What's it like out there?" We wanted to know how well prepared we were for the real world. I don't recall anyone pining for more Greek or Hebrew. Maybe a few wished they had more practice in homiletics. But by far the number one comment was "I wish I had more training in business and administration." Even a small church had a budget larger than what most of the seminarians ever managed in their personal lives. Whether their assignment was a solo post or included a staff, the novice pastors found human relation skills posed an ongoing challenge. One of the perks in joining the staff of Shades Mountain Independent Church was being led by a Pastor who came out of the business world. Dick Vigneulle sanctified his business acumen for kingdom work. I always

felt that in an era when most businesses were better run than most churches, SMI was better run than most businesses.

Dick's knack for business, an innate gift, began in childhood. His parents modeled hard work and expected their children to be industrious. The necessities of a large family in hard economic times demanded it. Dick acknowledges his father, Harold Vigneulle, as his first and most enduring model and mentor. If his dad was his first teacher, then Dick's first classroom in learning Economics 101 was in the streets of Wilmington, Delaware and on the paper route where he delivered copies of the *Wilmington Home Journal*. He worked hard to expand his route and in time garnered a good income. There was money for extras, even after setting aside money for a tithe and his savings account, as his father directed him to do.

As a college student needing direction to select a major, Dick turned to his father for advice. Harold pointed him to the field of business administration.

"Son, if you study business then you will be in good stead whether you go into the ministry or some profession. You can't go wrong there."

Dick heeded his father's advice and never regretted it. In the early 1950's when he was a student at Bob Jones University, the school ranked among the very top in the nation's schools of business. His training at BJU prepared him for a career in banking and gave an edge to his later calling to the pastorate.

While still in college, Dick demonstrated an exceptional ability at salesmanship. As a married student finishing his senior year, Dick went to work for the Mount Vernon Foundation (M.V.F.) selling their Memory-O-Matic system for filing and organization. He was a tremendous success, numbering among his customers university faculty and staff, as well as fellow students and preachers.

The company newsletter honored him with front page accolades, featuring a picture of Dick and under it the caption "Richard the Great: Lion of Leadership." The headline declared, "Dick Vigneulle: Greatest in M.V.P. History." The cover article challenged the national sales force to break young Vigneulle's sales record:

> *We all pitch our hats high in the air and shout a rousing skyrocket for Rich Vigneulle!!! Why? Why? Just listen to this.... In a single calendar week our Sir Richard of Lion Leadership enlisted*

91 Memberships for a total retail value of $7,247.50. Gentlemen, that is more than DOUBLE the greatest record in Mount Vernon Foundation history. The word TREMENDOUS exhausts itself trying to express this ASTOUNDING record.

Not even out of college, Dick became known as a go-getter of legendary reputation.

Dick's business feats continued in New York City when he turned around the struggling Christian bookstore at Calvary Baptist Church.

His parents' character training and his own growing faith kept the young man centered. A few years later, Dick arrived in Birmingham as a modern-day Joseph in his understanding of biblical stewardship. He was a goal-setter poised and eager to build on all the life skills and job experiences garnered since throwing newspapers in his hometown.

All he needed was the right opportunity or the right introduction. Mark Hodo provided both. A business legend in his time, Hodo recognized Dick's potential all the more shining because of his reputation as a young man of faith and character. Mr. Hodo became like a second father in his affection for Dick and commitment to mentor him in business, eventually choosing him to be his successor at City Federal.

In God's time and providence, parents, preachers, professors, and business presidents all had a hand in molding the banker-preacher God raised up to reach a mountain for Christ.

Many of Dick's supporters felt that his achievements in business gave him a secular pulpit for proclaiming his faith, one beyond most men of the cloth. He could command an audience with the secular as well as the faithful.

For that reason, when Dick announced his plan to leave City Federal to become the full-time Pastor of Shades Mountain Independent Church, some of his friends gave reluctant support or even outright disagreed. He already had an elevated pulpit of sorts in the business district so why give it up for a tiny church in the suburbs?

While grateful for his corporate experience, Dick came to realize, however, that in God's plan for his life, the business world was only a stopping-off point or a training camp. God had something more for him, and he found it in becoming SMI's Pastor.

Perhaps no one recognized the business edge Dick brought to kingdom work more than those pastors who encouraged him in his call to the church.

When Dick traveled to visit leading churches and pastors in the first weeks of his full-time pastorate, he felt affirmed and challenged during his visit with Lee Roberson, in Chattanooga, Tennessee. The Founder and President of Tennessee Temple University and Pastor of the mega Highland Park Baptist Church gave advice to the businessman-turned-pastor that called attention to the Board room as well as the pulpit.

Looking back, Dick summarized the advice from the revered patriarch of fundamentalism by repeating the elder pastor's familiar maxim: EVERYTHING RISES AND FALLS ON LEADERSHIP.

"When he spoke those words to me, I knew Dr. Roberson repeated that advice to his staff and students, and it was a creed by which he lived his life and led his people. I determined to live by it too. While I missed not having the seminary level training that many pastors have, I knew God schooled me through my life in business. Those lessons learned at the bank I took to the church, and they served me well."

As SMI's ministry expanded and grew, Dick led the staff and congregation with an executive's regimen that brought a corporate atmosphere to SMI's function. Despite the easy nature and charismatic thrill he brought to the church platform on Sunday mornings, the man at the ministry's helm worked behind the scenes with sober diligence and a demand for excellence not just sacrifice. He viewed mediocrity as a shortcoming, if not a sin. Lay leaders and staff pastors respected their Pastor for it.

Not discounting divine providence, the folks of SMI knew that God's blessings came as the fruit of their hard work and wise practices. As a Pastor, Dick never forgot what his father modeled and his Christian college professors taught: good business is rooted in Biblical truth. Moses, Nehemiah, and Paul were wise men of business as well as patriarchs and apostles of the Faith.

Over the years of Dick's ministry, journalists, students and fellow Christian workers came to SMI's Pastor's office to learn some of the mechanics of good ministry—what did he learn in business that helped him in ministry?

CHURCH BOARD

Dick Vigneulle organized for success. Assigning roles and maintaining accountability came second nature to him. From the church's very beginning,

SMI's internal organization reflected its heritage and creed, mixing evangelical zeal with the Methodist church's penchant for committees.

From SMI's inception and under Dick's guidance, the church Board was central to the church's organization and development of its leadership. SMI's Board formed and chaired church committees, an organizational model born out of conviction and necessity. In the church's early days, with no paid staff and no full-time pastor until years later, the laity were the church's ministers. There was no one else to oversee the work. Every church member appreciated Dick's example. He had a full-time job at City Federal and still filled the pulpit. Fired up by his leadership and grateful for his sacrifices, the

One of SMI's first Boards – pictured in Lew Bagwell's Memorial Prayer Garden

congregation developed a strong conviction about shared leadership.

The twelve-member Board included officers—chairman, vice chairman, and secretary/treasurer—who were joined by chairmen and vice chairmen of four key ministry areas—evangelism, Christian education, missions, and youth. One member at large rounded out the group. Board members served a total of three years, and then rotated off for at least a year's duration before being eligible for reelection. A minority of members rolled off at any one time, affording stability and continuity.

Limited tenure broadened the field of leaders, and likewise afforded time off after the grueling duties of Board service. The SMI Board met monthly for weekday evening meetings that could stretch to six or eight hours in length. The sessions began with a meal so the men could fellowship as well as be fed since many came straight from work to the church. Afterwards, before addressing the first agenda item, the men prayed, not offering a mere token invocation. In fact, a lengthy prayer meeting preceded the business meeting.

After Dick came to SMI full time, the focus on laity in leadership never abated, even after hired staff joined the pastoral staff. The group dynamic could dismay the insecure or novice minister. Many pastors' field work with a new assignment begins with trying to stir up laity's involvement. At SMI, however, the laymen and women of the church were like a healthy team of workhorses bridled, snorting and prancing, and ready to run! By keeping laity in primary leadership roles as partners with the pastoral staff, Dick furthered his mix of business-mindedness with ministry operations.

One lay leader recalls how, early on, the young congregation kept a vigilant lookout to secure its survival. More than once, established outside ministries tried to absorb the young church into their own organizations, thus claiming SMI's dynamic band of believers and absconding with its identity. In addition to the danger of these religious predators, there was always the risk of a well-meaning but divisive crusader intent on pressing his personal agenda.

Many SMI members were corporate professionals and business owners who came to church eager to work and feeling equipped to lead. Dick did not want to dampen their zeal. He prized their practical abilities and their positions in the community for spreading the Gospel. However, leadership in business did not automatically qualify a volunteer for leadership in the church. There had to be a time of proving and equipping before new believers held offices. Prerequisite to holding any post was proven spiritual maturity. Equally important, newcomers on the Board had to share the Pastor's vision for ministry.

Short-range security came with a tight agenda and stable leadership. Apprenticeship secured long-range precautions. Before any believer held leadership posts, there was a prerequisite of proven discipleship and hands-on ministry experience. As a result, SMI's volunteers saw their secular training honed for sacred service. Members of the congregation respected the fact that SMI required a test of time and servanthood.

Dick never wanted pastors on staff to displace the laity but rather to partner with them. Likewise, he wanted the congregation to respect the pastors' calls to ministry and to utilize their training and skills. At work was a fundamental New Testament principle of discipleship and church life: pastors were to train and equip faithful men and women for the work of the ministry. "And the things that you have heard from me among many witnesses, commit these to faithful men who will be able to teach others also" (II Timothy 2:2).

As the church grew and the pastoral staff expanded, SMI's Board and staff became two distinct but joined forces in ministry. Board members never attended staff meetings, and staff members rarely attended Board meetings. Dick, as Senior Pastor, became the link between the two, along with the Board representative partnering with the staff pastor in his assigned area. For example, the Board's Chairman of Christian Education linked with the Christian Education Minister, organizing their committee, setting goals, and recruiting and training volunteers for their specified ministry field. Not one given to micro-managing, Pastor Vigneulle released his ministry teams to do their work. He never abandoned staff or Board to ministry, building in checks and balances, whether through reports or meetings or budgets.

There was one grand exception to this separate but one approach to ministry: the Annual Board and Staff Retreat. A two-day event, usually held at a state park, brought together the church's pastors and Board members as well as their spouses. After a Friday afternoon of free time for recreation and casual fellowship, the folks gathered in the evening for a banquet. On Saturday the pastoral staff and Board members gathered for a combined meeting, the only time they would meet together.

Leroy Clark, who served several terms as Chairman of SMI's Board, described the importance of this annual meeting.

When Dick spoke at the annual retreat banquet, newcomers and returning members of the Board could be reminded of Dick's vision for ministry. We weren't here to do our own thing. We needed to hear our Pastor's goals. Also the Board needed to hear the different pastors—each one would recount what was happening in his life and ministry area. The Board needed to remember their job was to partner with the pastors. They were men with a calling and training to respect. The retreat gave some downtime together too so we could fellowship and get to know each other better.

201

Another practical purpose for the retreat was to provide instruction on the basics of Board life and ethics. It was an orientation meeting for husbands and their wives.

For example, one expectation communicated to the men and their spouses was a commitment to confidentiality. Ministry encompasses life's sorrows as well as joys and meets people at their lowest as well as high points of attitude and behavior. Unity in spirit and purpose headed off any damage from the surprises or disappointments of ministry life.

Dick insisted on a spirit of cooperation, often exhorting both staff and Board with his simple formula for success in ministry: "MUTUAL SUBMISSION." Like a husband and wife or father and mother, SMI's lay leaders and ministerial staff needed to maintain unity without sacrificing individual distinctions in gifts and calling. The unity of the body and peace within the family of God required it.

Leroy Clark reflected, "These people would pay a great price in personal sacrifice to serve, so it was important that the leaders and their families united in a common purpose. In business, things are pretty cut and dried. You make decisions and go on with your life. In church life, on the other hand, situations can get pretty emotional and disheartening."

The Friday night banquet featured a challenge from the Pastor and a word from the staff pastors, sharing updates on their areas of ministry. Then came the big event of the whole retreat—a prayer meeting. Peggy Vigneulle would lead the women to a separate area for their prayer time, and Dick would lead the men in their prayer vigil.

Each man was targeted with prayers of consecration, as the others gathered around and laid hands on a pastor or a layman one at a time. There were no quickie prayers. The intentional prayer effort in this annual commissioning and anointing of SMI's leaders resulted in a prayer meeting that often stretched into early morning hours. This start of a new year of church business began with prayer—pastors and lay leaders and their families on their knees before God. Dick knew good intentions alone meant nothing without God's favor and His divine direction to unite and energize the people.

Dick's business penchant to delegate and diversify would continue to guide his pastorate. As Shades Mountain Independent grew to over a thousand people in attendance, the church faced the challenge of keeping up with so many folks. Even a dedicated staff and hardworking Board could not keep up. Dick proposed a solution which the Board and congregation gladly adopted—the formation of an **ELDERS** ministry. While the Board and staff attended SMI's business and ministry matters, the elders would provide pastoral care for the church family.

Each elder was as carefully selected as a member of the Board or staff. These men accepted responsibility for a segment of the church membership, serving their assigned families in practical, caring ways. As part of their ministry, elders and their wives made home visits. If sickness or bereavement issues arose, the elders linked those in need to the church's care systems. They also hosted gatherings that brought together the families under their care, whether for prayer meetings or backyard cookouts.

As the first moderator of SMI's elders, Ed Baggett recalls a ministry that brought great personal joy to him and his wife, Mary Katherine.

"It was people serving people!"

Initially, the elder assignments were based on zip codes, but the geographic spread proved too cumbersome for effective service for some. A more successful approach, developed later, based elder groups on Sunday School classes. At least one elder was appointed to each class. Larger classes had two or more elders. The system matured into a network with multiple elders who, in turn, were aided in their duties by coordinators who oversaw smaller family units within the classes. In time, Lewis Moore joined Ed Baggett, and the two men served as co-moderators.

The elders provided a link between the Pastor and congregation. Just as the elders tied in SMI families to the church, so they also kept Dick informed on the needs and views of the congregation. The result was greater intimacy in the spirit and function of the church. More important, as the congregation grew, folks did not get lost in the crowd. Despite the church's growing numbers, individuals and families knew SMI was still a caring place.

The days of meeting in the Hoover insurance building or the Vestavia school library were long past. Church attendance was now counted in the hundreds not dozens. But keeping pace with an emerging, maturing ministry were the helping hands of SMI's Board, Pastors, and Elders. As a result, the church family kept alive the long-standing refrain that Shades Mountain Independent Church was *WHERE THE LOVE IS!*

STAFF

"When I hire someone to fill a staff position, I want a thoroughbred! I would rather pull the reins than have to push!" Dick once confided, both complimenting the caliber of his staff and revealing his standard for employment. With volunteers and paid staff, good intentions and lofty goals did not suffice.

Missionary veteran and lifelong Vigneulle family friend, Brom Cowser said, "Dick followed a principle that Dr. Bob Sr. repeated to his preacher boys—*Don't be afraid to borrow brains!*"

Dick valued godly counsel and would not hesitate to seek help or hire staff to cover the diversity as well as the volume of SMI's expanding ministry. He needed partners with gifts beyond his own. Dick's first Assistant Pastor, and the first employee hired after Dick went full time at SMI, was his brother-in-law, Jimmy Haley. Beyond their long-standing friendship and family ties, the two shared a Bob Jones Academy education as well as experience in ministry and business. With a bi-vocational background as a pastor and retail manager for a major department store, Jimmy was ready to provide daily oversight to church operations and help with teaching and pastoral duties.

Many of Dick's staff came upon recommendation of trusted family and co-workers.

When Rick and Mick were students at Liberty University, they told their father about a popular teacher on campus named Bob Stone who taught courses on family and personal relationships. Dick invited Bob to visit SMI and conduct one of his Family Life Seminars. Not long afterwards Bob joined the staff to head a counseling ministry while continuing to travel for his seminars. When the counseling load increased, at Bob Stone's urging, his former co-worker, Bob Palmer, was recruited to come to Birmingham and partner with Bob.

Likewise, when the church needed a staff pastor to oversee evangelism and discipleship, Dick found help with the recommendations of active lay workers Raymond and Faye Kelley. Faye worked on staff as a bookkeeper, and Raymond served on the church Board as Chairman of Evangelism. They told Dick about a former Birmingham research biologist who went into ministry and now served on the staff of Campus Crusade for Christ. Not long afterwards Drew Ramsay joined SMI's pastoral staff.

Dick's move from City Federal's executive suite to SMI's Pastor's office paralleled a larger change taking place in the American church culture. Emerging super churches of the 1970's fashioned a new role for the Senior Pastor. Dick was on the cusp of this paradigm shift to the Executive Pastor. With Sunday School classes larger than some entire congregations, and multiple tiers of employees, pastors now led more than a weekly Sunday School teachers meeting and managed more than a one-page budget. The pastor as CEO required his management skills to match his exegetical ones.

Dick came to the pulpit uniquely prepared, pioneering the role of Pastor as Executive. He was not alone. This new wave of leadership rose to the forefront leading large churches that became cultural and political influences, not just evangelistic ones. Congregations practically equated executive capacity with biblical scholarship. The complexity of ministries led by multiple staff pastors, as well as a congregation with multifaceted profiles and needs, demanded a pastor with administration function and communication skills. Dick Vigneulle was that kind of pastor—God spent the first half of Dick's life training him for just such a role.

Leading a group of Christians, as one dry wit suggested, is like "trying to herd cats!" They often refuse to march in single file, and you always have to chase strays! The same could be said for a pastoral staff. But Dick worked to keep a cohesive spirit among his staff and a unified vision in their various pursuits.

Dick was a no-nonsense boss, always well-groomed and immaculately dressed in a suit or sports coat with tie. His physical and spiritual stature commanded respect. Before and after church services, and even in the pulpit, Dick bantered with folks with a casual style that dispelled any air of formality. But in the workplace, while approachable and fun-loving, he led his pastoral staff with corporate intentionality and old-school expectations. He held a high performance standard and operated with corporate discipline. The business world marshaled his leadership style, while his core values and their outcropping standards came from Scripture not Wall Street.

Ever a focused multi-tasker, Dick lived with boundless energy. It showed in his fast-paced schedule and lively demeanor.

Drew Ramsay recalls, "The first word that comes to my mind when I think of Dick's personality is ENTHUSIASM. This describes the way he went about everything he did. Whether preaching, singing, or leading a meeting, Dick was enthusiastic."

The men serving under him knew Dick respected their abilities and expected them to take charge of their ministry areas. Other people's skills or attainments did not intimidate him. He respected them and valued what each person brought to the team. Unlike Saul, Israel's first king who grew jealous when young David won the cheers of the nation, Dick was not put off by any subordinate's popularity and influence.

One pastor recalls a staff meeting that addressed the issue.

"Dick looked at the men around the table and smiled as he said, 'I want you to know that I realize each of you has a following in the congregation, and that's fine and just as it should be. But what I want you to realize is that each man around the table has a following—you are not the only one. All I ask is that you make sure your following is following me as I lead the church in the task God has called us to do.'"

Prayer forged staff unity and so too did regular meetings. His door was always open to his staff, and he was a master of the working lunch. It was a special time when Dick singled out a staff member for a one-on-one exchange at his favorite local restaurant, a steak house on Montgomery Highway. Sometimes the invitations were spur-of-the- moment occasions for fellowship, but often those sessions meant there was a special project to pursue or a problem to solve. Dick accomplished a lot of mentoring, especially with the younger men, in those sessions. As an added perk, he always picked up the tab.

Regular staff meetings made up the work week. If not already on duty, all pastors were to be at work by 9:00 A.M to gather in the conference room. After a brief exchange of pleasantries and a review of any urgent announcements, Dick would read Scripture and lead in prayer. The men were dismissed within twenty minutes. Also the pastors submitted to their boss weekly staff reports which gave a daily account of work and events for the past work week.

One pastor, describing Dick's leadership, explained, "Dick was always prepared whatever the situation. He came to the table, so to speak, organized and with a planned pathway. His style of leadership, reflecting his corporate life, created a structured culture. There were responsibilities, reports, principles, and priorities. Things were carried out in a professional manner which meant 'do it right' and 'plan it well.' Excellence could be achieved and promoted through structure and planning."

The pastors also had regular private meetings with Dick to discuss personal or ministry events. In addition, once a week the entire pastoral staff met for expanded, agenda-led meetings, usually lasting a couple of hours. These gatherings kept the men informed of church events and long-range plans. In addition, each pastor was kept informed on what was happening outside his specific areas. The content and spirit of the meetings helped to maintain good will and a unified vision. At one of these meetings, the school administrator expressed frustration at a delay in getting classrooms set up for the new school year, just days away. Immediately after the meeting, all the pastors, including the Senior Pastor, went to classrooms to move and arrange desks and chairs.

There were two main lines of responsibility for each pastor—his budget and his calendar. Accountability for time and money would measure performance and prove trust. In Pastor Vigneulle's economy, capable time management and good planning proved as important as sound fiscal management.

One of the pastors serving under Dick recalls, "Not only did we learn to manage and be accountable for the finances of our ministry area, but we also gained a respect for the spiritual blessings and direction to be learned from biblical stewardship. A good cause did not warrant a blank check. There seemed to be an unspoken principle that a ministry had to pay its own way or sustain itself, in manpower and money. There might be funding from the budget or other resources, but if the ministry did not become self-sustaining, then perhaps its season had passed. There was a place for faith but not presumption. The staff learned to discern the difference."

Two annual events, critical to staff and ministry development, were the winter and summer staff retreats. In early January, right on the heel of the holidays, the staff gathered in Gatlinburg, Tennessee, the famed resort community in the Smokies. The off-season made the event more affordable even though the church paid all costs. Wives were invited to this winter retreat, giving the ladies time for fellowship and recreation as well as prayer. The two- or three-day event was devoted to calendar planning for the coming year. Each man arrived with his ministry area's twelve-month schedule, and Dick or Jimmy introduced church-wide events. Month by month sharing of dates and events assured a smooth coordination of people and facility resources. Sometimes there were slip-ups, such as the year a couples' retreat was scheduled for the same weekend as the annual Auburn-Alabama football game. The staff learned the hard way to keep open the Saturday for The Game.

Work and play made up the retreat, but in measured parts: two parts work to one part play. One day the men worked morning and afternoon, and so enjoyed the evening off, allowing the couples to share dinner together and then spend some downtime browsing in shops or chatting before a fireplace. The next day the sequence shifted, with planning sessions morning and evening and the afternoon off.

Some six months later, the summer retreat included only the pastors and was devoted to goal setting in addition to ministry planning and evaluation. The meeting site often was the vacation or lake home of a church member. Again there was a mix of work and fun and plenty of good food. Boat rides and water skiing eased any tension in muscles or attitudes after hours of discussion.

Whether in staff meetings, retreats, or private sessions, Dick loved to brainstorm, so much so that he could ignore the clock no matter how long the session continued or how late the night hours ticked by. Leading a ministry that was born by thinking outside the box, Dick encouraged creativity. But ideas meant nothing without a plan.

Like a traveler who wants only plain and simple directions, not wordy descriptions of local history, Dick tempered availability to his staff with an insistence on clear, concise communications—written or verbal. In personal exchanges, with family as well as staff, he would cut off the long-winded with his familiar dictum, "*What's the bottom line?*"

Dick not only wanted matters to be to the point, he preferred to keep the tone and topic positive. He did not avoid problems—he just did not want to dwell on them. He preferred ideas and solutions over complaints and naysaying. If someone brought him a problem, he appreciated a matching suggestion to solve it. He likely deputized someone else to "wear the black hat"—often the Chairman of the church Board or the Assistant Pastor. Dick operated best in a positive atmosphere. He wanted his staff and their ministries to be on track and harmonious. That desire led to another of his catchphrases, often repeated and wide in its appeal for unity and harmony: "*Guys, is everything copacetic?*" His delight was in goal-setting, formulating strategies, and planning celebrations.

Never one for wasting time, Dick kept staff meetings centered and moving along, and the staff kept them exciting. The meetings served to meld the leaders' hearts and to keep SMI on target in maintaining evangelism and discipleship the big priority. Diversity in personality and gifts could set up intense discussions. But one of the saving graces to unity and good will was a generous sense of humor among all the staff. Never coarse and rarely silly, good natured fun and teasing was common.

Once when a staff meeting drew to a close, one of the men asked what time it was. Dick forgot he was holding a cup of coffee. Turning his wrist to look at his watch, he spilled a Styrofoam cup of brew on his lap. Mercifully the coffee was tepid. Once the guys knew the Pastor was not burned, snickers gave way to outright laughter. The meeting was quickly adjourned.

OFFICE

Dick respected the power of appearance. He was old-school in his expectations of his staff and office management. His idea of casual Friday was a loose necktie.

Ancient Israel got in trouble after the nation chose its first king on the basis of appearance over character. The result was a fiasco under the reign of Saul. God chose an obscure shepherd boy to be Israel's second king, prioritizing a heart for God over appearance and popular opinion.

The Prophet Samuel, orchestrating the transition from man's choice to God's, summarized the experience: "man looks at the outward appearance, but the LORD looks at the heart" (I Samuel 16:7b).

In time, David, the Lord's anointed, grew in stature and proved his worth, but no doubt eventually his appearance too became regal, reflecting his high office and royal calling.

In the same way, Dick never sacrificed the priority of spiritual integrity and proven ability when selecting ministry leaders. He looked on the heart first. However, refined by the Old South traditions of his college and corporate life, Dick recognized the value of appearance. A rumpled suit and a cluttered office, he felt, detracted from the messenger and his message.

Leroy Clark recalls, "Dick was over-the-top on cleanliness and neatness. One year when the Board addressed staff salaries, Dick asked for money to be allotted to buy new suits for the pastors. He felt their suits were looking a little shabby or too casual."

Good order applied to the work environment as well as the workers' appearance. Dick lived his life in a well-ordered world, so naturally he projected the same at work, expecting if not requiring structure at work. The buzz word among the pastors was "Keep your office clean and your desk clear!"

One staff member warned the man taking his place about Dick's insistence on tidiness.

"I'm kind of messy and can't keep my desk straight, so here's a trick that works for me!"

With that he pulled out a cardboard box that he kept under his desk.

"Dick may open the door after hours to inspect—he will take a peek but never come in. So I just scoop all the stuff off my desk into this box at the end of the day and stash it down here. He'll never look *under* the desk!"

His reputation for neatness and order made Dick the brunt of pranksters. One of his idiosyncrasies was keeping the pen and pencil set on his desk in perfect alignment, like well-trained guardsmen at palace doors. The shafts of the pen and pencil had to angle in just-right parallel lines, without breaking rank. Fun-loving staff members would pass the desk and when Dick was not looking give a gentle tap to the pen or the pencil. When Dick turned around it would not be long before he sensed something was wrong. Without fail, with sonar-like efficiency, he would instinctively spot the offending guardsman and tap it back into a straight line. He was the same way when hanging a picture in his home or office. The top of the frame had to be perfectly aligned. Even the minutest tilt threw him off. He would stand up in the middle of a meeting, go over to the offending object, and shift it back in place—all without missing a beat as he spoke.

Shortly before his retirement, a reporter interviewed Dick for a "Church of the Week" article that appeared in *The Hoover Outlook* (June 29, 1995), and found a striking parallel between the appearance of the Pastor's office and the man who occupied it.

"The Pastor's office was a reflection of his personality, large, open, comfortable, and yet business like, rather than cluttered or over filled with religious mementos or icons."

Dick's office at the church was roomy and well-appointed. Peggy Vigneulle was her husband's decorator. It looked beautiful but not ostentatious. An executive desk stood before an entire wall of built-in bookcases and closet. Conference chairs faced the desk and across the room was a living room-like setting with sofa, upholstered chairs, tables, and lamps. The room looked like it belonged to someone with important responsibility. With the Prophet Samuel's insight to human nature, Dick wanted the church facility's appearance and maintenance to give honor to the message and not detract by being below par or neglected.

He confided to one of his pastors the usefulness of an office to command respect for the Lord's work. Long after he had been full time at SMI and his professional background forgotten by some, he escorted a visitor to his office.

"The man had been difficult and indifferent to Christian things, but when he walked in and saw a nice office, he suddenly found a new respect for what SMI stood for. It's sad that people are that way, but we need to be discerning and careful."

It was one thing for a ministry to make do with meager resources, but too often well-intentioned religious leaders unduly settle for less. Furthermore, after years in real estate development, Dick knew that well-cared-for facilities reflect good management. And good employees deserved the best environment and tools possible to do their job.

On the other hand, he held to a careful budget and conservative means. When one of the staff members submitted a proposal for decorating the church foyer with fancy furniture groupings, Dick vetoed the project as too expensive. He followed a plan of careful stewardship.

PASTOR'S STUDY

Pastor Vigneulle never studied at his church office. There were too many interruptions and distractions. He used his SMI office for appointments—to counsel or hold meetings. He had a secret "getaway" office where he did most of his studying and sermon preparation. One of the perks that City Federal afforded him after his departure was a private office at one of its branch locations. Few knew where it was. Some thought it was out in

Dick in his office early on as a pastor

211

Fairfield, and others guessed Mountain Brook. Other than his home office, this hideaway was the real Pastor's study for SMI's preacher.

The clandestine location served to protect Dick from himself, not just disrupting employees or parishioners. By his own admission, while Dick loved preaching, he chaffed at the hours spent in the study. He delighted in delivery, not preparation. A man of action finds it hard to be still. On Dick's study days, it was not unusual for staff pastors to receive a phone call from the boss. There was genuine business to discuss, and the random calls kept the staff alert and on call. But there was something else prompting the call, or so it seemed to one staff member.

"When Pastor would call me from his satellite office, I knew he was there to prepare a sermon. Once we covered the business that prompted the call, Dick would sigh and mention his struggle in hitting the books. Sometimes there was a tone in his voice that reminded me of a boy doing his homework and looking out a window watching his friends at play outside. He knew there was work to do, but he longed to be out where the action is!"

The struggle stemmed not only from the demands of his job and the bent of his interests, but also some suggest from the nature of his spiritual giftedness.

One of the pastors who served on SMI's staff suggested, "Dick's spiritual gift, I think, is exhortation not teaching. Those with the gift of teaching delight to hit the books, some tolerating the lectern or pulpit in order to get back to the study. Pastor Vigneulle, on the other hand, became energized by a crowd not books. He loved to challenge and encourage his audience, and so endured his hours in the study in order to get back in the pulpit. But the ultimate proof of his gift of exhortation was his undeniable power to impact his listeners. When folks listened to him preach, they left the building not only informed but ready to do something!"

His preaching style was kinetic, even when standing still his body seemed to move. Energy filled his voice as well as his body. Commanding in presence and volume, Dick never took on formal or ecclesiastical airs. He wanted to inspire, not pontificate. His messages, always Bible-centered and well-organized, kept to a layman's approach in simplicity and practicality.

Despite his lack of seminary training, he was a student of the Bible all his adult life. His knowledge, as well as his deep conviction that people needed to hear and heed the Word of God, gave him a freedom in the pulpit. Newcomers to faith and the church often felt intimidated by the Bible and embarrassed by their lack of knowledge. But Dick Vigneulle's simple, straightforward teaching informed his hearers and equipped them to study the Bible on their own.

Like a vocalist who speaks more than sings his lyrics, Dick preached with a different vocal pattern than most preachers. There was an agitated cadence that kept the words coming quickly and divulged the depth of his conviction. He spoke boldly. He often would throw his head back and lead with laughter, dispelling formality while drawing his audience further into his message. Dick never entered the pulpit without notes, simple and often hand-written ones, but he never was tied to notes. He kept 360-degree eye contact, so even the choir was never left out.

As he preached, Dick took on assorted likenesses. Sometimes, as he made his appeals for life-changing decisions, he sounded like a favorite uncle at the family reunion, regaling his kin with family history and destiny. The effect rallied the errant or discouraged, all the while inspiring the young.

Other times, though not one to raise his voice in a tirade, Dick often grew loud like a coach on the sidelines, exhorting church members as if they were players nearing half-time and every game was homecoming.

One admiring out-of-town guest, a repeat visitor, complimented both the preacher and congregation: "When I attended SMI, I never felt like I was in church. Even among the largest crowds, Dick Vigneulle made his audience feel they were part of an intimate conversation. Image, persona, presence—he had it all! When he preached, I wanted to be part of what he was doing because I sensed that something was happening and it was going to be successful!"

Responses like that made those hard times in the study worth it all!

CHAPTER SIXTEEN

Moral Majority

*I*n one of the most heated moments of the 1980 Alabama legislative year, crowds filled the Senate chamber in Montgomery's Capitol Building, and more witnesses packed the gallery. The Senate Rules Committee was conducting a hearing, as state leaders considered a resolution calling for a constitutional convention to write into Alabama's laws a prohibition against abortions.

A pastor from Dothan, Alabama spoke out: "Under our court rulings, a mother can put out a contract on her baby."

Advocates and opponents alike were present, energizing the room with formal declarations and impromptu outcries. The Senate Rules Committee Chairman, determined to avert chaos, maintained order, chastising those speaking out of turn. Mail bags overflowed his office, so he knew the importance of the issue to his constituency. He proposed a substitute resolution which asked the U.S. Congress—not the State of Alabama—to hold the constitutional convention. Some considered the substitute measure to be passing-the-buck, an unwanted side-stepping move. It passed unanimously.

Then a senator from Birmingham moved to put off the vote till later in the calendar. This motion passed unanimously too. The Chairman then suggested this would allow citizens time to write their congressmen, with one stipulation.

"But don't send me anymore letters!"

A fire storm of discussion followed, with fans and foes of the measure speaking out. The pro-abortion crowd, well represented, attempted to gain ground, citing figures and professionals favorable to their side.

But the people for life held their ground.

A reporter later described the scene, "The anti-abortionists, though, appeared to have carried the field. Wearing red roses, they out-applauded the ones who opposed the constitutional convention. Supporters of the resolution wore red roses, red ribbons, or red flowers which they said symbolized life. Opponents wore decals simply reading 'Choice.'"

One of the major speakers for life that day was SMI's Pastor. The reporter took note of him by name (in all caps) and went on to describe the stir he created in the Senate chamber.

"THE REV. DICK VIGNEULLE of Birmingham, one of the leadoff speakers for the resolution, got thunderous applause when he opened by saying he represents 'the moral majority of Alabama.' He said that the constitutional amendment is needed because 'the whole moral fiber of this nation is crumbling. These proponents of legalized murder do not speak for millions of God-fearing Americans,' he said, to another burst of applause."

An opponent to Dick, evidently watching the clock and not wanting him to have more than the allotted two minutes per speaker, edged near the committee table and shouted "Time!"

Not to be put off, Dick stood his ground, turned to the Senate Committee Chairman and after a quick appeal, continued with a brief prayer, closing "May these men and women do today what they will wish they had done when they stand before You! Amen!" Only then did the *Reverend* Vigneulle sit down, cheering crowds surrounding him.

A resurgence of activity by conservative Christians in American politics in the 1970's, spurred on in part by the nation's Bicentennial, culminated in the formation of MORAL MAJORITY. Founded by Jerry Falwell in 1979 as a political not church organization, MORAL MAJORITY undeniably impacted the cultural and political course of the nation. Many of its foes as well as supporters consider MORAL MAJORITY the era's foremost conservative organization.

Falwell and his supporters sought to inform and mobilize conservative Christians to "take back" America from encroaching liberalism. In time, Dr. Falwell sought to diversify the group by including religious folks outside the evangelical fold but who shared their Judeo-Christian values. Never officially connected to any one political party, MORAL MAJORITY emphasized moral issues over political ones. Their determined battlegrounds included voting booths and media outlets.

With the dawn of the Civil Rights era, Black clergymen and other stalwarts took courageous stands in the public arena to confront long-standing racial prejudice and discrimination. Braving public scorn and physical attack, leaders rallied supporters into a formidable voice and presence. A righteous cause united the rank and file until Washington, D. C. and the entire nation took notice and could no longer ignore their demands. When Civil Rights leaders took a stand against racism, determined to topple injustice, they reminded those ignored and disenfranchised just what could be accomplished by a people united in a cause.

Likewise, a wide spectrum of moral and political grievances prompted MORAL MAJORITY's formation and function. Conservative citizenry and church folks alike, alarmed by the unraveling of decency in America, rallied against a political hierarchy deaf to their cries and blind to their existence.

Common concerns and convictions united Dr. Falwell and his followers into a formidable army of champions. Their values-driven organization mounted a stand against such evils as abortion, the removal of prayer in public schools, pornography, and other enemies of traditional family values. More than just a voice for change, MORAL MAJORITY became a machine for change, uniting millions of American conservatives into a united voting block.

Above and independent of labels, by denominations or political parties, MORAL MAJORITY enlisted a membership in the millions and helped register voters in the tens of millions. In time, historians would credit MORAL MAJORITY with putting a man in the White House, an achievement Falwell himself described as "my finest moment."

As the organization's founder and chief spokesman, Jerry Falwell became a recognized figure of celebrity proportions, lauded by conservatives and demonized by liberals. The tenor of a man's message, let alone the measure of a man's influence, oftentimes surfaces from his enemies—who they are and what they say. Falwell's adversaries were vociferous, often notables among the nation's liberals in churches and congress. He wore their disdain as a badge of honor.

Nor was Dr. Falwell alone in the battle. Before, during, and after MORAL MAJORITY's lifespan, other Christian organizations and action groups were formed. Dr. Tim and Beverly LaHaye were valued friends to the Vigneulles and SMI. In 1988, Dr. LaHaye preached at the church every

Sunday night for nearly four months, forging a lasting tie with the Pastor and church. There were additional respected and influential voices in the country, including D. James Kennedy, Pat Robertson, and Charles Stanley.

Already a hometown hero in his native Lynchburg, Virginia, Falwell became a major figure in Fundamentalism after founding and building a mega church and Christian university. His influence widened with his nationwide television program—*The Old Time Gospel Hour*—elevating him to a national figure. Millions of Americans tuned in to watch their favorite television pastor, the strapping, blue-eyed preacher with a booming voice. Ultimately, however, after founding MORAL MAJORITY, Jerry Falwell became a political powerhouse the whole world took notice of.

Dr. Falwell and his preaching peers were just a generation removed from an era where the *innovative* tools for mass evangelism meant tents for itinerant preachers and radios for sermons over the air. Numeric success meant being able to count contacts and converts in the hundreds or perhaps thousands. But now a new breed of evangelists, outfitted with newer technology and innovative strategies, used television and mass marketing for getting out their message. With the whole world only a satellite broadcast away, success now meant numbers in the millions.

The preacher from Virginia stepped into the ring of national politics with a one-two punch against the devil: he would utilize mass media and develop a grass routes network. Falwell's national prominence positioned him to succeed at both. To accomplish the latter, he launched local chapters of Moral Majority, spinning his Rolodex of friends to recruit executive directors to lead state chapters. He knew people everywhere.

When it came to finding a leader for MORAL MAJORITY of ALABAMA, the choice must have been quick and easy. Jerry Falwell selected his old friend, Dick Vigneulle.

When Dick surrendered to God's call to leave his banking career to become the full-time Pastor of Shades Mountain Independent Church, one of the first he turned to for advice was Jerry Falwell. In fact, when Falwell learned that Dick planned to enter the ministry, he tried to recruit Dick for his own staff. Complimented but not tempted, Dick knew what and where God had called him to be. Besides, as both men's admirers' admit, the two were too much alike to yoke together—there can only be one designated quarterback per team.

Neither overshadowed the other in the size of his stature and persona, let alone drive and dreams. Like fraternal twins, Jerry Falwell and Dick Vigneulle were alike but not identical. Uncompromising biblical inerrantists, they agreed on theology and shared matching biblical values. Either one could fill a room with his outsize personality, and fascinate his listeners with storytelling and humor. Especially important for building the MORAL MAJORITY network, both leaders possessed refined organizational skills. Most importantly, both men loved the Lord, and loved to tell others about Jesus.

Jerry knew and loved Dick's whole family. The Vigneulle's twin sons were already students at Liberty University, the Christian school Falwell founded in Lynchburg in 1971. Rick and Mick Vigneulle became veteran Christian entertainers as they traveled the nation with Falwell's "I LOVE AMERICA" rallies. The rallies were spectacularly choreographed musical productions held on the steps of state capitols all around the country. Along with other school talents, the twins used their gifts for music and comedy to delight audiences.

One morning as the twins walked across the Liberty campus en route to class, they waved to their school's founder. Falwell was a familiar albeit famous pedestrian on campus. He delighted to walk among his students, frequently stopping to engage in one-on-one or small group exchanges. Never stuffy or put off, Dr. Falwell was a beloved pastor and respected father figure. It came as no surprise when the University President called the twins over to chat.

Looking down at the brothers, putting a hand on each one's shoulder, Falwell said, "Boys, how'd you like to fly to Birmingham and see your parents? I'm leaving in fifteen minutes—I've got a speaking engagement down that way. I'll drop you off."

It was a no-brainer. The brothers forgot class as they ran back to their room to pack quickly.

On another occasion, in another demonstration of the familiarity and friendship between the two pastors, it was the father not the sons who was the object of Falwell's attention—or, more accurately, the brunt of his pranks. At 1:00 a.m. the phone rang in the Vigneulle home, rousing Dick from a deep sleep. Figuring no good news comes at this hour, a bit alarmed, he picked up the receiver. The voice on the other end boomed with demands for information.

"Is this Rev. Vigneulle? Tell me about that church of yours up on the mountain. I might like to visit!"

Dick himself retells the moment, "I bit my lip at first—after all, it was 1:00 a.m. Then I recognized the voice and realized it was Jerry. He was in his plane, flying over Alabama, and he thought of me and wanted to call. That was like him—he never liked to be alone and he liked to talk, whether telling jokes or strategizing for ministry. I loved him."

But when Falwell recruited Dick to take the helm of MORAL MAJORITY of ALABAMA, the moment was sober and, after prayerful consideration, Dick said yes. One of the organization's tireless workers, however, insists that Dick did not know about his new post until Falwell announced it to a crowd.

Just as Jerry Falwell counted on a friend, in turn, Dick's first move was to call his best friend, Stu Gaines.

"Stu, have I got a job for you!"

Dick wanted his public service to enhance his ministry, not distract from it. But a disquieting predicament confronted SMI's Pastor: how not to let the patriot's stand in the public forum muffle the pastor's voice in the pulpit. Preparing political speeches should not distract from studying for sermons. Traveling the MORAL MAJORITY circuit could not justify long absences from SMI's pulpit. Dick purposed to protect and prioritize his calling as SMI's Pastor.

To keep his schedule from overload and his priorities in check, Dick would need help—from someone who would not be intimidated by him, by someone who knew him well, by someone he could trust. Stu Gaines was the perfect choice. The two enjoyed a long-standing spiritual, business, and social relationship. Their thoughts and work habits marched in unison. Already attuned to one another, they could hit the ground running. The two men shared a devout faith and great love for America and for the state of Alabama.

With Dick as Chairman and Stu the Executive Director, MORAL MAJORITY of ALABAMA would have a winning leadership team. Just about the only thing that separated the two were respective football loyalties: Dick was devoted to the Crimson Tide, while Stu remained a diehard Auburn fan.

STUART W. (Stu) GAINES

World War II interrupted Stu Gaines' college studies and football career. After a stint in the Marine Corps, he resumed his studies at Auburn University where he had earned a football scholarship to play quarterback. He graduated in 1948.

Dick with Stu Gaines

Diploma in hand, Stu Gaines returned to Birmingham, his hometown, determined to build his own real estate development business. The result was Developers Realty. Not till years later, when both men were already in midlife and established in their careers, did Stu Gaines meet Dick Vigneulle. The two got a late start on their lifelong friendship.

In the early 1970's, they met in the corridors of City Federal. Stu came into the bank's marble lobby and asked who he needed to see about getting a business loan—a really big loan. No ordinary loan officer would do, so a staffer directed Stu to the office of the Vice President in charge of the loan department, Dick Vigneulle.

After welcoming his guest and directing him to a chair across from his desk, Dick sized up his new client and immediately felt a brotherly connection.

Anyone who knew Stu Gaines knew he was a fanatical Auburn Tiger football fan, and in fact, Stu had the girth and roar of a tiger. Football and the Marine Corps taught the man to play fair but play hard. And that is exactly how Stu Gaines lived life, let alone conducted business.

Describing his friend, Dick recalls, "Stu had a big voice and whenever he said 'HELLO, DICK!' everyone heard him! He was a big man. And every-where he went he always wore his trademark Stetson—that big, white cowboy hat. Stu was friendly, open, and when he got down to business, he got down to business! I liked that! He was a straight shooter, and never cut corners. He was a great business partner."

Weeks later, aided by Dick's professional guidance and advance work, Stu got the bank loan he wanted. As head of the loan department, Dick had responsibility to watch out for the bank's investment and oversee the project. As the construction site progressed so too did the friendship.

There was more than business and collegiality at work. Only a few weeks before his first meeting with Dick, Stu had been converted. After accepting a colleague's invitation to attend a Bible study, Stu was led to the Lord by the group's leader, Howard Borland, a popular Birmingham Bible teacher. In Dick Vigneulle, Stu found both a banker and spiritual mentor. Dick invited Stu to attend the little church where he was the lay Pastor. The next Sunday Stu and his wife Bebe, along with their entire family, came to Shades Mountain Independent Church and never left.

In time Dick and Stu became business partners, most notably with the purchase of a shopping center. Stu was a pilot and part owner of a plane. It was not unusual for Dick to receive a phone call at the office from his buddy.

"Dick, the weather is beautiful—let's go flying this afternoon!"

The banker would accept, and as the two friends enjoyed above-the-clouds fellowship, they would also conduct business.

Dick explained, "Often there was property for the bank's consideration that I needed to check out. An aerial inspection often gave an advantage over just a walk across the property or a drive around it. I would see adjacent land or some element in the topography that sealed the deal or forewarned me of liabilities."

As Stu grew in the Lord, he became more and more active in church life. Over the years he served at SMI in various capacities: on the church Board, as an Elder, and Shades Mountain Christian Schools Board member. Ever the football fan, Stu was a member of the Jefferson County Football Association. He enjoyed refereeing high school games and for twenty years scouted and recruited players for the Auburn team. Stu dreamed of the day when Shades Mountain Christian Schools would have a football team.

Not only did the two men form a close bond so did their wives and children. Peggy Vigneulle and Bebe Gaines became best friends too.

"Peggy is the kind of friend in whom you can confide anything," Bebe testifies. "Even at the end of my weariest day, if Stuart said, 'Let's go over to Dick and Peg's house!' I was up and ready to go!"

For many years the two families vacationed together, sometimes taking long trips to Colonial Williamsburg, Disneyland, and Daytona Beach. Other times just the two couples slipped away to their favorite getaway spot in the Smokies—Gatlinburg, Tennessee.

Recalling those days, Bebe grins, "When we traveled, Stu would play country music just to aggravate Dick—songs like 'All My Ex'es Live in Texas' or 'Elvira' or whatever. While Peggy and I shopped, Stuart and Dick would sit in rocking chairs, talking and watching the passers-by. But the most special part of our shared history was watching the bond between my husband and Dick just grow stronger through years of shared business ventures, church involvement, Moral Majority, SMI miracles, and even squabbles! The Vigneulles were always there for the Gaines family. I love Dick and Peg. Friends? No. They are FAMILY to me."

When Dick surrendered to the call of God to leave the bank to pastor SMI, no one was more excited and affirming than Stu. The two were equals in business, but in spiritual matters, Dick was the elder brother. Stu wanted to do something to support Dick in this major life change, but what? Then the Lord gave him an idea, one he sprung on Dick as they traveled together in the car.

As they coasted down an Alabama highway with Dick behind the steering wheel of his Buick, and Stu stretched out on the passenger side, his Stetson resting on the back seat, he threw out his idea to the soon-to-be, full-time Pastor.

"Now, Dick, I want to be a part of your ministry. I own some property. You own some property. And we own some property together. Let's put it all together. You devote yourself to taking care of the church, and I'll take care of our business. I can do that for you and free you up. What do you say?"

A handshake sealed the deal.

A few years later, forming another partnership, this time for MORAL MAJORITY of ALABAMA, life only got better. Whether traveling Alabama roads for MORAL MAJORITY events or sharing steaks over restaurant tables for lunchtime strategy sessions, once more they were the perfect team. With so many shared interests and partnerships in business and the Lord's work, MORAL MAJORITY provided one of the happiest seasons of their lives and some of their most fulfilling work together.

Dick summed up the secret to their winning efforts with one word: trust.

"I could trust Stu. We thought alike, and we both loved the Lord. Stu was honorable and hardworking. That says it all—I trusted him like no one else."

The two became lifelong best friends, in the spirit of Old Testament heroes David and Jonathan. Bonded by their shared evangelical faith and love of family, Dick and Stu's personal relationship built on each man's innate good will and mutual respect for the other. Both men were strong-willed movers and shakers. Providence seemed to link the two to shake the foundations of government as well as the gates of hell.

As with all earthly ties, only death could separate the two. Sadly, that silver cord broke in 1999 when Stu died after a gutsy struggle with cancer.

His body weakened and tired, Stu refused further surgery. He opted for a few quality days to say his farewells. News circulated among his family and friends that the end was days if not hours away. Folks began stopping by Bebe and Stu's home, slipping into the family room where Stu sat propped up in his easy chair. They came to say their good-byes to their beloved Tiger Warrior.

Dick recalls that the day before Stu died, he tried to put together a musical tribute to his best buddy. He wanted to sing a song by Bill Gaither, "Old Friends."

"It's a great song and very apropos, but I just couldn't do it. Every time I'd start to sing, I'd choke up. Finally, I gave up. I spoke up, 'Stu, I wanted to sing for you, Friend, but I just can't make it. I get too emotional. But here's what I'm going to do—I'm gonna let someone else sing it for you.' And with that I played a recording, and we listened to the words together—a salute to Old Friends."

Stu loved the song—its words expressed what neither man could speak. As other friends called, sitting a spell, some stopping to pray, Stu would look at Dick and give a command.

"Dick, play that song for these folks."

Dick's message to Stu became his parting words to others.

The next day Dick returned to the Gaines' house. By this time very weak and near the end, Stu was confined to his bedroom.

"I sat in a chair beside his bed. He was fading, slipping in and out of consciousness. We played 'Old Friends' again."

As the song played, both men were crying. Dick knew Stu was dying and Stu knew it too. Stu rallied a bit. With a burst of strength but still breathing hard, he slapped the bed and gave Dick a command.

"Sit down here, Boy!"

Dick obeyed, like a compliant child.

"I told the Lord all morning that it is ridiculous that I'm hanging around! I'm ready to go!"

Then he looked up.

"Hurry up, Lord! Hurry up!"

Those were Stu's last words. All his bit of energy spent, Stu drifted off again.

The silent intervals grew longer and longer, the breathing more and more shallow. Dick and Peg, Bebe and the Gaines' children and their children huddled around the bed. Dick spoke softly.

"Let's sing."

Tears falling, the group moved from one hymn to the next, a holy serenade to an Old Friend. Song titles became a bedside testimonial: "Amazing Grace... It Is Well With My Soul...How Great Thou Art...How Firm A Foundation...Gentle Shepherd."

"In between songs, I'd read Scripture, then we'd sing some more. Stu's breathing got more and more shallow, till his chest grew still. He just stopped breathing."

Years later, recalling that final moment, Dick confided to a friend, "I think of Stu every day. I still miss him. My 'Old Friend!'"

———

Dick Vigneulle faced inquiry from laymen and at least a few pastors as well, repeating the same question: "Is there Scriptural basis for Moral Majority?" That question became the title of an article he wrote for the August 1980 issue of ON THE MORAL FRONT, the official newsletter of MORAL MAJORITY of ALABAMA. Before turning to Scripture, Dick pointed to the country's history.

"Revival of righteousness through God's people is nothing new, not even in these United States. At the turn of the last century corruption had laced the land at all levels—Teddy Roosevelt was police commissioner of New York City and had to walk the streets at night to fight police corruption. Politicians were after graft and involved in crooked deals from the beat to governors mansions. In this climate the influence of Dwight Moody and such evangelists as Billy Sunday brought about revival among God's people and once again God's 'salt' served its purpose [Matthew 5:13]....As throughout history God's people have been used as salt to influence government and society to turn back to God's moral laws."

As the article continued, Dick made an appeal to men and women willing to stand up and, if need be, stand alone. He pointed to the Prophet

Ezekiel's plea to ancient Israel, "So I sought for a man among them who would make a wall, and stand in the gap before Me on behalf of the land, that I should not destroy it; but I found no one" (Ezekiel 22:30).

Dick wrote further, "God seeks a man today to put up a hedge and stand in the gap for the land. We want him to find at least 1000 pastors and 50,000 followers in Alabama."

With a call to America to turn back to Judeo-Christian values, MORAL MAJORITY OF ALABAMA stated its goal in the same newsletter: "To give an effective voice to millions of Alabamians and fellow Americans who are disgusted with the way their state and country is being run. Where one voice seems to have little or no effect, this same voice becoming concerned with the issues and joining together with other concerned voices can change the very course of this land. How long have we sat and mumbled, not knowing what to do, while our nation and its Congress are being controlled by pressure groups seeking their own interests."

MORAL MAJORITY was a political organization, not a religious one. It cut across denominational and faith barriers to unite citizens with shared moral values.

In the same issue featuring Dick's article, ON THE MORAL FRONT printed a front-page declaration that defined Moral Majority's core values.

Pro-Life: Stand against infanticide, euthanasia and abortion.

Pro-Family: Stand against legislation and the cultural downslide that threatens the Judeo-Christian family.

Pro-Moral: Stem the tide of moral decay caused by increasing social acceptance of pornography, homosexuality, prostitution, and so on.

Pro-America: Protect America's freedoms by demanding a strong military and sound economic principles of government.

Without doubt, the public knew where MORAL MAJORITY stood. It seemed that believers from every corner of Alabama stood from bended knees and, energized by their own prayers, were ready to take a stand, putting their feet in motion to be an answer to their own petitions. A call to prayer culminated into a call for political action.

Despite Jerry Falwell's high profile and the public stand taken by Dick

Vigneulle and Stu Gaines, doubters and detractors seemed to outnumber believers in the cause. When MORAL MAJORITY, still in its early development, announced plans for a rally in Montgomery in the spring of 1980, one Alabama legislator mocked one of the pastors organizing the event.

"You Christians can't get together. You come out to fight on one issue and then crawl back in the woodwork."

The rally proved to be a great success, its giant crowd and stirring messengers gaining the attention of reporters and politicians alike. Shortly afterward, the same legislator who mocked the event before it happened now took a new view. In a stunning display of a new attitude, he turned to the same preacher he dismissed earlier.

"Pastor, we ought to get together and talk. I believe you folks have got something going!"

Within and without the organization, many consider the apex of MORAL MAJORITY's presence and influence was the 1980 presidential election that put Ronald Reagan in the White House. At the same time many entrenched liberals in congress were flushed out, and conservatives were swept in to replace them by a high turn out of voting evangelicals and other conservatives who rallied under MORAL MAJORITY's banner. Landslide issues included abortion and the family especially.

Part of the winning strategy for the conservative victors included efforts by MORAL MAJORITY's state level organizations, such as the Alabama group led by Dick and Stu. These state organizations helped to register imposing numbers of new voters, all the while raising more money and volunteers for the conservative cause. Some estimates maintain MORAL MAJORITY added three to four million registered voters to conservative efforts. Reporters in 1980, as well as political historians since then, cited three states in particular for stellar impact on the election's outcome: Alaska, Iowa, and Alabama.

Dick Vigneulle is the first in line to credit his partner at the helm of MORAL MAJORITY of ALABAMA. Stu Gaines remained a tireless worker to the end, traveling internationally on behalf of their organization. From Israel to the Caribbean there was a man in a Stetson hat with a Southern drawl giving voice for Alabama and MORAL MAJORITY. He worked hard behind the scenes, often in restaurant meetings or in the corridors of the State Capitol.

After Stu's passing, there were many tributes to the man that many regarded in their hearts as "Mr. Alabama." Some of Stu's friends learned of his death when a public announcement and tribute was made at the next Auburn/ Alabama game. His alma mater's flag flew at half-mast in respect for Stu and another distinguished alumnus being remembered that day. Also, the Mid-Alabama Republican Club, which Stu helped found, held a memorial program in his honor. During the program, Betty Bostwick, a well-known force in Alabama for conservative issues, paid special tribute to Stu's leadership and example.

> Most of you know Stuart was the Executive Director of Moral Majority and in that position he took a lot of guff— they really ridiculed him and he NEVER STOPPED and he NEVER RESPONDED IN KIND....He was a wonderful influence, not only on me personally, but also his vision of seeing that the Christian viewpoint had to be reflected in public policy...something that he never wavered on, and I appreciated him for that.

Stuart Gaines was so effective in his job that some wondered why he did not run for political office himself. But he preferred serving others. A particular prize for Stu Gaines was the victory won by his friend Jeremiah Denton Jr. for the United States Senate. Voters rallied to support Denton, a retired United States Navy Rear Admiral (the first ever elected) and former prisoner of war in Viet Nam. Denton authored a book describing his eight years of captivity and titled it *When Hell Was In Session*. He defeated Democrat Jim E. Folsom Jr., member of an old, distinguished Alabama political family. Folsom had defeated the incumbent in the primaries. A Roman Catholic and outspoken in his stand against abortion, Senator Denton went on to compile a solidly conservative voting record before narrowly losing reelection in 1986 to Richard Shelby.

In 1989, speaking before media hordes, Jerry Falwell announced the official disbanding of MORAL MAJORITY, while heralding the organization's lasting influence on America's political landscape and popular culture. After Dr. Falwell's death on May 17, 2007, tributes included his achievement in building the religious right into a political force. One obituary quoted Falwell when he spoke announcing the close of MORAL MAJORITY almost two decades earlier: "I shudder to think where the country would be right now if the religious right had not evolved."

At the bank, the church, and in public life: Dick Vigneulle recruited, mentored, and commissioned others not just to partner with him but to branch out and carry on his work and causes, like the Apostle Paul with his son in the ministry, Timothy.

Dick was not put off by talent different from or beyond his own. Good leaders discover and inspire new leaders. Whether in banking, ministry, or public service, Dick garnered respect for his ability to inspire and commission not just followers and workers but fellow leaders and visionaries. He maintained a lofty position of influence not because he held on to power but because he gave it away. He empowered others by example, rhetoric, and mentoring.

On Sunday, February 4, 1979, Dick stood in his pulpit at Shades Mountain Independent Church and preached a sermon that many in the congregation consider a hallmark of the man's convictions as a Christian and as a loyal American. Not only was the Pastor's heart full that Sunday, so too were his notes—it took two services for him to finish the sermon. Morning and evening that Sunday the sermon text and title were one and the same: *Wake Up and Stand Up, America!* (based on Romans 13:11-14).

"We must get our government back to its primary role of protecting our rights and freedoms and liberties, or we will no longer have any rights and freedoms to protect. Unless we clear up the confusion about (1) the type of government we have, (2) about where we receive our rights, and (3) the purpose of government, we will find ourselves ruled by an oligarchy—not a republic. We do not want another form of government. In the history of the world there has never been a people so free, so liberated, and so well ruled as we Americans. But if we don't begin to stand up for America and the principles upon which this great nation of ours has been built, I'm afraid we may very well lose it all!"

To help "Wake Up America" Dick prayed that mature, hardworking men and women might be led of God into political life. Just as Dick inspired countless men and women to follow God's lead into full-time ministry, he likewise worked to inspire and equip Christians to serve God and country in the public arena by running for government offices—on local, state, or even national levels.

Two sterling examples of Dick's answered prayer are a couple of laymen, right from the pews of SMI, inspired by their Pastor and led by God, who stepped out into the political fray. In the spirit and example of Old Testament government servants like Joseph and Nehemiah, they served God with secular titles and by fulfilling duties of state.

In the case of Dick Vigneulle's protégés, they braved personal risk and public doubt if not outright scorn, and succeeded, sometimes despite their own political party's expectations. In their Pastor's eyes, these two dedicated Christian men—one a state representative and the other a state senator—became lay ministers when they became elected officials.

THE HONORABLE GREG BEERS, Alabama State Representative (1983 - 1990)

As young believers, Greg and Evelyn Beers found personal friends and mentors in their Pastor and his wife. Peg and Dick lovingly invested in the young couple. Greg was especially fascinated because Dick had walked away from the business career most men only dream of. As a former banker, Dick nurtured believers to take the teachings of Christ with them to the marketplace, so that they would build their careers or businesses on the teachings of Christ. Greg Beers sought his Pastor's counsel in building his company as well as his faith.

Evelyn recalls, "Greg never thought about praying over his office or for his employees. He had never thought of making a profit to benefit his employees and not just the company or himself. He never thought of having a Bible study in his office or leading people to Christ there."

But Dick's mentoring, and Greg's open heart, changed all that. By the late 1970's the two had become especially close, their mentoring friendship formed on the tennis court as well as the church pew. Greg was an ace tennis player. Dick was beginning to have health and fitness issues, so Greg wanted to help Dick stay healthy. He began giving his Pastor tennis lessons. Over volleys and after sets, the exchange between the two continued.

Dick's expectations for his new believer buddy would go beyond the church house. As Greg learned to take Christ to the marketplace, Dick realized his disciple was capable of greater influence than he dared believe for himself.

In time, Greg was trusted with leadership positions at church.

"After a few years," Greg recalls, "Dick asked me to serve on the church Board and school Board. I learned how to kneel with other men and pray, and how to put my hard-headed opinions on the back burner and submit to God's direction. What an adventure."

Greg was learning servant leadership, the kind Jesus modeled and called for from His followers.

As Greg learned how to speak up for the Lord, willingly sharing his faith with family and co-workers, God was preparing Greg to speak up on public platforms outside his office or church. The moral integrity of faith and Scripture would equip Greg to build not just his family and business but also his state and country.

Greg explains, "Something that started burning in Dick's spirit in the early 80's was the decline in America's moral condition. Dick headed up MORAL MAJORITY for the state of Alabama. My enthusiasm for God found an outlet in politics. Through Dick's and my wife's encouragement I entered politics and won a seat as an Alabama State representative in 1983. To win this seat I had to learn to speak in public (another on a long list of miracles), run as a Republican in a district that had never elected a Republican and beat a twenty-year incumbent Democrat. God honored my step of faith, and I won a victory based on a platform of moral principles as taught in the Bible."

Representative Beers served two terms in the Alabama House before the press of a growing business led him to retire from politics. Greg started his company with a $5,000 loan, as his Pastor continued to mentor him in building a business for Christ. His company flourished along with his family, church, and political life. Annual sales reached above twenty-five million dollars. Furthermore, three hundred employees now looked to him for direction. Before leaving office, with God's help, Greg determined to see a particular law passed, one that confronted a moral evil.

"I spent years fighting to get a law passed that would prevent a minor girl from getting an abortion without the consent of her parents. In 1986 I stood on the floor of the state house of representatives and was able to see this bill become a law. Alabama was one of the first states to pass this type of legislation and it has stood the test of time. Again, God showed me that if I step out for Him, He will indeed perform mighty miracles."

Now a grandfather and reflective over his life and career, Greg Beers counts his blessings and blesses the minister who helped him build his faith and reorder his life.

> I can hardly imagine where I would be without Christ—probably divorced and, more than likely, waiting for my social security check. In all likelihood I would have lost contact with my three daughters and our seven grand-children. Instead, my time is spent with my wife, children, and grandchildren, and I get a chance to tell the grandkids stories about how Christ changed my life and about a special person named Dick who was my mentor. I do not know how much money Dick will leave behind when God calls him home, but I do know one thing that Dick will leave behind…thousands of changed lives spanning generations.

THE HONORABLE HENRY E. "HANK" ERWIN JR., Alabama State Senator (2002 -)

Hank Erwin and his wife, Shelia, were the first couple Dick married at Shades Mountain Independent Church. As the bride and groom exchanged their vows, they were distracted by a bee that landed and remained in Dick's perfectly combed and slick hair.

After graduating from Troy State University, Hank enrolled at Southeastern Bible College. Hank loved his Savior and wanted to serve the Lord. As he waited on the Lord's direction, Hank pursued a second college degree in Bible. At the same time, he and Shelia began attending a tiny church on the mountain, Shades Mountain Independent, still in its earliest days. They were eager volunteers and got busy in the Lord's work, serving shoulder to shoulder with Dick, Wales Goebel, and others in ministries to teens.

Having proved himself to be an invaluable worker, Hank was offered a job as Youth Minister at SMI. He loved his new job, and the

Dick and Peggy, Shelia and Senator Hank Erwin when Hank won the 2002 election for Alabama State Senate – Hank was SMI's first part-time employee as youth pastor starting in early 1970's

pay at $35 per week helped with Bible college expenses. With Shelia's high energy and quick, infectious laughter, she engaged youth and adults alike. Her organizational skills helped everyone who worked with her. When the youth ministry organized a visitation program, hundreds of teens showed up to go door-to-door and tell folks about Jesus.

Hank, with his boy-next-door good looks and quiet demeanor, won respect as a diligent Bible student and teacher. His fun, creative methods gained a larger following. The teens loved it when he planned what was labeled "Underground Church"—weekend youth outings where the participants came without knowing where their leaders would be taking them. The destination never failed to surprise and delight Hank's kids.

Committed to Dick's challenge to "Reach the Mountain for Christ," the Erwins made a winning team. More than witnesses, they were participants in Shades Mountain Independent Church's pioneer era. The Hoover insurance building services, gatherings in the Glenn and Vira Kennedy home, relocations to the school library and then the cafeteria, the "new site" on Tyler Road—Hank and Shelia remember it all with detail, like ecclesiastical historians. They can recite in poetic canter the names of places and programs that only SMI's pioneers fully understand: Hallelujah Hill, Buck-A-Brick, Round-Up Sunday, Last Chance, and Count It All Joy pins.

"In those first days," Hank recalls, "Dick would frequently say, 'I'm not a preacher. I'm a banker!' And in his heart-of-hearts, I think he was a musician first and a preacher second. But if Dick underestimated his homiletic skill, the congregation did not. His love for the Word of God and for people made everything he said worth remembering."

After graduation from Southeastern Bible College, Hank and Shelia moved to Texas so he could attend Dallas Theological Seminary. After receiving his master's degree, he returned to Birmingham and Shades Mountain Independent Church. But the Lord had opened doors to take Hank into a career in broadcasting. Hired by CBS News to be their local anchor, his face and voice became popular and authoritative with the Birmingham audience. His media career broadened the impact of his outspoken testimony for Christ.

From television newsman, Hank moved on to radio where he built a huge audience and fan base for his conservative talk show. He quickly became a fixture on Alabama radio and a respected spokesman for moral integrity in society and government.

In 2002, after much prayer with his wife and Pastor, and the urging of his friends and radio constituency, Hank decided to run for public office. He threw his hat in the political ring for the office of Alabama State Senator for the 14th District. His Bible training and broadcasting career made Hank a capable candidate as well as a capable office holder. But his path to the Alabama Senate chamber was neither broad nor obstacle free. Despite Hank's media popularity, some political warhorses considered him a young buck.

His wife and two sons, Andrew and Jonathan, in addition to his church family, knew Hank Erwin never did anything without careful consideration and a meticulous counting of the cost. A man of character and high standards, Hank found inspiration and resolve from his own father's example. His dad— Henry E. "Red" Erwin—was a World War II war hero and recipient of the Congressional Medal of Honor "for heroism above and beyond the call of duty." Sensing his own call to duty, Hank announced his candidacy.

During one of Major Ian Thomas's preaching visits to SMI, he said something that inspired Hank, a challenge he seemed to memorize upon his first hearing. Hank recited it countless times through the political campaign:

"Go where you are sent, stay where you are put, and give them what you've got!"

Two other men vied for the senate office with Hank. The political race, rugged and brutal, demanded that Hank stand bravely like David doing battle with not one but two Goliaths. And just as it happened in the Old Testament contest, Goliath lost—both of them!

Hank prevailed, winning 54% of the vote, despite modest campaign funds and two opponents. His campaign speeches repeated Hank's promise to foster moral and spiritual renewal for his beloved state. Voters liked what they heard. They have returned him to office for a second term.

Dick is the first to salute Senator Erwin's public example and public service.

"Hank is a leader among leaders. He is straight-shooting, and a Christian example among fellow legislators—and they look to him as that. And he is a dear friend!"

Senator Erwin would be the first to give God the glory for His blessings. Likewise, his Pastor's personal encouragement and practical assistance benefited the winning candidate. But long before Hank's run for office, Dick Vigneulle helped prepare the way as the head of MORAL MAJORITY of ALABAMA.

Years later, the veteran senator pays tribute to his Pastor's lasting legacy.

"Thanks to the work of Jerry Falwell and Dick Vigneulle, MORAL MAJORITY set up a state dominance on moral issues and remained a dominant force in Alabama for over twenty years. Dick's influence was widespread and the political organization he headed up had a profound influence on Alabama's laws and lawmakers. MORAL MAJORITY of ALABAMA was feared and respected by legislators. What Dick started had a lasting effect on the thinking, laws, and running of state government in Alabama!"

Church members at Shades Mountain Independent Church sometimes ribbed one another, "I bet you hate to go on vacation and miss church here at home 'cause you just know something good is going to happen, and you don't want to miss out on it!" And it was true.

The norm for life at SMI was the spontaneous and unexpected. A rabbit puppet was known to pop up from the baptistery once to make an announcement (even at relaxed SMI, some members failed to see the humor and the bunny never appeared again!). Unexpected celebrity guests, or even announced ones, came to the platform to sing or preach. The surprise might come from the home crowd not visitors: such as an SMI volunteer team of adults just returned home from the mission field or youth group teens back from a marathon bicycle evangelism trip. Passing the microphone back and forth, the gaggle of excited believers lined across the front of the auditorium, giving stirring impromptu testimonies that squeezed more hearts than a theologian's sermon. Sometimes even those planning the unexpected for worship services would be taken by surprise.

In the spring of 1981, in an evening service, the Pastor was taken by surprise. Leroy Clark, Chairman of the church Board, unexpectedly came to the pulpit. He tapped into the microphone, got everyone's attention, and then introduced another Board member, Jim Braswell.

A tall, congenial man, and respected furniture store owner, Jim looked out at the congregation, all the time making sure he kept Pastor Dick in the corner of his eye.

"Folks, I've been working for days to make this special moment possible. My crew of helpers and I just got the technology all in place at 2:00 this afternoon so that we could introduce to you tonight a very special guest. He wants to speak to you tonight via telephone hookup from his office in Lynchburg, Virginia. Ladies and gentleman, here is Dr. Jerry Falwell to make a very important announcement."

With that even Dick was sitting on the edge of his seat.

"Hello, Dick. Greetings to you too, Peg, and all the good folks of Shades Mountain Independent Church. This is Jerry Falwell speaking to you from my office here on Liberty Mountain. I am excited to bring you a very important and distinguished announcement about your Pastor."

The unmistakable voice of Thomas Road Baptist Church and MORAL MAJORITY immediately filled SMI's auditorium. The man needed no introduction. Everyone knew who he was.

Falwell continued, "Dick, this afternoon the Board of Liberty University met and voted unanimously to award you an honorary doctorate. We're going to fly you up here for this spring's commencement and make you 'DOCTOR' Vigneulle!"

The rest of the message was lost in the congregation's hoopla. Like a mini-rapture, all the saints flew in the air, standing to their feet and applauding. With laughter and tears, hugs and handshakes, all SMI rejoiced!

On May 11, the Vigneulle family, along with Stu and Bebe Gaines, attended the Liberty University graduation. Following a message by the commencement speaker, Dr. W. A. Criswell, the noted Dallas Pastor and Baptist statesman, the University's Founder took center stage. Accompanied by Dr. Pierre Guillerman, Dr. Falwell called SMI's Pastor to the platform.

Outfitted in a cap and gown, Dick walked up to the dais and stood silently before the thousands in attendance, graduates and their families, students and faculty, guests and dignitaries. His mind raced like a videotape on super fast forward. He thought about his little high school in Delaware. He grinned to think of the principal who reprimanded him for truancy. Dr. Bob Senior's voice echoed in his mind, declaring one of his proverbs, "Boys, do right till the stars fall."
And Dick's parents, Harold and Marjorie Vigneulle, marched into his thoughts—a son is never too old to want to please his folks. Peg caught his eye as he looked past the sea of graduates. She was still as pretty as the first day he saw her in high school.

Dr. Jerry Falwell presenting Dick with an honorary doctorate at Liberty University May 11, 1981

Whatever the honoree's reverie that moment, Dr. Falwell's words brought him back to the present.

In formal proclamation, the school leaders heralded Dick Vigneulle for his accomplishments as a Christian businessman in Birmingham and as the Pastor of Shades Mountain Independent Church. But added special recognition centered on his leadership as head of MORAL MAJORITY of ALABAMA. Prompted by friendship and shared conviction, Dick had rendered service that aided Jerry Falwell and others in their shared fight for the soul of America.

Dr. Falwell and the Liberty family could not have been kinder and more gracious, but Dick was eager to get back home and celebrate this special life moment with his SMI family.

The great champion of the new birth, Dick Vigneulle through his work for MORAL MAJORITY rose to stand as a warrior for the unborn. Even after the demise of MORAL MAJORITY and after his title of Pastor passed to another, Dick would continue to be a voice for life. The cause of the unborn and speaking for those who could not speak for themselves became the lingering cause on Dick's personal agenda.

On Sunday, January 19, 1997, Dick spoke at a meeting sponsored by the North Alabama group Choose Life/Sav-A-Life. The annual event was held on or near the January 22 anniversary of the Roe vs. Wade Supreme Court's decision legalizing abortion. Dick was one of the featured speakers

The Huntsville Times reported on the event the next day. In an article titled *Praying for Life*, the Times staff writer, Thomas W. Krause, described the gathering.

> *Speakers Sunday offered strong words in the fight against legalized abortions.*
>
> *Richard Vigneulle, a former banker and a Birmingham preacher, used passages from the Bible, legal case history and medical experts to condemn abortion.*
>
> *The Bible, he said, offers many examples of the unborn with names and personalities. This, he said, proves a fetus is a life. Court cases, he said, have allowed unborn babies to sue for damages and have received social security benefits. And, in 1967, at a Washington, D.C., international conference on abortion, he said, many medical experts concluded human life began at conception.*
>
> *Vigneulle openly condemned society for allowing abortions to take place.*
>
> *"Only a perverted society could make laws to protect little eagle eggs but not to protect unborn human life," he said.*
>
> *The crowd Sunday—totaling about 1,000—agreed with Vigneulle.*

Even as the nation's statistics worsened, his message remained unchanged, his convictions unwavering, his voice still heard.

It is sweet irony that the former banker's legacy stretched from the church house to the state house, bringing the law of God to shape the laws of men.

CHAPTER SEVENTEEN

Miss America

One of the church pastoral staff members recalls Peggy Vigneulle with admiration as the "First Lady of the Church" and described how she carried out her role as the Pastor's wife in perfect harmony with her husband and the congregation.

He said, "When SMI first contacted me about coming on staff, I had just earned my last seminary degree and continued to teach undergraduates as I pondered my future. The opportunity to work with this dynamic banker-turned-pastor both intrigued and scared me. One point of curiosity was the Pastor's wife, no doubt a person of influence considering her husband's position and personality. I wondered if she would be a person who missed the country club life I envisioned was hers as the wife of a big executive. Would the church house be a stretch? Then I met Mrs. Vigneulle, and in time as I got to know her, first impressions were confirmed: she was far more comfortable in home and church life than anywhere else."

Peg was Dick's college sweetheart, and he never lost his young suitor's fascination, and she always looked the part. The collegian from Delaware won the belle from Birmingham, Alabama. The summer before Dick's college senior year, they married. She took his name and in time he took her hometown. With the look and charms of a genteel Southern lady, Peg achieved big impact very gently.

She is the picture of femininity without ever being fussy. Her striking appearance, always immaculate and fresh, even in maturity, is eye-catching, a pretty lady with carefully coiffed hair and stylish clothes. Even so she has a calming, welcoming presence with friends and strangers alike. Never one to want to draw attention to herself, never with an agenda of her own to push, Mrs. Vigneulle delighted in her family and home, a priority lived out quietly.

Dick took a rightful pride in his wife, sometimes paying her public tribute. One of Dick's pet names for her is "Miss America" and that is how he often referred to her from the pulpit. Family and friends who knew and loved Peg believed she could have won the title in Atlantic City if she had tried, but winning the title from her admiring husband was sufficient. She was happier hearing Dick say it than Bert Parks.

As one staff member recalls, there was one tribute the Pastor gave his wife that stood out.

"Dick was preaching on the home and family. As he spoke of the virtues of a godly wife, in a spontaneous aside, he looked at Peg sitting in the choir and then to the audience and said 'I'm never ashamed for my wife to take my arm in public.' That compliment stayed with me. It pictured perfectly a good wife and a grateful husband. It gave us confidence as a congregation too, kind of like children when they spy their parents hugging or affirming their love. Dick set a good standard for family appreciation for us husbands too."

Church was part of Peggy's life all her life. Her love for the Lord expressed itself in her love for church life and ministries. Raising up her four

children in the nurture and admonition of the Lord meant faithful church attendance. Even as a corporate wife, she remained a faithful church worker.

When Dick wrestled with his call to leave the business world for full-time ministry, Peggy was his primary confidante and prayer partner. In private life her partnership with her husband might have defied public perceptions. After all, Peg is petite and quiet. Dick is big and booming. She defers. He insists. Her manner is always kind, never speaking ill of anyone. She never intruded,

Peggy loved to serve others – January 1975

but her presence—in public or private—was always welcomed. If Dick could be barbed at times in the discharge of his duties, Peggy was the velvet wrap that padded any pointed edges.

Even so, no one knew her husband better, and there was no one he trusted more than his wife. She had long been his partner in personal business and family life, and now her input proved critical once more in her husband's discerning God's will and finding personal peace. When he finally made the decision, no one was happier than Peggy.

Peggy and Dick singing at 10th Anniversary of his pastorate. Choir robes had been provided by Mr. Mark Hodo. – 1984

Dick knew that leaving the bank would forfeit financial rewards and increase risks. But Peggy encouraged her husband with a ready answer.

"Honey, we have no security except in God's will."

As a Pastor's wife, Peggy Vigneulle carved out her own niche in the church, free of expectations—real or imagined—of what a Pastor's wife should be. Personal respect from her husband and church family won her this freedom, and besides that she was part of a congregation without traditions and that often defied ecclesiastical norms.

Peg shared Dick's gift for music and so naturally the church choir was a central part of her public role, shying away from any solo spotlight while taking her seat in the alto section. She loved children and enjoyed children's ministries. She frequently accompanied Dick on evangelistic calls. One of her favorite roles was as a hostess for events in her home or the church.

Peggy Vigneulle's life has not been without severe trial.

When their son, Tom, was born in 1961, Peggy almost died. Delivery complications left the delivery room medical team working feverishly to save the young mother's life. Dick prayed frantically, desolate at the thought of raising four children alone, without their mother. While under anesthesia, by her own testimony, Peggy saw the Lord. She told the story later.

"Jesus was walking toward me, and I pleaded with the Lord, 'Please let me stay and raise my baby.' With that, He turned and walked away from me. The Lord let me live."

Later in life, Peggy endured and eventually won out over an extended battle with depression. She wrote openly and candidly about her personal struggle in an article for *The Joyful Woman* magazine (October 1980). The piece was later reprinted in the *Shades Mountain Messenger* newspaper.

"I want to share with you the time in my life I call *The DARK DAYS*.... Many people do not believe Christians ever go through depression and trials like I went through, but the Lord uses our trials and dark days to make us stronger and to teach us to have faith when we have no sight or feeling."

She went on to cite verses that became God's promises to hold on to, especially I Peter 4:12, 13 (KJV), "Beloved, think it not strange concerning the fiery trial which is to try you, as though some strange thing happened unto you: But rejoice, inasmuch as ye are partakers of Christ's sufferings; that, when his glory shall be revealed, ye may be glad also with exceeding joy."

Reflecting on her Bible promises, Peggy wrote, "The Lord taught me what it meant to trust Him no matter what the circumstances."

Her struggle with depression seemed to creep up on her and once gaining a stranglehold on her spirit, it would not let go. She persevered in prayer and medical treatment, continuously supported by a loving husband and family. No doubt God worked through prayer and medicine and family love, but a turning point came when a friend gifted her with a book.

A friend of ours had given me the book, *The Christian's Secret of a Happy Life* by Hannah Whitehall Smith. One night, back home from my hospital stays, I went up to my bedroom with a very heavy heart. I was crying—no, I was sobbing my heart out. I felt my heart had been crushed into a billion pieces. I picked up that book, lying on my bedside table, and began to read it. I came to a prayer in that book that exactly fitted the need of my life. I read it, reread it. Finally I told the Lord that the best I knew how I wanted to really pray that prayer and mean it with all my heart. Here is a part of it.

Lord Jesus, I believe that Thou art able and willing to deliver me from all the unrest and bondage of my Christian life. I believe Thou didst die to set me free, not only in the future but NOW and HERE. I believe Thou art stronger than sin, and that Thou canst keep me, even me, in my extreme weakness from falling into snares or yielding obedience to its commands. And Lord, I am going to trust Thee to keep Me. I have tried keeping myself and have failed and failed most grievously. I am absolutely helpless. So now, I will trust Thee. I give myself to Thee. I keep back no reserves: body, soul and spirit. I present myself to thee as a piece of clay to be fashioned into anything Thy love and Thy wisdom shall choose. And now, I am Thine. I believe Thou dost accept that which I present to Thee. I believe that this poor, weak, foolish heart has been taken possession of by Thee, and that Thou hast even at this very moment begun to work in me to will and to do of Thy good pleasure. I trust Thee utterly and I trust Thee NOW.

The burden lifted, and God gave a reprieve from the dark days. Peggy sensed an immediate change. There might be more battles to withstand, but the war was won.

"All my problems didn't end overnight, but I was willing and able to face life and its problems with the Lord's help with total confidence and strength."

Family soon heard the news and saw the change.

My! What a relief! That weight I had carried on my chest for months literally lifted. It was GONE! The Lord used that prayer and my complete, total yieldedness to change my life. I called my mother and my aunt the next day. They both said the same thing: 'Everything's going to be all right now.' I said, 'I know it.' I prayed the Lord would let Dick see the difference in me, and that I wouldn't have to tell him. He did, almost immediately. After that, songs bubbled up from my heart. I went around singing everyday. There had been months I couldn't really sing, nor did I want to hear anyone else sing.

Peggy continued to describe her path to recovery.

"The Lord taught me so much through my trials and dark days and showed me I could not be a good Christian, a good wife, a good mother, and especially not even a good preacher's wife except as I yield myself to Him each day and allow Him to live His life through me....I thought I had to work for victory, and He showed me I just had to apply what He had already accomplished in my life. Christ had already done all for me on the cross when He said, 'It is finished.'"

Sometimes dreams that seem to die turn out to have been delayed. That is what happened with Dick and Peggy Vigneulle's *dream house*.

In the early 80's the Vigneulles began discussing a move from their Sceptor Lane home. They prized their old homeplace, a storehouse of family memories. The Vigneulle children, now with kids of their own, still prized the backyard tree house built by Pop Vigneulle, Dick's father. But it was time for something new, or so they thought. Both loved architecture, design, and building, and their creative fancy yearned for a new outlet. After purchasing a lot in Hoover, with a mountaintop view looking out to Oak Mountain State Park, the couple stoked their planning efforts. Urged on by Peggy, Dick visited Hiram Gilbert, a noted Over the Mountain builder of fine homes.

After Dick led Hiram to the Lord, friendship and discipleship brought a new, precious meaning to building the dream house. Plans were drawn, studied, altered, and then drawn yet again to be pondered over a while longer. The Vigneulles even started purchasing prized furniture pieces and little treasures that would go into the dream house. The living room in the Sceptor Lane house grew crowded, almost resembling a furniture showroom. But the inconvenience would be only for

Dick and Peggy – mid-1980's

a little while, or so they thought.

Then unexpectedly, plans changed, and the dream seemed to die. With economic shifts, pressing ministry needs, changes in family priorities, or whatever, the prized lot on the mountainside was put up for sale and sold. The architectural plans for the Gilbert-built dream house put away.

The Vigneulles were never possessed by their possessions. Dick repeatedly reminded admiring guests in his home, "It's all gonna burn someday anyway!" They proved that free spirit time and again.

For example, in the 1980's, while enjoying a Florida vacation, high up in a hotel tower, Dick and Peggy endured a scare and a loss with grace. Dick had left the hotel room's sliding doors ajar to catch the ocean breeze at nighttime. As they slept, a cat burglar rifled their room, stealing Peggy's precious jewelry, gifts from Dick's corporate days. Peggy was disappointed but not undone. Life goes on, and that is how the two of them felt about their dream house too.

In 1988, long after Dick and Peggy gave up the idea of moving from Sceptor Lane, life took a surprise turn. A staff member, knowing Dick's love of architecture and the building trade, urged the Pastor to take a drive with him on their lunch hour. He had seen a house that Dick might like enough to want to buy it.

Put off by the suggestion at first, Dick insisted, "I'm not looking for a house."

But, with gentle urging, he yielded and drove to a high point in Hoover and walked into a house on Pavillon Drive. The lot and house were beautiful, though the outside failed to stir him at first.

"It's too contemporary looking," Dick thought to himself.

He and Peg loved traditional design. Even so, it was a handsome house, perfectly situated on a wooded site, and obviously very well-constructed. One fact was unmistakable. After surveying the house and its setting, with a wide sweep of his eyes, Dick identified the builder without having to be told.

"No doubt about it—this is a Gilbert-built. I can tell. Hiram Gilbert built this house."

This was a commendation, not just nostalgia. Hiram was Dick and Peg's builder of choice from years before. A Gilbert-built house was considered by many to be like a work of art because Hiram held to fastidious standards in design and craftsmanship. His admirers considered him a proven genius in situating a house on its building site for maximum WOW factor.

Once inside the house on Pavillon Drive, Dick had a moment of déjà vu: a house he had never entered before was as familiar as if he had been in it a hundred times. The feeling was almost haunting, and then it dawned on him. The layout and design was an exact match to the plans he and Peg had labored over years ago in planning their dream house.

What appeared to be a single story from the front actually opened into a three-story structure in the back. The expansive home's soaring views looked out to Oak Mountain and upper Shelby County. Stepping out onto the deck, Dick felt transported by the glorious view to his favorite getaway place, Gatlinburg, Tennessee.

Vigneulle's third home in Birmingham – Pavillon Drive

The lunch hour went long that day. Dick returned shortly with Peg in tow to share in his discovery. Days later the house was theirs.

When the Vigneulles took occupancy of their dream house, the couple enjoyed making it their own. Peggy was always Dick's interior decorator of choice, whether for home or his private office. Here was ample room for their growing family and congregation.

The Pavillon Drive house became a place for expansive hospitality ministries. Whether on short notice or with advance planning, Peggy has always been the gracious hostess. Dignitaries in business and Christendom have sat at her table. Once Dick invited the entire church congregation to "come on over to our house!" Fortunately for Peg and the neighbors, this was no spontaneous invitation. Days of planning and lots of prayer pulled off the perfect reception. All the neighbors received invitations too, and church families signed up for thirty-minute segments. Thankfully, no traffic jams resulted, nor overloads in electrical outlets or peoples' tempers.

The house also gave place to the owners' special interests. The lower level family room was large enough for Dick to leave his train collection on permanent display. His office was in a quiet area and large enough to include an inner sanctum, a room within the room that was wrapped in bookcases to hold the Pastor's library. He was just as thrilled with another space that is his domain—the garage. Outfitted with built-in cupboards and painted floor, Dick's garage is as immaculate as his Sunday suit. Also, he designed the landscape for the new house.

Peggy found her special places too—especially her craft room. Huge closets held an array of silk flowers and a florist's equipment. A gifted floral arranger, Peg provides arrangements for many family members' and friends' weddings and special occasions. Another of her hobbies is jewelry making. Peggy honed skills as a jewelry designer, and her workroom held drawers and trays of Austrian crystals used to fashion her special pieces. Like a good wife of biblical fame, her costume jewelry gifts are prized "above rubies."

In 2004 the Vigneulles celebrated their 50th wedding anniversary. Dick and Peg could celebrate a life of shared faith and love, a marriage lived out in a lifetime of Christian service and shared commitment to the Lord Jesus Christ. God's hand graciously guided and provided for them.

Now their offspring spread out over three generations of children, grandchildren and great-grandchildren. Dick and Peg earned new names: Gran Gran and Big Daddy. Their

Dick and Peggy's 50th Anniversary celebrated August 11, 2002

247

family had not escaped the tests and trials common to modern generations, but their faith in Christ and confidence in the Bible's promises gave the Vigneulle clan a sure foundation.

As a wife, mother, business executive's wife and then Pastor's wife, Peg had been tested by the thorns and thistles of life. Recurring health issues, a runaway teenage son, the unending demands and opportunities for a pastor's wife: a plethora of heartbreaking and heartwarming episodes played out her days. In addition, a growing congregation called for her husband's pastoral attention morning, noon, and night. A banker's hours were long but at least had limits. A pastor is on call twenty-four hours a day, seven days a week.

But her trials seemed to enhance her natural gift for caring and nurturing, especially the young or the afflicted. Unlike her husband, who carried out his ministry publicly before a huge congregation, Peggy often ministered privately and behind closed doors. She repeatedly found solace in her prayer closet.

As her children grew to adulthood, Peggy grew heartier as a woman of great faith, proven and improved by her trials. Throughout her adult life, Peg has been a woman of prayer. With the succeeding seasons of life, her valor and victory in intercessory prayer became family legend.

By her own family's testimony, Peg is the Vigneulle kinfolk's most heroic prayer warrior, a respect proven by a dramatic prayer intervention for one of her own grandchildren.

Diane Vigneulle Stough recalls desperate days of her adult daughter Selah's drug addiction. Independent in spirit and routine, she seemed beyond her mother's grasp in every way.

> I had struggled with Selah's lifestyle choices for quite some time, but her addiction left her strung out and wasting away. She was five feet and nine inches tall, but now weighed only eighty-five pounds. As a Christian mother, I was confident that my Heavenly Father would help me help my daughter. So I prayed and prayed, asking the Lord for wisdom to know how to deal with my struggling Selah. But I still had no idea how to reach her. Then one day the Lord spoke to my heart with a clear command. 'Treat her like Jesus. Treat her like she's already walking with God.'

Immediately Diane felt a release in her own spirit and a freedom to do what until now had been unthinkable.

"I felt assured and no longer weighed down. I no longer focused on her drugs and tattoos. Instead, I would follow the Lord's counsel: treat her like she already walks with Jesus."

For a period of time the two drifted apart, talking on the phone occasionally but never visiting. Diane felt led to go to her daughter's apartment, a half-hour drive away. She pulled into the parking lot, closed the car door, and took slow but deliberate steps to Selah's front door. Excited and full of faith, Diane knocked and waited, and then knocked again. Finally, the door slowly swung open. The figure that opened the door startled her. Dangerously thin and covered with bruises, Selah looked up with two black eyes.

"Honey, can I take you out to lunch?" Diane asked, focusing on her mission and not her daughter's appearance.

"Mother, look at me. You would take me out even though I look like this?"

"It's okay. Everyone has to eat, right? It just doesn't matter—let's go."

Although their relationship had been strained, and the two had not spoken to each other in days, the moment turned hopeful when Selah smiled.

"O.K. Mom, let's go!"

Selah seemed to get excited. She slid into her flip-flops and put on dark sunglasses, and the two went for a mother-daughter outing.

Diane whispered to herself as she closed the apartment door behind them, "Lord, I never want to bring her back here again. Give me the strength and help me to speak words from Your heart. Jesus, speak through me!"

Diane drove to a nearby IHOP restaurant. Once inside, the two settled into a booth. Sitting quietly, neither spoke a word for a spell. When the food arrived, Diane was not hungry, but her daughter chowed down, eating to make up for days of hunger. While Selah ate, her mother prayed.

Finally, Diane spoke, her voice calm but direct.

"Honey, you need to get help."

Over the restaurant table she continued to confront Selah with the need to make an immediate break. After an exchange of excuses and appeals, protests and rebuttals, to Diane's happy surprise, her daughter softened.

Finally, Selah agreed.

"I know, Mom. I'm going to clean up and get some help soon…real soon. I don't know where, but I will get some help."

Like a folk ballad refrain, she kept repeating the promise over and over.

Diane spoke up, offering assurance and support.

"I will take care of you, Selah. You can come home with me. No worries—just come home with me."

Then she repeated the promise, "I will take care of you!"

"Mother, you would let me come back, knowing the shape I'm in?"

"Yes, Sweetie! You need help and you need it now."

After repeatedly questioning and testing her mother's offer, Selah agreed, her reluctance draining away.

"All right, Mom, but what do I have to do?"

"Nothing. There will be some rules."

"What kind of rules?"

Diane gave a terse reply, looking her daughter in the eye, "No drugs, no friends, no phone."

After an awkward silence, Selah looked up and nodded her head in agreement.

Diane was excited and scared. She had spoken with such confidence, but actually she had no plan. What should she do next?

Selah wanted to go back to her place to pick up a few things. But Diane felt it would not be a safe move. Not only was she apprehensive for her daughter's physical safety, she feared Selah might relapse and decide not to make the break after all.

Diane kept shooting quick prayers heavenward.

"God, give me guidance! God, help me!"

Her heart kept beating rapidly. Trying to keep calm before her daughter, Diane found her thoughts turning toward her own parents.

"Every daughter needs her mom at certain life intervals. Just as Selah needed me right now, I needed my mother too."

Minutes later Peggy Vigneulle heard her phone ring. She answered and smiled to hear the voice of her daughter. Then suddenly she could tell by the tone of Diane's voice that something was seriously wrong.

"Hi, Mom! It's Diane. I have a big favor to ask of you and Daddy. God has answered our prayers—Selah has agreed to get help. But I need somewhere to go—we need a safe place. Would you and Daddy take us in for the night? I have no idea what we're going to face, but Mom, I need your help."

Peg relayed the news to Dick and quickly came back with their answer, "Yes, Honey. Come on home."

Dick and Peg welcomed their daughter and granddaughter. Sitting on the living room sofa, Big Daddy welcomed Selah, assuring her of his love and delight to see her.

Peggy joined the group, and Selah looked up and softly spoke, "Hi, Gran Gran."

Noticing how agitated and fidgety Selah grew by the minute, Peggy softly suggested the two women move to her guest bedroom for rest.

Diane promised not to leave Selah alone.

"I'll stay with you till you fall asleep, then I'll come back and check on you every five minutes. I promise."

Comforted by her mother's pledge, Selah relaxed and soon fell asleep. Diane slipped out to rejoin her parents in the living room. True to her word, in a short time, she went back to the bedroom to check on Selah. What she saw horrified her.

"Selah was sitting straight up, her eyes were wide, and her mouth open in a silent scream. I threw my arms around my girl, asking over and over, 'Selah, what is it?'"

In the throes of withdrawal, tormented in soul and body, Selah soon found her voice. A piercing scream filled the house.

"They're coming to get me! They're coming to get me!" she cried, pointing to the ceiling."

Peg rushed back into the room. Like an emergency room doctor in a crisis triage, she took charge as she knelt by the young woman's bed and began to pray.

As Diane later gave account, "As she joined me in prayer, my mom took command of the spirit and space in her house. She claimed spiritual authority over my daughter's tormentors."

"In the name of Jesus, let Selah go! We pull down every stronghold!"

She commanded demons to leave and called for Christ to free her.

Mother and Grandmother continued to pray.

"Wow! What a change—for my daughter and me! That day, my mother's prayer became a turning point for both Selah and me. We had a long road to recovery ahead of us, but the journey began that day. God would lead us to doctors and counselors, family and friends to help and support us, but

Selah's deliverance began that day when my mother prayed us through."

The whole Vigneulle family celebrates the years of sobriety that have followed. Selah has remained drug free.

"We both owe a debt to my mother," Diane often testifies. "Mom is a woman filled with the Holy Spirit, and she has a strength that you don't know is there until it is needed."

Diane recalls one other lesson she learned that day in her parents' home, watching her mother intervene for a prodigal granddaughter.

"A few days earlier, when the Lord told me to love my daughter as if she already walked with God, I did not fully understand how to do that. I wanted to put aside my own hurts and disappointments. That's what led me to go to her apartment for an intervention. Even then, however, I didn't know exactly how to live out the Lord's command until that night when I watched my mom in action, loving Selah and praying powerfully for her deliverance. Then I knew fully what the Lord meant when He said, 'Treat her like Jesus.'"

Peggy Vigneulle, by her words and actions, set a godly example of what the love of God looks like—a proactive love, unconditional and full of mercy.

Peg Vigneulle's maternal example not only captured the compassion and power of her own spirit, but also summarized her ongoing legacy. Whether with family, friends, or strangers—the kind-hearted or ill-tempered—Peggy Vigneulle loves them all the same. She treats them like Jesus.

CHAPTER EIGHTEEN

Family Treasure

"*U*nderstand this SMI folks, Peg and I did not do everything right as parents. No, we made many mistakes, but we were committed to raising our children for the Lord. God heard our prayers and honored our commitment. I speak from experience—the Lord will give wisdom to those believers who humbly seek His help. God did it for my family, and the Lord will do it for you and yours!"

GOD'S BLUEPRINT FOR THE FAMILY

In the fall of 1995, just weeks after becoming Pastor Emeritus, Dick Vigneulle was back in SMI's pulpit, preaching on a theme precious to him— "The Family." He spoke with a patriarch's perspective, reflecting on his own experiences as a husband and father. The solid Christian testimonies of his four adult children, three sons and a daughter, gave moral authority to his sermon.

Likewise, he spoke transparently of his own shortcomings and his family's everyday struggles throughout the generations. He did not feign perfection for himself or his kids' upbringing, and so gained a ready audience. Facing their own challenges, parents and grandparents sitting in the pews did not feel offended. Their Pastor once more took them to God's Word, and then used the text to springboard into an unusually personal testimonial. Sweeping aside any hesitancy about safeguarding his privacy, Dick used his own life experiences for candid illustrations.

Throughout the twenty-five years of his pastoral ministry, in his preaching and ministry strategies, Dick stood as a family advocate. In SMI's early years he recruited Bob Stone to lead a counseling and seminar ministry that championed the family. When Dick led the congregation in establishing Shades Mountain Christian Schools, he envisioned more than just a top-notch

Dick and Peggy with children
Rick, Mick, Diane, and Tom – July 21, 1979

academic institution. He wanted a Christ-centered school that functioned in partnership with the home and local church. To build families, he built a school.

The man known as "Pop" or "Dad" to his children and now "Big Daddy" to his grandkids, preached to safeguard more than his family circle and the families in his congregation. Dick felt strongly that modern-day culture seemed to be on a seek-and-destroy mission to bring down the institution of the family as God created it and the Bible explained it.

As he spoke, Dick delivered a message of hope not despair. Times were critical but not hopeless.

> Families all over America are dying. Satan's strategy is to divide the husband and wife and thus destroy the family. But I believe that when God renews lives He also brings healing and restoration to families and relationships. When a husband and wife determine to follow God's blueprint and refuse to allow anything to divide them, then they become an impregnable force to withstand Satan's war on their family. Marriages can survive and thrive! Fathers and mothers can lead their children with confidence. All we have to do is follow God's blueprint. And here it is!

With that, Dick pointed to the Bible and read his sermon text—Colossians 3:17-22.

"Folks, we have looked at this passage a number of times, but it has such an important message that we need to look at it again. Here, I believe, is God's blueprint or pattern for the family."

Then he listed fundamentals.

254

"The father is the head of the family. Men, we need to remember that we are to be an earthly example of the Heavenly Father—and that one day we will give account for our kids to the Heavenly Father. Together with his wife a man raises his children in a home where Jesus Christ is the focus. The Bible should be the most important book in the home. Read it to your wife and kids. Explain what it means. And live it. Seek to bring your children to a personal relationship with Jesus Christ as personal Savior."

Dick moved on to the major thrust of his sermon. With his folksy, down-home approach, he resorted not to exegesis but personal example. Almost confessional in tone, Dick pulled back the curtain on his private life. He shared his experiences as Dad to Rick and Mick, Diane, and Tom.

"Here are twelve lessons I learned as a father. These are major pointers for executing God's blueprint for the family—the godly family."

1. PROVISION: There is a lot more to raising a family than just making a living. I learned you can be a good provider and a lousy dad. Being a father is a huge responsibility. It is not a part-time job. To all you dads listening to me, remember that your family needs you, and every day is important. I could not succeed in my own strength. I needed help—God's help. You do too.

2. FAMILY DEVOTIONS: There is irreplaceable value to family devotions. Peg and I regularly gathered our children to read the Bible and pray together. By example we showed our kids that God was number one in our home. We taught the Bible, and we taught them how to pray. The kids saw God answer our prayers and that strengthened their own faith. They realized that God cared about them and their problems or desires.

3. FUN: As a father I learned how important it is to have fun with my children. We enjoyed games, played basketball in the driveway, and went fishing. We even rode motorcycles together! I tried to make my kids' special events a priority, going to their swim meets, ball games, and wrestling matches. Not only did we share fun times, we grew closer and created memories our family still cherishes.

4. GOD'S HOUSE: Commitment to God's House was a top priority for Peg and me. Even my life at the bank did not keep us away from church services—Sunday morning and evening and Wednesday night. NOT attending church, or even youth group activities, was NEVER an option.

The local church is the family's best friend. The Bible upholds the role of parents: "Honor your father and your mother, that your days may be long upon the land which the LORD your God is giving you" (Exodus 20:12). Bring your kids to SMI, and we're going to teach them to honor and respect you, parents.

Sunday starts the week, and when you go to church you make the Lord the priority of your life. Church ministries offer something for every family member, with Sunday School classes and youth activities as well as opportunities for the whole family to be together in worship.

Let me say again, keeping God's House a priority was one of the greatest decisions Peg and I ever made. Our whole family continues to be beneficiaries of that choice.

5. PARTNERS IN PARENTING: Over the years God brought many individuals into our family life who played important roles in helping Peg and me raise our children: grandparents, aunts and uncles and other family members, school teachers and coaches, and youth pastors. Build a support group around your family to encourage and counsel you as parents and to partner in reaching your kids for Christ. Expose your children to godly people who will impact their lives. My kids sat under SMI's guest speakers so they got to hear great men and women of God.

6. CONSISTENCY—NOT PERFECTION: I learned quickly and often that there is no such thing as perfect parents. Humility and honesty matter. Learn from your mistakes, parents, and keep asking for God's grace and wisdom. I don't think our children expect perfection, but they do want us to be honest and not hypocritical. Family integrity leads to my next point.

7. APOLOGIES: There is a great exercise that keeps us real with the Lord and with our families—it is learning to admit wrongs and to ask for forgiveness. In learning to say "I was wrong, and I am sorry—please forgive me," we keep ourselves accountable. I learned that if I ever wanted our children to admit when they were wrong, then I had to do it also.

8. CHARACTER DEVELOPMENT: As a father, I learned that the development of Christian character in my children is a process—not an event. It takes years, and so, most importantly, I had to learn to be the proper role model and to be consistent. Go for the long haul!

9. FRIENDS: Remember, folks, that I did not become your full-time

Pastor until the age of forty-three, and by that time my three oldest children were college-age. Rick and Mick and my son-in-law were all three students at Liberty University. So when our older children were growing up, Peg and I did not have Shades Mountain Independent Church or Shades Mountain Christian Schools, or other Christian influences that we have here now.

My oldest three attended public schools, and consequently many of their friends were not Christians. As a father I quickly learned that our children's friends had a powerful influence, and that wrong friends can cause irreparable harm.

As a safety measure to decrease harmful influences, first, Peg and I made our home the gathering place for our children and their friends.

Second, we rarely permitted our kids to spend the night away from home You cannot control the atmosphere in someone else's home. Certainly, there were exceptions, and we did allow them to have their friends stay with us. In fact, there seemed to be someone dropping in or staying over most of the time! And we loved it!

Third, let me encourage you, parents, to know who your children's friends are. Take control. Your children more often than not are influenced more by their friends than by you. And that's wrong! Parents, you need to be the greater influence in their lives. Be creative, but be protective. Your children will thank you later.

10. CHORES: My mother and father taught me to work. Part of normal family life was doing our chores. It built discipline as well as good character. I taught my children the same lesson. As a father I learned how important it is that the whole family participates in household chores. My kids learned to make their beds and clean their rooms, scrub the bathroom and wash the dishes, mow the lawn and rake the leaves.

After one of the kids scrubbed the kitchen floor, I heard him calling out to siblings and friends in the house, "Don't step on the kitchen floor—I just mopped it!"

That showed me that kids' good work habits result in a healthy sense of pride and ownership of their home and family. Hard work developed responsibility and appreciation.

Peg and I taught the kids that work and a job well done is right and acceptable to the Lord. It is vital that everyone do something regularly for the benefit of all. Everybody shares. As a result, you teach your children responsibility and an appreciation for the things you parents have done for them.

11. ZERO TOLERANCE for REBELLION: Rebellion in any form has to be dealt with immediately and thoroughly. Listen, if we want to raise children with moral and godly character, we must start with the clear understanding that all of us are children of Adam. We inherited a sin nature—a bent or tendency toward evil. It is in all of us, folks.

This may come as a shock to some of you grandparents, but the fact is there are no perfect children! We don't need to ask when our children misbehave, "*Why does that child behave that way?*" The answer is that he got it from you! And you got from your parents, and they got it from their parents, and so it goes all the way back to Adam and Eve.

We all come into this world with an appetite to do wrong, so don't be surprised when your children do things that you know to be wrong. Anger, lies, stealing, rebelling—when our kids behave this way, they are just behaving according to their sin nature.

Because of our sin, Christ came into the world to die on the cross, and with His own blood purchase our redemption. Every child, as well as every adult, needs the Savior. When a person accepts Christ as personal Savior, God gives that one a new nature—one alive to God, eager and able to do His will.

Even after our children are born again, they need to be surrounded with parental prayer and role models. Children need direction, affirmation, and support to develop godliness in their own lives.

Back to my main point: rebellion is a terrible sin. The Bible says, "Rebellion is as the sin of witchcraft" (I Samuel 15:23). Confront the sin, and do not ignore it. If you fail here, the result will be heartache and God's judgment. How do we handle rebellion? Bring the rebel into submission through prayer and godly discipline—including corporal punishment (Proverbs 22:15; 23:13-14).

12. OBEDIENCE: As a father, I learned the importance of teaching our children to obey. God's Word says, "Children, obey your parents in the Lord, for this is right" (Ephesians 6:1). Parents must help their children do just that by making disobedience an unpleasant experience. Disobedience is always wrong!

If your children learn obedience, then when it is time for them to leave home and go out on their own, obedience turns to honor. Peg and I are so blessed because today all four of our children honor their mother and father. They not only are our children, but now they have become our best friends.

A familiar adage among Christian educators reminds teachers and parents of education's higher purpose: *Teach children how to live, not just how to make a living.* Dick echoed that higher purpose.

"Parents, our task is to make sure our children grow up in an environment that will equip our sons and daughters to one day become competent, responsible parents in their own right."

As Dick poured out his heart, surely the godly example of his own parents spurred him on. Through all his own joys and stresses as a dad, Dick was guided by the standards and memories Harold and Marjorie Vigneulle built. Dick's folks gave him a living model that guided him as a young father.

Years later, now a grandfather and great-grandfather, Dick refined and proved a godly heritage. In seeking to be a good father, he became a better man and a stronger Christian and more compassionate pastor.

The most important success in life was passing his Christian legacy to the next generations of Vigneulles. Dick's greatest wealth was not held in tangibles like money or land or awards. The dearest assets in his and Peg's life were Rick, Mick, Diane, and Tom. His cherished children—his FAMILY TREASURE—would always be life's greatest gifts. Children are the lasting treasure earth allows the faithful.

Three sets of Vigneulle twins – Rick and Mick, Joy and Judi (daughters of Tom and Ginger), Anna and Abby (daughters of Mick and Sue) – December 2006

Dick and Peggy with extended family – children and grandchildren – 1992 (Anna and Abby not born yet).

RICK & MICK VIGNEULLE

Dick's twin sons are over ten feet tall—if stacked one on top of the other. To be exact, the stack would measure ten feet and eight inches. If Rick and Mick were "vertically challenged" in stature, they were giants in energy, motion, and mischief. From their birth in 1954 in New York City, to their childhood and adulthood in Alabama, the two were inseparable and identical. Even as toddlers, the boys displayed their father's zeal for life and charismatic personality. Lovable and unstoppable, Rick and Mick won the hearts of everyone they met, and still do.

The twins enjoyed a happy childhood, but their teen years took a gradual turn. Truancy and breaking boundaries displaced childish pranks, testing the relationship with their mom and dad. Looking back, both sons agree that peer pressure and self-esteem struggles prompted their misbehavior. Whether quiet or overt, the twins wrangled with authority issues and expectations, whether from parents, teachers, or even friends.

Rick and Mick have "performed" together since boyhood

In tenth grade, at the end of the year, Mick brought home a failing report card. The attendance column noted 30 days of unexcused absences. Dick had no idea his son was skipping school and was failing.

"Son, you got all F's and one D! What happened?"

"Sorry, Pop! I guess I spent too much time on one subject."

The weekend after the report card, Mick Vigneulle mulled over his worries about his life's direction. On Sunday, May 30, just four days after his seventeenth birthday, as Mick got ready to go to church, he confronted his own need for change.

"I had been a quiet rebel, not wanting to disappoint Mom and Dad. I was at a fork in the road. I remember looking in the mirror as I was shaving

261

and saying to myself, 'Something's gonna happened to you today!'"

SMI was still meeting in the high school lunchroom. Mick took his place in one of the folding chairs in the youth section, and sat back ready to listen to his father preach. But when the song service ended and Dick read his Bible text, the Pastor startled his son with a message on hell. On the last stanza of *Just As I Am*, Mick went forward. Lew Wheeler was his counselor. He took the teen aside and read Ephesians 2:8-9.

"After Lew read the Scripture and explained it to me, it helped me with my assurance. We prayed, and I still remember the peace that came over me."

As summer unfolded, Mick held to his commitment to the Lord. He distanced himself from his twin brother and their worldly friends. As much as he loved Rick, Mick needed to safeguard himself from temptations to go back to the old life. Near summer's end and just days before school began, Rick invited Mick to join him and his buddies in an end-of-summer fling. There was going to be an overnight campout. Mick declined.

The next day, busy with their own activities, none of the Vigneulle family members, at first anyway, noticed that Rick had not returned from the campout. By late in the afternoon, however, Dick and Peg, now aware of their son's failure to come home, grew more concerned with each passing hour. Then a phone call brought alarming news from the parents of one of Rick's camping buddies.

"Our boys have run away from home! They are hitchhiking to California!"

Rick felt like a young Christopher Columbus, out to discover America. The spirit of adventure blinded him to any thought of causing his parents alarm. Just the same, he still said his prayers, giving some evidence that he knew he was breaking boundaries and testing limits—whether God's or his parents or both.

"Lord, please protect me from this stupidity! Let my parents' prayers protect me."

Not until the second day did Rick call home. Well aware of her son's ongoing spiritual struggles, Peggy heightened her prayers for her runaway adventurer.

"Lord, whatever it takes—do what You have to do to make my son right with God."

News of the Pastor's son's escapade soon spread, and a few tongues wagged. Peggy overheard a church member express disapproval, as if a minister's family must be perfect. Typically, she was apt to ignore such a comment, but not this time. She confronted her family's critic.

"My son is no different than your son."

She stood up for her son, but even so took issue with his choices.

Speaking of Rick and his fellow travelers, she later reflected, "They had been taught right, but they were just being rebellious."

Contrived excuses and desperate pleas, all the more convincing with their gritty smiles and dusty clothes, garnered free rides. Dozens of cars stopped, one after another, to pick up the motley teens standing by the roadside. Some nights they slept outdoors. Once they reached Arizona, a Good Samaritan allowed the weary young travelers the use of an empty trailer with two beds, modest accommodations the teens gratefully accepted. Gradually, the young men came to a sober realization that the Lord was watching over them. It was God's provision that kept them, not their own inventiveness.

Rick even witnessed to one of their drivers who gave them a lift. She was so impressed that she took the boys to her home to feed them and wash their clothes.

Their Westward trail carried on through Texas, beyond Arizona, and finally to California. Once on the West Coast, Rick called home, prompted by his need for money, not repentance. The teens wanted to visit Disneyland and, if they could raise the funds, go on to holiday in Hawaii. Truthfully, the young men were not ready to ditch their adventure, let alone return home and face the music.

In a ploy to get cash, Rick asked his dad for the plane fare to come home.

Dick agreed. So did the other boys' parents. But Dick offered advice.

"These boys all have savings accounts. This escapade should cost them something. Let's pay for their plane tickets with their money!"

All agreed.

After Rick received his one-way plane ticket for a direct flight home, he went to the airport to transfer the ticket to Alabama for a ticket to Hawaii.

"I'm sorry, Sir," the ticket agent explained, "but your ticket is nonrefundable and nontransferable."

Not only disappointed that his adventure was ending, he winced at the realization that his dad, anticipating Rick's move, had outfoxed him.

Peggy remembers the day Rick arrived back home.

"Dick was too upset to go to the airport. He sent me alone to pick up our son. As Rick walked down the plane's stair ramp and across the tarmac, he looked pathetic. His clothes were all disheveled, and the soles of his shoes were so worn out that four layers flapped as he walked. Even so, I was so glad to see him—put out but glad to see him!"

When Rick arrived home, his father was waiting for him out on the patio. Rick walked out to meet him, wondering how his dad would respond. Dick remained seated and calm. His first words surprised his son.

"Rick, you did a gutsy thing. I am proud of you. I only wish I could have gone with you!" Then, moving forward ever so slightly in his chair, Dick leaned toward his son and added, "But I don't want you ever to put your mother through this kind of suffering again. If you want to leave home, Son, then go pack your bags right now. I will give you some money and drive you down to the bottom of the hill."

"Oh, no, Dad!" Rick assured him. "I want to stay home."

Days later, lying across the bed in his room, Rick began to recount to his mother his runaway escapade. Some stories were humorous, others moving as he reflected on people's kindnesses and God's watchcare.

"Mom, even though I ran away, I could not get away from God. I've known truth too long."

A spiritual turnaround was coming, but not just yet. For three months after Rick's return from California, he was still angry that his Westward adventure ended before he wanted it to. A stubborn spirit dragged out his resistance to God, and delayed a surrender that he and his parents both knew was coming.

For many years, Wales Goebel's after-Christmas winter retreat in Gatlinburg, Tennessee drew hundreds of teens to the Smoky Mountains. Even youth uninterested in spiritual life matters would sign up for a fun-time in the snow. As 1971 came to a close, Rick signed up for the retreat.

The twins were raised in church, always under the sound of preachers and Gospel singers, including their father. Over the years there had been half-hearted efforts by Rick to clean up his act, but none of the changes lasted. After arriving at the retreat, he heard great Bible teaching, but even before the first service, something else grabbed at his soul. Rick was moved by the godly teenagers surrounding him. Their love for Christ seemed real, their testimonies genuine.

He began to pray.

"I want what these people have. If You are real, God, change me. I've heard about You my whole life."

Then it came—that peace that passes all understanding.

"Afterwards, I told my friend, 'I've yielded my life to Christ. Don't tell anyone. I want to see if it will last.'"

Once Rick was back home, the biggest proof of his changed heart, was a consuming burden for lost people.

"I did not want my friends to go to hell. I started telling them about Christ, including the guys who ran away to California with me. I led each of them to the Lord."

The bond between brothers was back. The twins encouraged one another in spiritual pursuits. They purposed to separate themselves from the world and held each other accountable.

After high school graduation, Mick enrolled in Liberty University, the new Christian college in Lynchburg, Virginia, founded by his father's good friend, Jerry Falwell. Rick would join him a year later, but first he enjoyed being at home a year longer.

"For the first time in my life, I found out how it was to be a twin by myself."

At Liberty University, the twins would not only find their future mates, they would also discover their future vocation.

The first time Mick saw his future wife, Sue, on the campus of Liberty University, his heart skipped.

"I knew she was the marrying kind!"

Every young man wants to make a good impression on the first date, but for Mick things went awry. He took Sue to a bowling alley, popular with students and near the campus. She was a great bowler. But his game was wasted. Even more humiliating, after a sloppy release of the bowling ball, he watched it amble down the lane only to make a soft landing. Most of the pins tottered and finally toppled over. But one popped out of place. The lone wayward pin kept spinning until coming to a stop some fifteen feet out on the lane. Out of reach for the reset machine, it blocked the lane and delayed the game.

Whether prompted by chivalry or embarrassment, Mick ran out on to the bowling lane to retrieve the pin so that he and Sue could resume playing.

Then a voice bellowed over the loudspeaker, "Get off the bowling lane! Do not walk on the bowling lane!"

All eyes turned to Mick with unwanted attention. His face turning red, he tried to ignore the public reprimand. At first he just scooted the pin along, and then he finally kicked it. To his surprise, the pin was heavy, and it bounced hard, back against his foot, tearing loose his big toenail. As his sock filled with blood, he limped back to his date. He was crestfallen. Sue was in giggles.

Mick lost the game but won the girl. Love triumphed, despite a lackluster start and a long courtship lasting over three years. Sue was shy and Mick unsure. The two endured a long separation while Mick completed a summer youth ministry assignment in Hawaii. Love letters and poetry swayed hearts. Not long after his return to Virginia, Mick proposed to Sue.

The couple prepared for a summer wedding at the end of the school year. But God had one more test, one more separation.

Randy Rebold, a ministry leader for Dr. Falwell, approached the Vigneulle twins with a ministry opportunity. Even under ordinary circumstances, folks found it hard to say no to Randy. This time he came with compelling evidence that the Lord had sent him. He approached Rick first with his amazing mandate.

"I've been on a fast for forty days. The Lord has laid on my heart to ask you and your brother to travel with me this year."

The offer barely out of Randy's mouth, Rick gave an immediate answer—"No!"

Both twins already had plenty of travel experience under their belts, and life on the road is never easy. Besides, Rick had one more year of college.

Again, Rick reinforced his answer—"No!"

"You can't say no, Rick, until you and your brother have sought counsel and prayed. You have to do both, and only after that can I accept your answer."

A few days later, the two men ran into each other late at night in the Kroger Supermarket.

"I need an answer," Randy reminded Rick. "Have you prayed about my offer?"

"No."

"Then I cannot accept your refusal until you have sought counsel and prayed. The same goes for Mick."

Rick had to admit to himself that he felt under conviction—God wanted him to go. When he finally sought counsel from his dad, Dick encouraged him to accept Randy's offer.

"It will be good for you to get away and get some perspective on life decisions you have to make. You need to go on the road. I think then God is going to answer some of the bigger questions you're wrestling with, Son."

After his father's counsel, followed by serious prayer times, Rick accepted the job.

Randy had won one twin, but the second would be no easier to convince.

"Mick, how about joining a traveling ministry team to represent Thomas Road Baptist Church and Liberty University? You would be perfect! Your talent for music and comedy would be a great addition to the team. Besides, your brother, Rick, has already agreed to join the team. You two could serve and travel together!"

Mick's answer was simple and easy.

"No, thanks! I appreciate the offer, Randy. I really do. But I'm getting married this summer!"

Despite his refusal, Mick could not get away from the offer. His unrest grew, so too did Sue's. God kept prompting him to accept the offer. The couple talked and prayed together.

"Mick, you have to do this."

Sue insisted that her fiancé accept the ministry opportunity, even if it delayed their plans. Her love for Mick and the Lord made her willing to wait. As Paul reminded the Corinthians in the New Testament's "Love Chapter" (I Corinthians 13), true love "bears all things…endures all things."

"I received seven job offers that year," Mick recalls. "And this was the only one that did not pay any money and required me to delay my wedding. But it was God's will. If Rick and I had not accepted the job and listened to God's prompting, we would not have the ministry that we share today."

Randy Rebold's call from the Lord to join his ministry team may have required Mick to leave behind his wife-to-be, but in Rick's case, the ministry led right to the girl who would become Mrs. Rick Vigneulle.

Rick's future wife, Debbie, a fellow Liberty student, was part of the team. In the spring prior to the tour's start, the two first met for a team publicity photo shoot. Rick was immediately taken with the pretty redhead.

"I liked her spunk and personality," he said.

One of the other team members, noticing the mutual attraction, teased the couple by saying, "You two are gonna fall in love and get married!"

Rick was already fighting his growing feelings for Debbie, and the taunt only caused him to struggle all the more. But love prevailed. By Christmas holidays the two were engaged to be married the following summer.

The itinerant summer ministry unfolded one of the most memorable evangelistic and public relations efforts of Dr. Jerry Falwell's ministry to date. The "I LOVE AMERICA" campaigns took the student team of musicians and entertainers to state capitals throughout the country. In the mid-1970's patriotism surged with America's bicentennial celebrations. The ministry team gathered huge crowds and gained celebrity with television and video broadcasts, mixing evangelistic outreach and patriotic challenges.

After graduation and the finish of the twins' ministry for their alma mater, the Lord led them into their own brand of ministry, born out of their yearlong tour experiences. The two brothers founded RICK and MICK VIGNEULLE MINISTRIES, operating from their home base at the family compound in Wilsonville, Alabama. The men combine side-splitting comedy and inspirational contemporary music for an outside-the-box approach to an evangelistic meeting.

"Now we get paid to do what we used to get spankings for!" Rick laughs.

Debbie and Sue are integral parts of their husbands' ministries. Their college courtships and on-the-road ministries for Liberty University initiated the young women for the special demands of their husbands' calling.

As their website celebrates, now beyond their ministry's twenty-fifth anniversary, Rick and Mick have served as internationally known Christian comedians and contemporary music artists, performing in all fifty states and fourteen foreign countries.

RICK+MICK, as their logo identifies them, have been featured on television, performed in the White House, and conducted chapels for professional baseball teams. *LIFE* magazine featured them in its *20TH CENTURY HIGHLIGHTS* book.

The twins have appeared with David Jeremiah on *TURNING POINT*, Charles Stanley on *IN TOUCH*, as well as Jerry Falwell for the *OLD TIME*

GOSPEL HOUR. The brothers have shared the ministry platform with such notables as the late Adrian Rogers, Zig Ziglar, Tim and Beverly LaHaye, and Josh McDowell.

Rick and Mick – 2008

Noted California Pastor David Jeremiah commends their work, saying "I don't know two fellows who enjoy ministry more than my good friends Rick and Mick Vigneulle. They accomplish this through the medium of comedy and laughter. If laughter is like a *good medicine* then you will overdose with these brothers."

The heart of their ministry is evangelism. Statistical evidence, the twins point out, shows that 64% of people who make a profession of faith in Jesus Christ will do so before their eighteenth birthday. The Vigneulles have committed their lives to winning teens for Christ.

As they travel to towns and cities, the twins often conduct their highly acclaimed high school assembly programs called "ATTITUDE CHECK," which

Typical scene where Rick and Mick sing and play guitars for their outreach ministry to young people.

is a motivational program, utilizing their humor and songs, to build teen's self-esteem and encourage healthy lifestyle choices. From gym floors or high school podiums, Rick and Mick bring middle and high school teens a relevant message on topics that include suicide, teen pregnancy, drug and alcohol abuse, and bullying.

Their community outreach includes a public invitation to a Thursday night "PIZZA BLAST" where students receive free pizza and soft drinks, and a Gospel message. Tens of thousands have received Christ through the Vigneulle twins' evangelistic ministry.

The brothers are dedicated fathers too. Mick and Sue have five children, a son and four daughters. Rick and Debbie are parents of three, two

Rick and Debbie's family at son Brandon's wedding August 2008
L-R Tiffany (Steve), Rick, Jocelyn (wife of Brandon), Brandon, Debbie, and Joshua

Mick and Sue's family December 2006
Mick, Sue, Mandi (Joel), Ashley, Drew, Anna, and Abby

sons and a daughter. The twins are quick to credit their parents for helping them to succeed in life as family men and ministers.

In 1997, RICK AND MICK MINISTRIES sent out a thank-you letter to ministry supporters. One letter got a hand-written postscript. The letter addressed to Dick and Peggy included a love note from their grateful sons. The twins' salute pays tribute to the Christian legacy Dick and Peg pass on to all their children. Likewise, many of their spiritual children would add an "Amen" to Rick and Mick's tribute.

P.S. We love you for ALL you are and do for us. You're our Number One heroes and know without a doubt that we are an extension of you to the 20,000 – 25,000 who've committed their lives to Christ through us. We learned by example and life-style and honor you with what we've become (all that is GOOD, that is!). Thank You for giving to our ministry through all the years we've been in existence and for the confidence you had in us even when we didn't have it in ourselves. Like the song says, "Love them while you can"—and we do! We've changed our roles from children to BEST FRIENDS!

Thanks for being our parents, our counselors, our example, our Pastor, our Pastor's wife, our financial advisor, our cheerleaders, our supporters, our wind beneath our wings, our heroes, and for giving us Jesus, and for beating the devil out of us when we needed it! WE'RE GRATEFUL!!

DIANE VIGNEULLE STOUGH

Dick's home was his castle, and a princess lived there—his daughter, Diane.

"My Daddy called me 'Princess' or 'Baby' every day of my life growing up, and he treated me like royalty. He was my hero from childhood, and in my eyes he could do nothing wrong. My father always encouraged me and probably spoiled me. He almost never spanked me—that kind of discipline was left up to Mom."

Only one other man eclipsed the princess's love for her father, and that was the young man who would become her husband.

A school friend of the twins, Wayne Stough was part of the neighborhood brood of teenagers that hung out at the Vigneulle household. He began attending Shades Mountain Independent when the church still met in the school library. Dick's sermon series on the book of Revelation gripped his heart with fear and concern for his soul's condition. After church one evening, Wayne lingered in order to talk to one of the youth leaders. The impact of weeks of listening to Dick's preaching and the counselor's careful explanation of the Gospel came together. The claims of the Gospel suddenly became clear and irresistible to Wayne.

"I see it now!" he exclaimed, and then prayed to receive Christ as his personal Savior.

Not long afterwards, Wayne's parents, already attending SMI, got saved and became faithful church members.

Still a part-time Pastor, Dick found time to be a spiritual mentor to his children's good buddy. Wayne confided his teen struggles with alcohol and drug abuse. Christ had set him free, and he wanted to stay on a clean path. Dick enjoyed his time with the young man who showed so much promise for the Lord.

With such close ties to the Vigneulle family, he began spending more and more time with the twins and their sister, Diane. The SMI youth group traveled in swarms, meeting on basketball courts or taking over a local pizza joint. After a few months, Diane became more than Rick and Mick's little sister to Wayne. He was in love. Friendship led to courtship.

Diane recalls, "Wayne would come to my house almost every night. When it was time to leave, he would hop into his little green Volkswagen Beetle, and with the windows rolled down, as he drove away, Wayne would begin shouting, 'I love you, D!' And he would keep on shouting and honking his car horn at the same time! His voice filled the night air, so we could hear him as he wound down the hill from our house on Sceptor Lane until he reached Tyler Road. I was swept away by his romantic antic, but now when I think back, I wonder what the neighbors must have thought!"

Midway through her senior year, Diane and Wayne were engaged. With their parents' blessing, a wedding was planned to follow her graduation. Wayne had finished his sophomore year of college. For a year he skipped lunch to save money to buy an engagement ring. Diane wore her mother's wedding dress. Peg had worked for weeks sewing to add seed pearls and lace, making sure the dress fit perfectly for her daughter's special day.

Six months after their honeymoon, Wayne and Diane moved to Lynchburg so he could study at Liberty University. Diane audited classes and worked at a local bank.

"Not only did my dad teach me about God and the Bible, he also tutored me in money management and practical business principles. Wayne felt that God was leading him into a career in business, and Dad mentored him too. My husband had wonderful parents, but I think Daddy played a special place in his life as a spiritual and career advisor."

Even though she grew up in a Christian home, and sat through family devotions every day of her girlhood, Diane struggled for many years to gain an assurance of her salvation.

> I can't remember a time I didn't love God. I prayed to receive Christ as a child, but had doubts. I would talk to Shelia Erwin, who worked with the youth in our church's early days with her husband, Hank. Shelia would walk me through the salvation message and pray with me, without ever getting frustrated or putting me down. I had all the knowledge, but I would worry that I had left out a word when I prayed to be saved. I prayed the Sinner's Prayer at such a young age that there was no outward dramatic change in my life to prove my conversion. Sometimes the issue seemed to be settled, and then the doubts would pop up again.

Adding to her stress was a strong desire not to fail her beloved father.

"My love and reverence for my dad made me feel guiltier for my ongoing struggle to understand a believer's security in Christ. I did not want to disappoint my mom or daddy."

The witness and prayers of family and friends were not without effect. As a young married woman in her twenties, Diane experienced a climactic prayer moment that ended the struggle.

"Wayne had left to run to the store. I dropped to my knees on the kitchen floor and cried out to the Lord. 'If this is the abundant life, I don't want it! But God I long for You in my heart! If You are out there, I need You to meet with me and fill me with assurance.' Even before I got up off my knees, the assurance came. I knew without a doubt that I was a child of God!"

Minutes later Wayne walked in the back door. Immediately he sensed a change in his wife's countenance and spirit.

"What happened?" he asked. "Something is different!"

Diane loves sharing her faith, and she does so with confidence.

"What the Lord was teaching me, I feel, is that salvation comes not from merely reciting a prayer but in establishing a personal relationship with the living God through His Son."

The Stoughs continued faithful in local church life, following the pattern Dick and Peg established for family worship, even in the earliest days of his business life. But several years into their marriage, Wayne and Diane sensed the Lord leading them into a whole new ministry, one different from anything either had ever known.

Wayne grew up in a Southern family that squelched any discussion of their Jewish ancestry. Some distant family members became vitriolic when insisting on silence on the issue.

When their son Stuart was a young boy, he was hospitalized after being severely burned while playing with a friend. He spent months in the hospital. During their frequent trips to the hospital, the couple's route passed a synagogue. Daily sight of the place awakened in Wayne a desire to explore his Jewish heritage.

When the couple learned of a Messianic synagogue in town, a Jewish house of worship made up of born-again believers in Jesus Christ as Messiah, the Stough family began attending. For Wayne especially, Davidic-style worship fulfilled a spiritual hunger. He relished the liturgical services rich in the prayers and traditions of biblical Judaism.

While he was on a quest to discover his ancestral roots, Diane was advancing a spiritual one of her own. Her maternal grandmother, Louise Haley, held a reverential love for God's chosen people, the Jews, and became an avid student of the nation of Israel in Scripture and current events. Dick Vigneulle's love of Israel and prophetic studies came, in part, from Mrs. Haley. The Stoughs, therefore, followed a natural bent from both families.

Wherever the Stoughs have lived, through the transfers and relocations mandated by his business life, Wayne and Diane have joined a Messianic synagogue.

For many years now the two have been active members of Birmingham's Beth Hallel—"House of Praise." Serving alongside their rabbi, Wayne is the Service Leader, guiding worshipers through the liturgy and reading the Hebrew Scriptures. Diane is the Praise and Worship Leader.

Diane explains what "Messianic Judaism" means, quoting her synagogue's website.

> Messianic Judaism is "biblical" Judaism. We believe the Word
> of G-D is true from Genesis to Revelation. The first believers
> in Yeshua (Jesus), the Messiah, were Jewish and believed,

as we do, that the Messiah prophesied about in the Old Covenant Scriptures had come and will return. We believe in G-D's end-time plan for the nation of Israel and the world. A central part of Messianic Judaism is belief in the physical and spiritual restoration of Israel, as taught in the Scriptures. We are committed to bringing a deeper understanding of G-D's Word to the "Body of Messiah"—Jewish and Gentile.

Wayne and Diane (Vigneulle) Stough's family – 1991
Wayne, Diane, Stacey, Stephen, Stuart, Selah, Seleste, and Shannon

Business life and their own homing instincts brought the Stoughs back to Alabama. Today they live in Wilsonville, on the Vigneulle family compound where all Dick and Peg's children own homes. Despite being born and bred a city girl, Diane loves country life. She and Wayne now have six children and eleven grandchildren. Every day renews her appreciation for the godly legacy God gave her.

Diane's hand-written note in the 50th wedding anniversary card sent to her parents paid tribute to her Christlike parents.

"I certainly must be one of the most blessed people in the world. You have been there for me all through my life and I would like to say thank you. But, most of all, your heart of love has led me to the Father, but it was also your life that led me to Jesus. You are wonderful parents, and I praise God every day for my heritage."

TOM VIGNEULLE

Tom Vigneulle, the last of Dick and Peg's four children, was the only one to be raised largely by a pastor-father, not a businessman. He grew up in a preacher's home, not a banker's. Yet ironically, by his own account, he is the only son Dick almost lost.

Tom recalls, "My dad was losing me. My junior year there was very little communication between us. He seemed to be busy all the time, whether it was Youth for Christ or Keswick Conventions or the church. I felt like I never had personal time with my father."

Unlike his older brother Rick, the overt rebel, here was a quiet, brooding dissenter. In a surprising twist, the three older children, largely raised by a businessman father, have warm memories of a childhood where their dad was actively engaged in their lives and playtimes. On the other hand, the child raised by a preacher-father felt neglected and disconnected.

Perhaps the bank's defined hours and off days versus the endless 24/7 demands on a preacher account for the difference. Multiple factors perhaps account for the troubling reversal of childhood experiences: differences in personality and temperament, or changing times in the country and culture, or even heightened spiritual warfare against clergy families.

By the time Dick caught on to Tom's plight, it seemed almost too late. Dick recruited the youth pastor and church peers to help him in reaching out to Tom. The turnaround came during Tom's senior year. Not discounting the prevailing power of prayer, Dick found a practical remedy for his father-son disconnect: he bought season tickets for UAB basketball for Tom and him.

"We attended every game—my dad and me—no matter how busy his schedule or whatever ministry demands on him. And that year the team played in the NCAA tournament, and we even got to attend those games."

Dick poured more attention on Tom. For his senior trip, he joined his parents on a trip to Israel.

But one special father-son outing stands out in Tom's memory because it was an extraordinary demonstration of love, one that took Dick way out of his comfort zone.

Dick was not a moviegoer. Brought up in a religious childhood home and trained in a strict fundamentalist college, he did not go to "picture shows." Worldly entertainments were forbidden. Years later, as a father he permitted his children to go to movies. As a Pastor he did not preach against movies, though he certainly advocated caution and parental censorship regarding what kids watched on television or at the movies. But even on a personal level, going to movies just did not interest him—he would rather attend a sports event.

During Tom's senior year a blockbuster movie caught the whole nation's attention—*JAWS*. Tom wanted to see it, and to his surprised delight, his dad offered to take him.

"This was a big deal that my dad would even go to the movies, let alone take me—just the two of us for a father-son outing. I already started to feel important when Dad made the offer, but even more amazing to me, he was going to skip Sunday night church to take me. He got someone else to fill the pulpit. I don't know what excuse he gave for not being there."

"Even so," Tom laughs, "Dad drove to a movie theater clear on the other side of town where hopefully no one would see him at the movies on a Sunday night."

By the time Tom graduated from high school, he was not sure where he would go to college. But he certainly knew where he would NOT go— Liberty University. The school's Founder and President, Jerry Falwell, was his father's close friend, and besides his older brothers attended there. Tom wanted to make his own way—out from under the shadow of his father or older brothers.

"Just having the name Vigneulle would immediately give me a lot to live up to—or live down!"

A Liberty staff member visiting SMI took a personal interest in Tom and challenged him to reconsider his refusal to come to Lynchburg. To his own surprise, Tom changed his mind and enrolled. Within hours of arriving on campus, he was recruited for leadership duties, sometimes without getting a chance to refuse. His classmates elected him class president. He quickly established his own presence. Nurtured by godly teachers and classmates,

Tom grew in the Lord and found his way.

As a boy he prayed to receive Christ as his Savior while sitting in the balcony at SMI as his father preached. But years of doubts plagued him.

"When you don't have a specific date to claim, sometimes Satan has a victory," Tom acknowledged.

But at Liberty, as he grew in understanding God's Word, he settled the matter. Assurance displaced his doubts.

After college graduation, Tom returned home to Birmingham.

A self-described "Momma's boy," Tom is quick to point out that when it comes to business acumen and love of corporate life, he is the most like his father of any of the Vigneulle kids.

"But I also have my mother's tender-hearted ways," Tom explains, "so that means I charge into a board meeting but shed tears when making the hard decisions."

In 1987, Tom started his own business in Pelham, Alabama—Royal Bedding, Inc. The company's website points out that the company is Alabama's largest mattress manufacturer that sells directly to the public.

Ginger Vigneulle, Tom's wife, was a school teacher at Shades Mountain Christian Schools when they met. Her love of athletics and personal fitness training made Ginger a natural as a physical education teacher.

Dick remembers the day Ginger came into his church office to be interviewed for the SMCS job. A single girl and recent college graduate, she

Tom and Ginger's family – 2000 Tom, Ginger, Tom Jr. (TJ), Joy, and Judi

was very nervous.

"Ginger was great! I knew right away she would be a great teacher, a real asset to our school," Dick recalls. "But bless her heart, she was so tense that she could not relax. I wanted to calm her so, trying to be reassuring, I said, 'Young lady, I want you to know that I am going to take care of you!' After she later met and married my son, she would grin and remind me of my promise to her!"

Tom and Ginger are active members in a Baptist church in the Greater Birmingham area. They have passed on to their three children, a son and two daughters, a love for Christ and great interest in missions. Tom delights to pass on more of the lessons his father taught him.

"Dad taught me to tithe when I was a young paperboy. 'You don't rob God, you tithe!' he told me. It is a principle I'm now teaching my kids."

Certainly Tom has his father's head for business, but there is more. He has his father's heart for God.

For Christmas 2008, the extended Vigneulle family gathered at Gran Gran and Big Daddy's home on Pavillon Drive, a cherished but expansive annual holiday tradition. Peggy's skill at decorating and floral arranging transforms the home into a Christmas wonderland. Dick's extensive train collection and Christmas village fascinate young and old. It was wonderful to have almost everyone home!

Four generations of Vigneulles gathered in Dick and Peg's living room after dinner. It was a joyous family reunion, as children and grandchildren, siblings and cousins, and aunts and uncles celebrated the bonds of family and faith. The climax of the reverie was a devotional led by Dick as he challenged his children, their children, and their children one more time on the urgency of the Gospel, sharing the Good News as if telling it for the first time.

Their daughter, Diane, journaled a description of the event.

There were 37 in all, with each one bringing lots of food and smiles. We all ate until we could not move and then retired into the living room for fun, laughter, and singing. The only ones not there were two grandsons and their families, who were unable to drive in from out of town.

For days my dad had such a burden to make sure all of his family would go to heaven and not one would be missing. He wanted to share the Gospel and make sure everyone knew his or her salvation was sure. He shared his heart and gave the salvation message.

After my dad had spoken and asked the family to pray, my mom had her own petite address.

Mom said, "I just want all of you to know that Gran Gran loves you. It is wonderful to have all of you here. Your Big Daddy and I know that we are going to heaven, and it is our heart's desire to see each person in our family there too."

Then Mom began to tear up, but managed to continue. "Everything that your Big Daddy said earlier was to share with you all the love we have for each one of you and to be sure you are saved so we can spend eternity with each one of you in heaven."

Dick and Peggy's family passion, after nearly sixty years of marriage, still delights in telling the "Old, Old Story of Jesus and His Love!" Despite a lifetime of Christian witness, they do not take for granted the soul needs of their own loved ones. No one gets to heaven on someone else's coattail. A new generation needs to hear and the older generations need to be reminded of Jesus' words, "You must be born again" (John 3:7b). The greatest love bequest this couple could offer is a testament of love—their own as well as the love of the Savior who died for all.

"For God so loved the world that He gave His only begotten Son, that whoever believes in Him should not perish but have everlasting life. For God did not send His Son into the world to condemn the world, but that the world through Him might be saved. He who believes in Him is not condemned; but he who does not believe is condemned already, because he has not believed in the name of the only begotten Son of God" (John 3:16-18).

CHAPTER NINETEEN

Transitions

*O*lympic athletes running a relay race are not the only champions to lose the prize because they dropped the baton at hand-off. Sadly, sometimes modern-day churches and religious institutions flounder with the departure of tenured founding pastors or charismatic chief executives. These heroes arrived at their pantheon stature because of genuine achievement or long tenure or their status as the "founder." All three points applied to Dick Vigneulle and his ministry as Pastor of Shades Mountain Independent Church.

As early as the mid-1980's, Dick knew that he must prepare himself and the church for the day when he would no longer be at the helm. His desire to minister would never wane, and his soul energy seemed boundless. But in fact, his body was tired. A 1984 heart attack reminded him of his own mortality. No one is promised tomorrow. Ultimately poor health would thrust him from the pulpit.

Too often Dick watched once legendary ministries falter because leaders did not know when to quit or how to go "gently into the night." A few spiritual giants even suffered tarnished legacies because they stumbled when handing the leadership baton to a successor. He determined that, by God's grace, such a fate would not fall to him or SMI.

Understandably, transitions inevitably require sharp adjustments. It would be unrealistic to expect none, so Dick aimed to minimize any fallout when a leadership change occurred at SMI. The tight bond between pastor and people that made his pastorate so joyous could become a liability. His son, Tom, pointed out that for many in the church family, including himself, his dad was the only pastor they ever knew. Dick wanted the church to realize that, when the time came, embracing their new pastor would not diminish the bond shared with him. He wanted continuity without rivalry.

The early church, even in its infancy, came to grips with the distractions and even outright division resulting from partisan loyalties and personnel changes.

Paul reprimanded the Corinthian church for such a breach of unity.

For it has been declared to me concerning you, my brethren…
that there are contentions among you. Now I say this, that each
of you says, "I am of Paul," or "I am of Apollos," or "I am of Ce-
phas," or "I am of Christ." Is Christ divided? Was Paul crucified
for you? Or were you baptized in the name of Paul? I thank
God that I baptized none of you…(I Corinthians 1:11-14a).

Paul is a model leader, in part, by refusing a congregation's adoration and pointing them to the Lord. Nor did he hold on to ministry but rather gave it away to disciples trained to lead. For example, he recruited Timothy to assume the helm of his pastorate. When gathering and delivering an offering for the poor that he labored long to collect, Paul assigned a reputable team to deliver the gift. The Lord's approval not man's mattered most.

Even so, the great Apostle himself became embroiled in controversy. A schism between Paul and Barnabas, his earliest mentor, ended one of the early church's stellar missionary teams. The two parted over opposing views of young John Mark's potential.

In great measure, SMI's ability to break from its past would determine its future. Furthermore, some might argue, the endurance of Dick's own legacy rested with the one who took his place. Proof of a job well done relied on making the right choice. In the natural course of life, an elder's success, as well as proof of a youth's maturity, shines on the moment when it is time to let go: such as a father giving his daughter's hand to her husband on her wedding day, or packing up a son to head off to college or an out-of-town job.

The secure and settled pastor usually has two advantages to leverage church issues: time and the pulpit. There was no need for haste. Dick would be careful and deliberate. His preaching would prepare the people to recognize and accept his successor.

Eventually, the most inescapable signal that told Dick he must prepare for this inevitable transition came from his own body. Serious illness weakened his once lion-like stamina. For several years Dick did not take a vacation, except for brief getaways with Peggy to the mountains or the beach. She continually urged her husband to slow down.

The twins especially, by this time middle-aged and ministry veterans themselves, could speak with authority, insisting "Dad, you need to back off." All four of his children tried to nudge their father to make the hard choice.

Dick would never tire of the dynamics of sharing the Gospel and interacting with people. But everyday staying power failed him with the daily tasks of a pastor: meetings, counseling, sermon preparation. Other matters nagged at Dick. True or not, he felt as though he was losing his ability to reach career people or connect with high school students.

Counsel from trusted friends and advisors echoed family sentiment—"Dick, it is time."

Most of all Dick prayed. From the very start of his SMI ministry, Dick prayed for the good sense to know when to quit. More than once, he shared publicly his private prayer.

"Lord, if it's a year or fifty years, give me enough wisdom to know when it is time. It will be the most difficult thing I ever have to do, but when it is God's time for me to step down, it will be the right time. And the right man will be in place."

He later confided, "I've always felt that a pastor has a responsibility never to leave his people without a shepherd. The Lord will send us that individual."

Ten years before Dick's final Sunday in the pulpit, he had begun to pray for God's man to take his place. He was concerned but not driven. God would guide. God would provide. Reflecting on his own life story, Dick found strength of heart.

The God of his salvation directed his path from college to career, leading him from New York City to Birmingham, from City Federal to SMI.

Whether listening to a family member or staff member, Dick often abbreviated the conversation by asking, "What's the bottom line?" At this stage of his life, Dick knew the "bottom line" was not between a man and his job but rather a servant and his God. "What is God's will? What path should I take?" As much as he loved his family and trusted his friends, ultimately only God could give an answer governed by peace.

The healthy state of the church confirmed Dick's acceptance of his exit strategy. The "Church on the Mountain" experienced mountaintop achievements that signaled it was a good time to step aside. The church had no debt. Faith Promise had climbed to $600,000. Shades Mountain Christian Schools' enrollment hit 600. The spirit of the congregation was positive. In other words, the climate was perfect for a new man to have an advantageous start. Dick wanted his successor to be free to dream and plan without being sidetracked by inherited problems.

When the time came to transition, the decision was not made lightly or quickly. Dick Vigneulle's love for SMI, like his vision for it, would never die. But the ultimate proof of his loyalty to God and his love for the church would be to let go when his successor was ready, releasing his life's work to a new and younger generation. Like Moses, Dick would let go of God's people, but first he had to find SMI's Joshua.

The transition would be played out over several years. As the Lord continued to enable Dick to let go, God also was refining Dick's successor and readying the congregation.

By his own account, Dick recalls making the decision to select a successor in 1988, but Dick's "Final Sunday" would not come until 1995. The church's Silver Anniversary on July 2, 1995 would mark more than twenty-five years of achievement, for it would be the end of an era—Dick Vigneulle's era.

God's master transition plan unfolded first in Dick's heart and later would be confirmed in the congregation's acceptance. Once Dick settled in the conviction that God's time had come for him to begin the separation process from the church, the next step would be to find his successor and broaden that man's shoulders for the mantle to fall on them.

Dick's successor, when eventually made known, would be in-house and familiar to the congregation. Long before the congregation knew, Dick chose Harry Walls to succeed him as Pastor of Shades Mountain Independent Church. His selection, once announced, found acceptance without even a vote from the congregation. History repeated itself: Dick was never voted on by the congregation, and neither was Harry. Dick's confidence spoke for all, a privilege unique to founding pastors, as Dick himself suggested.

Harry Walls first visited SMI on a summer Sunday in 1986. He stopped in Birmingham to visit a college buddy from his days at Liberty University. Harry was en route to Los Angeles, California where he had just taken a position with Dr. John MacArthur Jr. at The Master's College. After the evening service, Harry met Pastor Vigneulle. The two shook hands and briefly chatted. Dick took an instant liking to the young man and so invited him to lunch that Wednesday. Their mealtime meeting stretched out over three hours as the two men shared their stories. Both felt a connection as two men called of God with a love for the local church and a passion for lost souls.

That midweek appointment, in fact, was the golden moment in Dick's search for a successor—like the Prophet Samuel searching out Israel's next king and finally encountering young David, the last of the farmer Jesse's sons. Dick long harbored the idea that God's choice would be obvious when he met the man whose vision and heart beat with his. At that noon hour Dick knew he had met God's next man for SMI.

Dick was as ready as Samuel to pour out the anointing oil. And as with Israel's future king, the Prophet may have anointed David, but his succession would be years off.

During the restaurant exchange, Dick confided his intention to retire. He spoke at length about his long-standing search for a successor and the qualities needed to lead a church like SMI. Harry was open, interested, but hesitant. He only recently accepted the Dean of Students position at The Master's College, so he did not feel it was God's season for him to come to SMI.

Another meeting followed that night after Wednesday night Prayer Meeting, and this one included Karon, Harry's wife. Before the evening ended, even more resolved, Dick made a job offer.

Dick respected Harry's desire not to disappoint Dr. MacArthur. A compromise was worked out. Harry would travel back and forth from Los Angeles to Birmingham, for periodic ministry visits at SMI, sometimes even filling the pulpit for Dick. After a year of cross-country ministry, Harry accepted Dick's offer to join SMI's staff in 1988. He would serve as Assistant Pastor of Evangelism and Discipleship. Dick's motivation was clearly understood. Harry knew that in accepting the position to join Dick at SMI, he also was accepting Dick's commission to succeed him as the church's Pastor.

Neither man knew the transition would stretch over so long a period, but both agree today it was God's perfect plan from the beginning. For one thing, with an able assistant to share his pastoral load, Dick was reenergized.

Harry Walls' gifts, like Dick's, were abundant and obvious. Harry was studying pre-med at Brown University when he was led to grow in the Lord by a disciple-making lay pastor. Harry sensed God's call to ministry and so transferred to Liberty University. He pursued a rigorous course of study in pastoral ministries with a minor in Greek theology, completing undergraduate and seminary studies at Liberty in 1982.

Harry was educated, a natural-born leader, and a man confident in any circle. While working under authority, Harry was not stifled in freedom of thought or creative approaches to ministry. Here was a mix of moxie and holiness that qualified him to lead the next generation, just as Dick had led his. Both men pushed the envelope and forged their approach to ministry unhindered by tradition. Dick's strong temperament and forceful presence did not intimidate Harry and never compromised his views nor his courage to present them. In other words, Harry was the kind of leader Dick admired, the sort SMI would require in the 21st century.

Harry's extended SMI apprenticeship allowed him to learn the subtleties of the people and the expansiveness of the work. Also it gave ample time for the people to get to know him and naturally grow in their love for him and his family.

The transition from founder to his first successor rarely succeeds without struggle. Legendary heroes cast long shadows as well as wide ones, so whether a man succeeds Bear Bryant or Dick Vigneulle, the task is daunting. As in athletic competition, so in the Christian life, timing and pacing sort losers from winners. Time would give Dick and Harry both an advantage.

True to his pattern with staff, Dick outlined a vision and delegated responsibility, but it was up to his point man to make it happen. Dick required accountability from employees at all levels, but he never dogged them with oversight and micromanagement. The same was true for Harry, only on a much grander scale. Both men grew secure in God's plan: for Dick to step aside and for Harry to step up as SMI's next Pastor. Their personalities and ultimately their approaches to ministry might vary, but greater were their shared loves: love of God, love of witnessing and reaching the lost, love of a pastor's call, and a love for SMI.

In 1994, Dick formally turned over the church's daily operations to Harry. That same year Dick traveled to Europe to visit SMI missionary posts, turning over extended pulpit duties to Harry. Upon his return home, Dick heard repeated, spontaneous compliments for the young man's ministry in his absence.

"You would have been proud of him, Dick!"

This high praise warmed Dick's heart and only affirmed his choice of a successor.

One year later, July 2, 1995, the hand-over was complete. The date was SMI's Birthday Sunday and the celebration of 25 years of ministry. Dick presided over his farewell Sunday, a grand day of celebration.

Sharing in the day's festivities was Steve McKinney, an attorney and longtime church member. As Chairman of the church Board, Steve worked closely with Dick and Harry over several years as the pastors worked out the changeover.

> I've had a ringside seat as God worked His will. The story of these two men testifies to God and His way of working in this ministry. It is the story of willing hearts submitted to God's will—in peace even with tough decisions. Thank you, Dick, for answering God's call twenty-five years ago, for being faithful and setting the course regardless of the circumstances. Thank you for having vision beyond today and tomorrow and causing us to reach further...for living a sanctified life of integrity and courage. Thank you for caring about our future particularly more than you care about yourself.

As the service ended, the mantle was passed and Harry F. Walls III officially became the Pastor of Shades Mountain Independent Church. Dick achieved his final and certainly one of the most critical assignments of his ministry—putting his life's work in the hands of the next generation. The hand-off was complete.

Well over a decade has passed since Dick's "Final Sunday" and the church's transition from founder to chosen successor. He successfully let go and artfully executed the hand-off. Proof of God's blessing and Dick's obedience is the fact that the Vigneulles still worship at SMI, and that Harry has held the post all these years. Pastor Walls continues the heritage of a church committed to winning the lost and discipling believers—on the mountain and around the world. Today Dick Vigneulle is still his respected confidant and appreciated mentor. SMI's Founding Pastor is not forgotten and remains a much-loved hero of the faith.

Pastor Harry Walls becomes Senior Pastor of SMI – July 1995

CHAPTER TWENTY

Aftermath: A Matter of the Heart

"*D*ick, you don't look well. Are you feeling okay?"

As Executive Director of World Reach, Tim Prewitt knew the Chairman of the Board very well, enough to know that something was drastically wrong. Dick never missed a Board meeting, and always made a point to arrive early and review the agenda with Tim. But today, Dick's ashen color and inability to focus his thoughts sounded an alarm.

"You know, Tim, I haven't felt well all week. Even when I was singing in church last Sunday, my wife could tell I wasn't up to par. Peg didn't want me to come this morning, and Mick stopped by the house to insist I go to the doctor."

His sense of humor in tact, Dick added, "We compromised—I still came to this meeting but my son drove me."

Then in a more serious tone, and trying to allay Tim's concern, Dick put a hand on his shoulder, and said, "You know, Tim, I would rather be at this World Reach meeting than anywhere else. And that includes days like today when I don't feel so good."

As other Board members arrived, Dick took his place at the head of the conference table and called the meeting to order. But an hour or so into the meeting, Dick's condition took a rapid decline.

Tim recalls, "Dick became lethargic, and any trace of color drained from his face. He couldn't focus. His words and thoughts drifted. It was like he was there, but he wasn't there. The other men took notice, and the whole group soon reached the same consensus—he's got to go to the doctor, and right now!"

DAY OF CRISIS

The events of Thursday, January 15, 1998, remain etched in the Vigneulle family history, a date to remember like Dick and Peg's wedding anniversary or the birthdates of their four children.

Three years earlier, Dick had retired as Pastor of Shades Mountain Independent Church, but he remained active in various ministries as well as with travel and family life. On Sunday, January 11, just a few days before the fateful Thursday Board meeting for World Reach, Dick had sung a solo for the morning service at SMI. He chose a Gaither song and one of his favorites— *He Touched Me*. Within hours and for many months to come, that song title became the theme of Dick Vigneulle's fight for life. It was a battle he would not, indeed could not, face alone.

Mick Vigneulle responded quickly to the summons to transport his dad to the doctor. Dick protested all the way down Montgomery Highway from World Reach's Hoover headquarters to Brookwood Medical Center.

"Mick, I don't think I can even walk from the parking lot to the front door of the doctor's office. Besides, I don't think there's anything more doctors can do for me."

Cardiac problems had plagued Dick for fifteen years. In the early 1980's he visited the famed Pritikin Clinic in Florida for treatment, hoping to avert bypass surgery. He found the diet and regimen difficult to maintain. Then in 1983, after much resistance, he yielded to heart surgery. But now, fifteen years later, the old warning signs returned, such as shortness of breath and angina pain. Since the Christmas holidays, Dick's family noticed him popping nitroglycerin tablets like candy mints.

The blunt fact of the matter is that Vigneulle never liked hospitals. He avoided them.

"They make me sick," he would seriously protest.

Even as a pastor, he rarely made hospital calls, preferring to delegate the task to his staff.

As he aged and health issues began to recur, Dick still stalled going to the doctor's office, let alone going under the surgeon's knife. Dick's feisty resistance, even as his son drove him to the hospital, was rooted in more than willfulness. He earnestly believed that he had exhausted all his medical options.

"Son, I'm telling you that there's nothing more doctors can do for me," he kept insisting.

The battle did not end even after Mick situated his father into a waiting room chair. To no one's surprise except Dick's, he had to wait and wait a long time.

"Mick, take me back to the Board meeting. I'm just wasting time here."

Thanks to humor and a deaf ear, Mick would not budge. Finally, the nurse called for "Mr. Vigneulle," and Dick was escorted to an examination room. The doctor hooked him up to a heart monitor and found an irregular heart beat. Upon further examination, he gave a dire report.

"Rev. Vigneulle, you have had a heart attack. It could have been yesterday or even much earlier. In fact, you could be experiencing a heart attack right now. I am going to admit you. I've already ordered a wheelchair."

The news did not dampen Dick's determination to go home. He protested.

"But I've walked into this hospital on my own!"

"Well, you're not walking out!" the doctor shot back. "I'm consulting cardiology to see you as soon as possible.

Dick underwent heart catherization and demonstrated narrowed bypass grafts and progression of his coronary artery disease. After evaluation by cardiac surgery, Dick was scheduled for an operation for the next morning to redo coronary artery bypass grafting.

Less than twelve hours later, all the immediate family convened at Brookwood Medical Center. Peg and all four of their children—Rick and Mick, Diane, and Tom—gathered around Dick's hospital bed. Encouraged by Dick's relaxed manner and even jovial spirit, the family bantered to pass the time, laughing at Big Daddy's jokes. The Vigneulles felt assured knowing that the surgery was routine, even commonplace nowadays. After a three- or four-day hospital stay, he would be back home.

On Friday morning, January 16, as the hospital attendant began to wheel the gurney carrying Dick from his hospital room to the operating room, he looked up at Diane.

Noticing her distress, her daddy said with a reassuring smile, "Don't look so serious! I'm going to be fine."

Then surveying the entire family, he gave one more confident testimonial, "Guys, I'm at total peace."

His good spirits and assurances allayed their fears. The family remained together at the hospital to keep a shared vigil until the surgery was over. There was no place else they wanted to be, and besides, staying close to each other made them feel close to Dick.

Admittedly, for some years now they had been swayed by Dick's pessimistic outlook that nothing more could be done for him. Today's surgery hopefully meant not only a longer life but a more active one. Dick's cardiac surgeon, Dr. Wade Lamberth, ranked tops in his field, so Peggy and the children knew Dick was in good hands, both earthly and heavenly. Their hopes were high, and their guard was down.

The waiting room clock ticked off the hours. The surgery's normal time frame came and went. The clock's hour hand continued long past the expected hour when the surgery should have ended. Finally, a nurse came out to give a report.

"Mr. Vigneulle has experienced a set back. The doctor completed three bypasses. That part of the surgery was successful. But once in a while a patient's heart has difficulty restarting after surgery, and that is what has happened. His heart would not beat on its own, and each attempt to remove him from the bypass machine leaves his heart weaker. The doctor is working very hard. That's all I can tell you right now."

Nearly two more hours passed. Growing more and more anxious, the family found a spokesman in Tom. He demanded to know what was happening.

A staff person appeared, trying to give a straightforward explanation of a complicated medical situation. The prospects were glum, but the nurse spoke calmly and without emotion, trying to brace the family for the worst.

"The team was closing the chest when things began to go wrong. Mr. Vigneulle's heart rate dropped, and his heart rhythm became disorganized. That's when the team reopened his chest and put him back on bypass. After a couple of hours the team tried to take him off. But once again the Reverend's heart was unable to sustain cardiovascular function, and he had to be placed back on bypass. He is in grave condition, but the doctors are doing all they can."

While the waiting room grew deathly still, the operating room scene must have been frantic as Dr. Lamberth stubbornly refused to give up on a near lifeless patient. At one point, he literally held Dick's heart in his hands as he massaged it. His efforts were relentless, as the family learned later with more detail provided by support staff and the doctor himself.

"Dick is still in there," he said, pointing to the body on the table. "I can't let him go."

Dennis Butler, the nurse attending Dick, lauded the doctor's valiant efforts. A born-again believer as well as a dedicated medical worker, Dennis later included an account of Dick Vigneulle's case in his book titled *CROSSROADS: Where the Paths of Nurse and Patient Meet*.

"I saw God working here. Dr. Lamberth was a bulldog. He did not know the meaning of quit. If you were his patient, he would hang on to you and fight to the very end. Anyone else would probably have given up and let him die on the table."

Later acknowledging his own dogged determination, Lamberth likened himself to a sports team determined to play, no matter the disadvantage, and refusing to surrender before the clock ran out.

"If in a football game the team was playing in the fourth quarter, behind in the scoring and with only two minutes left to play in the game, the team would not take the ball and go home. They would keep playing."

Lamberth and his team played on, even after repeated attempts to get Dick off the bypass machine failed. Dennis Butler recalled the ongoing battle for life that moved from the operating room to the intensive care unit.

"Dr. Lamberth fought a seesaw battle all afternoon. Nine hours after a routine, three-hour surgery had begun, a fourth attempt was made to get the patient off the bypass. Few were optimistic about his chances for recovery, but many people were praying."

Already persisting beyond the normal efforts, Dr. Lamberth kept trying to get Dick's heart to start beating on its own. It was like trying to jumpstart a battery that would not spark and turn over. Then the doctor tried an experimental procedure, giving the patient drugs to thin his blood and slow down the heart so that it could rest for an hour or so in the hopes it would start up. Finally the procedure worked.

Nurse Butler recalls receiving his new patient.

"At eight o'clock that night—eleven hours after surgery began—I received Dick Vigneulle into Bed 2 of the Cardiovascular ICU. As he arrived in the unit, I remember being struck with the thought that this was not a living being. This was a corpse being kept alive against his will."

Mick Vigneulle later wrote an account of his father's grim situation in an article that appeared in *Lighthouse*, a supplement provided by Shades Mountain Independent Church and appearing in a Hoover/Vestavia neighborhood newspaper (June/July 1998).

"Normally, the third attempt to take a patient off the machine is the last. Most patients don't survive and the ones who do survive the ordeal usually die within a few days from trauma. Dad is the only patient, according to his doctor, that has ever been attempted a fourth time, and it wasn't until the sixth or seventh time that they were successful."

Like an army braving defeat, rallied by a great general, the medical team persisted in Dr. Lamberth's campaign to save Dick's life.

Nurse Butler described his patient's condition.

"He had more IV drips and machines than I had seen in one patient in a long time. He was on not one but four drugs used to raise blood pressure, all of them at maximum therapeutic doses. His heart was also being assisted with an intra-aortic balloon pump. It works by inflating like a balloon when the heart is resting to give an extra 'bump' to the blood pressure and cardiac output. It collapses and 'rests' while the heart pumps. The balloon pump was set for maximum output."

Several wires protruded out of the chest wall, attached to an external pacemaker. Set to drive Dick's heartbeat at one hundred times per minute, increasing his cardiac output and blood pressure, the pacemaker had to be coordinated with the balloon pump.

Complications multiplied along with remedies, almost outrunning the medical team's ability to keep up. Dick's heart swelled, so much so that the doctor could not close his chest after surgery without compromising cardiac output. There was nothing else to do but leave his chest open.

Once again Dennis Butler describes the eerie scene.

"A sterile surgical towel was placed over the open chest and a clear, plastic, adhesive dressing covering most of the chest went over that. The rib spreaders used to keep the breastbone apart during surgery remained in place. The actual heart was covered with only a sterile surgical towel and a thin plastic dressing. Pull back the sheet and you could see the ripples under the dressing every time his heart beat. It is a most peculiar sensation to watch something like that even after years of intensive care work."

Despite his constant medical attention and strong personal faith, Nurse Butler was not hopeful for Dick Vigneulle's next hours. As the family later learned, Dennis stood over their loved one for twelve hours straight, working almost nonstop to keep him alive.

"When he arrived in the unit, his blood pressure was 70/30—just barely compatible with life. We had already hit the upper limit of everything we could do for this man, and he was just barely alive. Any slide in the wrong direction, and he was a goner. I had never presided over the death of a fresh open-heart patient. I prepared myself to witness my first."

As he kept a vigilant watch, Dennis and the two nurses assisting him had to be ready for anything. For example, one medication would be administered only to create an allergic reaction. A countermeasure necessitated almost divine anticipation of varied body function responses. With every second counting in a battle to keep Dick alive, the nurse would call for a medication and another would run to fetch it. Again and again there would be a desperate order and a hasty run.

These life and death deployments continued throughout the night as Nurse Butler countered and anticipated one crisis after another. One misstep could have deadly consequences. Tested to his limits, it was as if Dennis played an intense game of chess with the grim reaper, with Dick's life the prize trophy.

The nurse kept up a bedside vigil. At 3:00 a.m., after a co-worker insisted he break for some food intake, Dennis gobbled down his lunch while standing at the foot of his patient's bed.

"I have never been so busy. Vital signs. Monitoring the bleeding from the chest tubes. Watching the changes in the blood pressure and heart rhythm. Timing the balloon pump with the pacemaker. Watching and adjusting the IV drips. Drawing labs. Giving blood and medications. During all this, I never took my eyes off the monitor for more than a few seconds at a time."

Another nurse later told the Vigneulle family that if Dennis had not been on duty that night, Dick would have died on at least two different occasions.

The light of dawn began to creep through the hospital windows. As the darkness gave way to light, the staff felt victorious just knowing the patient had survived the night, a small victory in a war not yet won, but a victory just the same. Then to their horror, they noticed the patient beginning to shift and move. Suddenly Dick opened his eyes, definitely not a good thing in a patient whose chest is still open from surgery. The agitated movements could cause serious harm, and if he became aware of his gruesome state, the emotional trauma could be damaging too.

Nurse Butler bent over the head of the bed and practically yelled in Dick's ear in order to be heard above the ICU background noise.

"Your surgery is over."

While another nurse ran for more morphine, Dennis spoke a command.

"Wiggle your toes!"

Dick wiggled both feet.

"Squeeze my hand!"

The patient complied with a strong squeeze. Dick's response was a small gesture but an important positive sign. After prolonged reduction of blood pressure, there can be brain damage. But Dick's mental status was strong enough to hear and respond to spoken commands, so he had not suffered a stroke or severe brain damage.

With six milligrams of morphine, the patient went back to sleep.

As the new day unfolded, the day after surgery, complications continued. The one bit of good news was that the doctor was able to close Dick's chest.

However, in another reversal, the patient's kidneys showed signs of shutting down, due to low blood pressure. In fact, during the course of the next seventy-two hours, every major organ would shut down. The medical team could not humanly explain why Dick did not die. Dr. Lamberth insisted on keeping his patient in the Cardiovascular Surgery Unit (CVSU) and so under his charge.

Nurse Butler described the yet-unfolding medical crisis.

"Dick Vigneulle's long siege of low blood pressure had stunned his kidneys and his liver. The kidneys quit working and dialysis followed. His liver enzymes began to rise and functions regulated by the liver became deranged. At one point his bilirubin was so high his skin began to turn yellow with jaundice."

The medical team began a new form called *continuous dialysis*. The more familiar traditional dialysis is done a few hours at a time, every other day or so with quick shifts of blood. But with continuous dialysis, the blood is slowly cleansed nonstop, around-the-clock. By avoiding huge shifts in blood volume, blood pressure drops are averted, lessening disturbance to organ function. Such machines are not a rarity today, but in 1998 they represented emerging technology. These machines typically were only available in larger medical centers and only on a limited basis. Brookwood's inventory included at least two.

By mid-February, his recovery faced another wave of complications. The latest life-threatening problem came to his lungs. He developed ARDS— Adult Respiratory Distress Syndrome—also known as *shock lung*. The condition results when a patient's lung tissue is flooded with fluid. Some estimate the survival rate of ARDS patients at that time at about 20%.

To manage the latest crisis, Dr. Gustavo DuBois was called in. A critical care specialist and pulmonologist, he was familiar with ARDS patients. The post-operative condition, sometimes part of a domino effect in medical complications, often results in patients who have suffered severe trauma, such as auto crash survivors, bombing victims, or battlefield-wounded soldiers. During the Viet Nam War era, doctors discovered the use of respirators significantly increased the survival rate of ARDS patients.

But use of a respirator was not a guarantee of the patient's survival. In fact, the likelihood of added complications increases.

Dr. DuBois explained, "The respirator is a two-edged sword. In order for the patient's major organs to function properly, the oxygen level needs to be high enough to fuel necessary functions, but if the oxygen level gets too high, then the lungs may develop an oxygen toxicity. There is a fine line between how much oxygen to provide for normal functioning versus too much that might *fry the lung*, so to speak, and cause irreparable damage. There must be a careful balance."

Dick's survival rate remained low for many weeks, due to his age, type of surgery, the number of failing organs, and continuing risk of further complications. One doctor estimated a slim or less than 10% chance of survival. At one point, his cardiac surgeon, Dr. Lamberth, conceded a 1% probability of survival.

As one of the doctors pointed out, a huge and diverse medical staff worked on Dick Vigneulle. The dedicated team included many more beyond his loyal primary doctors. In addition to a dozen or so doctors, key players included nurses, pharmacists, respiratory and physical therapists, nephrologists, nutritionists, and others. Furthermore, personnel from housekeeping and foodservice did their part.

When Dick finally came out of a coma, weeks after his initial surgery, his children were there for the special moment. Joyous and spontaneous, they gently whispered words of love and support.

"Dad, people are praying for you!"

Dick managed a one-word response: "Fabulous!"

Mick Vigneulle recalled the family's own struggle, dealing with pessimistic reports while clinging to hope.

"The days were long, but after about six weeks, Dad began to respond to us by lifting a finger or blinking an eye on command….we hung on to anything to increase our faith that he would survive. And survive he did! Dad began to turn the corner slowly. Sometimes he would smile at us, and even mouth words on good days. We lived for those few moments! Over the next six to eight weeks he improved to the place where he was no longer considered in critical condition. The doctors now classified his status as recovering!"

By March, while still a CICU patient, Dick was taken off dialysis.

In late April, doctors removed Dick's tracheotomy. After 103 days in ICU, Dick was transferred to the hospital's rehabilitation center. He still had a long way to go before he could return to his home, but he was closer.

Dick in Brookwood Hospital with rehab staff after his heart crisis – May 1998

Weeks of therapy would follow. Dedicated therapists worked hard, keeping Dick encouraged and working to bring strength and stamina to his limbs, to his whole body.

On May 7, Dick was able to sit up in a chair. The man who once pounded piano keys and pulpits, who raced across church platforms and tennis courts, who once raised a strong voice in song and sermons, now spoke softly and counted sitting in a chair an accomplishment to celebrate. And it was. His family anticipated the day when they could take Big Daddy home.

Later that month, on May 26, the hospital discharged him, sending him home with a feeding tube and oxygen supply for nighttime. Still unsteady on his feet, he rode in a wheelchair out to the family car.

One of his well-wishers was Dr. Lamberth, who was moved to give a personal salute to Dick and to the Vigneulle family's courage. In a solemn testimonial to his patient's miraculous recovery, his words were simple and his judgment straightforward.

"Mr. Vigneulle, you went beyond the point of no return and came back!"

CARING HEARTS

The medical miracle of Dick Vigneulle's recovery unfolded over the long months in the Brookwood Medical Center's Cardiac Intensive Care Unit. At the same time, another witness for the Lord was lived out in the hospital's waiting rooms—a testimony to the power of prayer. The eyes of the medical community focused on Peggy Vigneulle and her children and their families. Supported by a loyal church congregation, this family would not surrender their loved one, nor let go of their hope. The family's tenacity was not the result of denial or naivety. Quite simply, the family believed in the power of prevailing prayer—a lesson taught to them by the husband and father upstairs in the ICU hovering between earth and heaven.

Dick's cardiac surgeon, Dr. Lamberth, was among the many paying tribute to the power of the Vigneulle family's faith, family love, and prayers.

"Every imaginable thing went wrong. By all probability, Dick should not have survived. Then a true miracle happened. The Lord decided a good man who had done good works would survive. It took a strong family and friends to get the doctors to keep working to get Dick well. Sometimes when a patient is so sick, the family will get stressed out or even say, 'My dad would not want to live and be in this shape.' But the Vigneulle family insisted that the doctors continue trying."

The crisis certainly tested the family's faith. The constant waiting kept their emotions tautly stretched and gnawed at their physical stamina too.

"My faith felt like it had a hole in it the size of the Titanic," Mick later wrote. "I flinched every time the elevator bell sounded, picturing the doctor stepping out alone, apologizing for not being able to pull Dad through."

On the first day of the crisis, when an expected routine surgery went horribly awry, Peggy immediately contacted her Shades Mountain

Independent Church family to call the prayer chain to emergency action. A church family already in prayer now hit crisis mode.

Within a few hours, the hospital's telephone switchboard lit up with incoming calls from across the country and around the world—people wanted updates on Dick Vigneulle's condition. Within the first three days of Dick's hospitalization, Brookwood received over 10,000 phone calls. Pastor Harry Walls and SMI arranged for the installation of a special phone line—a hot line—to handle the overload of telephone inquiries.

One of the first to call was Dick's old buddy and family friend from Lynchburg, Virginia, Jerry Falwell. With the clarity and confidence of an Old Testament prophet, he made a simple declaration to the family.

"Your daddy will live! God's not through with him yet."

A prayer network of churches crisscrossed the entire nation. Birmingham's local Christian radio stations began to announce updates on Dick's condition.

Scores and then hundreds of folks came to the hospital daily, without letup. In an efficiency move that was both hospitable and practical, the hospital staff set up a make-shift private waiting room for the Vigneulle family and their many visitors. A storage area was cleared out and furnished to accommodate the family and their many well-wishers. Food was brought in to feed the family and guests, such a bounty that meals were shared with staff and others in the waiting room areas.

The children still marvel at their mother's strong faith. Her confidence became a deep well that refreshed others as they drew on her strength. Peggy reached a turning point when she made a prayer closet out of a hospital bathroom. She closed the door for privacy as she knelt before her Heavenly Father. When she emerged from that moment of solitude, even her family took notice of the champion spirit that filled her, and never left.

One of her sons later said, "Mom's faith was incredible. She was willing to let Dad go but felt God wasn't finished with him yet. She got alone and prayed, 'Okay, God, this may be it, but if you want my husband to live, please encourage the doctor so he can encourage us.'"

One hospital worker expressed the respect so many felt for Peggy and the whole family, saying, "They knew the outlook was very grim, but they never lost their faith or their hope or their poise."

In a heavenly twist, the doctors would concede that it was Peggy who encouraged them. Dr. Dubois, the pulmonologist, was one of them.

I was impressed with how each member of the Vigneulle family played a role and was vital in reinforcing the fact that, as a deeply religious family, they held out hope. And certainly you could tell how prayer made a difference, not only in holding the family together, but also in Dick's recovery. I truly believe it. I could see it in his family. There were trying times when things were not going well. Even as physicians we even doubted the possibility that he would live, and then the next thing we knew he would get well and things looked bright.

Dr. Lamberth, the cardiac surgeon, noted Dick's strong will to live, "Survivors survive because they want to."

Then acknowledging the key role of the patient's loved ones, he said further, "Most families wear out before the patient wears out. As long as we were working, the family was working. In time, we all won!"

As the days of Dick's unfolding medical disaster became weeks, and then months, Peggy and the children still maintained their prayer vigil at the hospital. Rick and Mick kept some of their ministry obligations, knowing their father would want God's work to continue unhindered. Otherwise, they kept a vigil too. Peggy, accompanied by her daughter, Diane, remained at Brookwood for six weeks straight. The family eventually worked out a calendar and rotation so that at least one family member was with Dick at all times. For example, Tom preferred to come in the mornings, and so that became his special time with his dad. Day in and day out, Dick was never alone.

After he was taken to the Cardiac Intensive Care Unit and the early crises were under control, Nurse Dennis Butler allowed the family to make visits. Peg would stand and pray over Dick. Placing one hand on his leg, she would intercede with thanksgiving, believing God for the unseen.

"Thank You, Lord, that Dick is being healed. Please give the doctors wisdom."

The children later recalled her quiet moments with their father.

"After talking to God, Mom would talk to Dad, calming and assuring him, expressing her love. She might be upset at times, but never shaken.

301

Mom was solid as a rock. She was quiet but so strong in her faith."

Mick further described their efforts.

"During the first two months, there were many times we could not tell if Dad could hear us or was aware of our presence. But we stayed by his bedside singing his favorite hymns and choruses, reading the Bible, and talking to him."

Diane recalls a prayer the family repeated at the close of every visit, at the end of every day.

"We would repeat the prayer God gave Moses and Aaron for blessing Israel."

> The LORD bless you and keep you;
> The LORD make His face shine upon you, and be gracious to you;
> The LORD lift up His countenance upon you, And give you peace (Numbers 6:24-26).

When Dick began to awake out of his long coma, he spoke first with his eyes, even before gaining the feeblest powers of speech. His nurse, Dennis Butler, described his first eye-to-eye encounter.

"When he awoke from the coma, I first saw what I called 'the look.' Mr. Vigneulle was sixty-five years old and had snow-white hair and piercing blue eyes that gave those of us around him a kind but knowing look. If you ever wanted to see someone who could look right through you, it was Dick Vigneulle. He had a piercing gaze—not threatening, just knowing and *aware*."

Medication and medical instruments, essential to sustaining his life, limited the patient's ability to speak. Even so, Dick made efforts to talk with those around him. Just one spoken word or even a single gesture rallied the hopes of his family and caregivers.

His visitors increased.

Stu and Bebe Gaines visited often, Stu insisting, "Dick, you've got to make it. I want you to preach my funeral."

Cornerstone, the much-loved SMI quartet, repeatedly visited for bedside concerts, serenading their Pastor Emeritus with the hymns he loved. On one visit, as the men sang, Dick lifted his arm and tried to direct the music. Nurses, hospital staff, and even other patients and their families would come around to listen in to the Cornerstone mini-concerts. The singers visited other patients, as staff and family members made requests. Toward the end of his hospitalization, Dick managed to sing along with Cornerstone—a musical milestone in his recovery.

Folks came to comfort and be comforted once more by the one they had called "Pastor" for so long. More than well-wishers, countless Christians shared the family's vigil in a public demonstration of Christian graces and spiritual gifts. Their ministry of presence bolstered the patient, his family, and his caregivers.

Dick had given himself freely and sacrificially to many as friend and pastor, and now, as one friend noted, "What he did for so many came back to him."

In critical moments, Peggy and the children called the church elders to Dick's bedside to lay hands on him and pray. Dr. Lamberth took special notice.

"A group of men came one night to pray when Dick was on a ventilator. That was unique in that I had never witnessed that in my entire practice. Dick's church was supportive as well as his family and friends. Dick knew a lot of people and had touched a lot of people, and they in turn had touched others."

In fact, the church elders came to pray over Dick on three different occasions, each time in response to a medical crisis. The first time was for his kidneys when facing renal failure, the second time after his lungs succumbed to ARDS, and the third time when the medical team struggled to get Dick off the respirator.

One of the Vigneulle children commented, "Once the SMI elders prayed about an issue, it never surfaced again."

The bedside visitors never knew when Dick might awaken again and speak. Sometimes he surprised them. One afternoon the twins were talking with their father's nurse. As they chatted she shared that she was engaged and would soon be married. Bob Palmer was also present and described the brief and unexpected conversation that ensued.

"Dick had been totally out of it to this point. He had not said anything. Suddenly, after hearing mention of her fiancé, Dick spoke to the nurse and asked, 'Does he know Christ?' The nurse began to cry and said, 'I'm not sure.' Then Dick said, 'He's got to know the Lord.' Dick did not say anything else and was out of it again."

King Solomon's godly wisdom prescribes laughter for healing: "A merry heart does good, like medicine" (Proverbs 17:22a). There were moments when humor sustained both family and staff in their long vigil.

When Dick first learned he had already been in the hospital for seventy-two days, he looked at his wife with a puzzled face and asked, "Peg, did you know that?"

While Peg was out of the room, Dick confided to a nurse, "I've been asleep so long that I've missed my wife's birthday!"

Eager to please, the nurse ordered a birthday cake so Dick could surprise his wife and make amends. When Peggy returned, a "Happy Birthday" party welcomed her. She graciously joined in the celebration and thanked her husband, even though her birthday was still months away. He had not missed it at all.

Much later Dick would learn more about his family's months of devotion, but equally pleasing to him was hearing about his family's devotion to others as well. The family ministered to staff and patients alike, praying, singing, and sharing their faith. Countless people came to Christ. Even as Dick lay silent on his sickbed, his life was touching others, bringing folks to Jesus.

For many years, Dick kept on his desk a favorite saying. More than a motto, it was a promise for him to live by, a simple creed to repeat and encourage others: "MAN'S IMPOSSIBILITIES ARE GOD'S OPPORTUNITIES!"

Throughout his life, he had experienced this simple truth lived out over and over, but his medical miracle took it to a whole new level.

The beloved Dick Vigneulle's recovery was a medical miracle that would be documented and retold by physicians and clergy alike. Believing prayer and inspiring faith held together a family and medical team, a congregation and larger faith community. A godly man's illness and near death created an occasion for people of faith to prove God's great power. With honor to his family and gratitude to a dedicated medical staff, Dick would be the first to say that the promise is true: *MAN'S IMPOSSIBILITIES ARE GOD'S OPPORTUNITIES!*

THE ROAD HOME

Three special stops or events marked the route to Dick's recovery and the praise celebrations that heralded his homecoming.

The first was on the very day he went home from the hospital on May 26, 1998. Despite ongoing confinement to a wheelchair, Dick was elated the day he was wheeled out of Brookwood's Rehabilitation Center for the short drive to Hoover and his home on Pavillon Drive. But the driver did not take the shortest route. Down Highway 31, Dick passed familiar sights and storefronts that had been hidden for months. Then the car took an unexpected turn off the highway and up Tyler Road. The family arranged a special treat— a drive by his beloved church at the fork in Old Tyler Road and Tyler Road. Dick quickly realized where he was headed, but his excitement turned to alarm. As Shades Mountain Independent Church came into sight, there were hundreds and hundreds of people standing outside the buildings.

"Was there a fire or bomb scare? What was wrong?" Dick wondered to himself. "My first thought is that there had been an accident. Then I looked at Tom and he smiled. Then as my car got closer, I saw the crowd clapping and cheering—that's when I got emotional! And I've been emotional ever since!"

More than just a hero's welcome, the crowd's jubilation must have echoed the joy of Lazarus' friends when he walked out of his tomb and

came back to them from the dead. The throng of church folks, for all their shouting and clapping and waving, were a worshipful bunch. This was a praise-gathering as well as a homecoming.

The car did not stop and resumed speed,

Top: Tom drove Dick home from hospital. As a surprise to Dick, Tom drove past SMI where church members waited – May 1998 ***Bottom:*** Driving past SMI while going home from hospital, alongside car are celebrating, emotional church greeters.

305

but not before Dick could wave and smile in return. As much as he would have loved to hop out of the car and start hugging and high-fiving his friends, Dick knew he could not. His doctors would not have approved, and he knew that the needed strength was not in him. In fact, it was all he could do to summon the stamina to handle the ride home. The longed-for reunion with his church family would have to wait.

As the waving crowd dimmed from view, Dick purposed in his heart, "I'll be back, and soon! I want to be back for Birthday Sunday in July! Yes, that's it! I'm gonna work so I can be back for Birthday Sunday!"

Dick Vigneulle was a man who always kept his word, who fulfilled all his promises—even to himself. True to the commitment he made earlier, he pushed and pushed his rehabilitation therapy with one goal in mind—to get strong enough to be back in church on the first Sunday in July.

Throughout SMI's history, Birthday Sunday, the annual celebration of the church's founding, always featured famous guest preachers and singers. The arrival of these illustrious visitors made the day even more special. But on July 5, 1998, the congregation's anticipation had never been greater as they prepared to welcome to their midst one more precious than a visiting celebrity.

Those in the pews expecting to see their former Pastor as they remembered him would be shocked, not just disappointed. Confined to a wheelchair, an oxygen tube attached to his face, and eighty pounds lighter, Dick drew a few gasps amid the cheers. The weak figure being rolled down the aisle by his sons looked like a ghostly version of the mighty figure who once strode across the platform.

As if the church orchestra had begun to play Handel's *Hallelujah Chorus*, the entire congregation rose to its feet. Thunderous applause continued as the Vigneulle sons lifted their father's wheelchair, with him still in it, to the top of the platform. All the while the overflow crowd continued to roar its approval.

Once the crowd stilled, at least enough for Dick to be heard, he began to speak. The body and voice might have been weak, but the fire was still there. The Founding Pastor indeed was back.

Still seated in his wheelchair, trying to ignore the oxygen tube dangling before him, Dick flooded the people with his love and appreciation.

"You wanna know what a little heaven on earth is like? It's being here with you folks today—you are great!"

He went on to thank his Pastor, Harry Walls, and all the staff and congregation for their outpouring of love, expressed in so many varied ways.

"This has got to be the greatest congregation! You're the most loving and most giving, most wonderful people! It blew me away when you met me out front here when I came home from the hospital."

He then recapped his medical drama. Most of the crowd could have recited the events like familiar Scripture, but this was their first time to hear the account from the man himself. He concluded with a blunt summary of the whole narrative.

"Everything was heading south, and it looked as if I would see my Savior very soon."

He went on to thank publicly Brookwood Hospital and its staff. Many from the medical team who cared for Dick were in the audience that very morning, including Dr. Lamberth and his wife. He acknowledged them all and asked them to stand, joining the congregation in another round of applause. This time they celebrated the human hands that fought for Dick's life and worked for his ongoing recovery.

"The doctors and nurses were phenomenal. On numerous occasions they saved my life. I was in the hospital for over 130 days. My recovery was slow and arduous. My muscles atrophied, so I had to learn how to walk and use my fingers."

There were others to thank, including his loving family and church. Their prayers made the difference. When he was unconscious and too ill to pray for himself, they carried the burden.

Making sure that folks knew what the celebration was really about, Dick reminded the crowd of God's faithfulness. The Lord hears and answers prayer. He honors faith.

"Some of you have asked if when I was in a coma, if I saw any angels. Well the answer is yes, but they wouldn't let me in because of all your prayers. Think of it—I could have been in glory today. But because of your prayers, I'm here, and apparently God's not through with me yet!"

Turning to a preaching mode, Dick called the congregation's attention to the Gospel of Mark, chapter two.

"Here is the story of a palsied man whose friends could not get him to Jesus. So they made a hole in the roof and they let him down on a cot. After seeing their faith, Jesus forgave the palsied man and healed him. It wasn't just the sick man's faith but his friends' faith that God honored. And I say to you this morning that it wasn't my faith, because I was out of it in a coma. It was your faith. Every one of you who believed God on my behalf—that's why I'm here this morning."

Then Dick asked his sons to pick up his wheelchair and lower him back down off the platform to the sanctuary's main level. The men quickly but carefully obliged their father's request. Once on the main level, before his sons could wheel their dad out of the auditorium, Dick spoke up. There was one more thing he wanted to say . . . and do.

"For any doubters who said I would never live, for any who said I would never get out of bed, who said I would never get out of a wheelchair, who said I would never walk again . . . and then for ALL of you who prayed believing . . . ."

To his sons' dismay, Dick looked up and asked to be lifted up out of the wheelchair.

"Dad, are you sure?" they all whispered.

Dick nodded his head up and down. The sons obeyed. Then, with one on each side standing guard and the third behind him pushing an empty wheelchair, Dick began a shaky but determined walk down the aisle, one tiny and unsteady step at a time. At that moment, even the brawniest men in the room recognized that the strongest man in their midst was the frail figure slow stepping out the door.

A CHRISTMAS PARTY

As the Vigneulle family anticipated Christmas 1998, Dick made a special request.

"Let's throw a party!"

"Well, Honey, that's a great idea," Peggy answered.

Long admired as a gracious hostess, Peg loved opening her home for gatherings big or small. After her husband's repeated near-death experiences earlier in the year, Peg felt as though every day was Christmas now that Dick was back home. Not since the twins were toddlers watching for Santa Claus had she been so excited about December 25. She was ready to party too, but best of all was seeing Dick so spirited.

Smiling big, Peg asked, "What kind of party do you want?"

"I want to have a THANK YOU CELEBRATION here at the house for all those doctors and nurses who took care of me. I can't get it out of my mind how God used them to save my life. We could invite them and their spouses, and then I could thank them once more—each one of them. And most of all I want to tell them about Christ."

Without a moment of hesitation, Peggy agreed. When the Vigneulle children and their spouses heard about the party, they all signed-on to help. This would be a party with a mission—a Great Commission cause.

Dick had made great strides in his recovery, but there was still a long way to go. Some compromises to his health and stamina might, in fact, be permanent. There were many days of discouragement and a few low-spirited moments. But the Christmas party stoked his enthusiasm.

Plans fell into place. A caterer, a family friend, planned a sumptuous buffet for the guests, a spread New Testament hostesses Mary and Martha would have envied. Peggy spent hours in her basement flower room, working on holiday floral arrangements and decorations to fill every level and every room of the house. This year there would be more Christmas trees and lights and garland than ever before. When Peggy and her helper elves finished, Pavillon Drive would make the North Pole look drab.

Dick insisted on writing out the evening's schedule and planning the inspirational program. He even helped address the invitations.

One of his sons chuckled and said, "Dad, you're back! You're in charge again!"

On the night of the party, Dick and Peg stood at their front door, warmly greeting everyone with handshakes and hugs. Nearly a hundred guests crossed the threshold. Among them were Dr. Wade Lamberth and his wife. He acknowl-

Dick and Peggy with Dr. and Mrs. Wade Lamberth (the heart surgeon God used to save Dick's life) – December 1998

309

edged later that this was the first time he ever had dinner with a patient.

"It was a neat evening," he recalled years later. "It was more than unique because Dick had been on the verge of death for so long and in so many ways during his hospital stay. Now, months later, here he was with his family, saying thank you to us all."

The party took place just a few weeks shy of the first anniversary of the start of Dick's crisis. Now, as the year ended, surely everyone in the room marveled to be sharing a party and not a funeral with the Vigneulle family. And no one was more alive that evening than the miracle survivor who had invited them all into his home.

Amidst all the festivity, the real purpose of Dick and Peg's "Thank You Celebration" was not lost on the guests. Every doctor, nurse, or medical worker present that night might have felt like the lone guest of honor, and rightly so. But these dedicated men and women knew the evening celebrated a team effort, not any one person's solo performance. Besides, most if not all recognized that higher hands had guided them.

Medical spouses, who must share in the interruptions and sacrifices required by their loved ones' career in medicine, took a shine to the evening's events. They appreciated the recognition given to their husbands and wives. When Jesus healed ten lepers, only one returned to say thank you. Evidently the ratio of grateful patients has not improved in two thousand years.

Guests circulated in the great room, many standing before the giant stone fireplace, warmed by the heat and sound of a crackling fire. Others gathered across the room in front of the wall of floor-to-ceiling windows that looked out over the mountainside. A night sky illuminated by stars and Christmas lights charmed guests, as Christmas hymns played in the background.

As the evening unfolded, the doctors and nurses engaged their hosts by swapping stories and anecdotes back and forth, retelling Dick's amazing recovery. Some stories Dick heard for the first time.

Dr. Lamberth would say, for years to come, "Dick Vigneulle is THE person I quote all the time as being my modern-day miracle. That's what I say, that's what I believe. If you didn't believe in God, you have to say this is unexplainable by common sense and statistics. We don't have many burning bushes today, but this was a miracle. If you didn't believe in a Creator up there, this would make you start to pay attention."

A few guests, detained from sharing in the mealtime, arrived just in time for the special program the Vigneulle family prepared. With coffee cups and punch glasses in hand, folks gathered again in the great room.

Rick and Mick kicked off the entertainment segment with their inspirational antics.

Drawing from their comedy routine, the twins performed their "Chipmunks Skit," and then turned to song with their version of a Christmas classic, "The Twelve Days of Christmas."

After singing carols, the crowd listened to each of the Vigneulle children, along with their mother, share a personal testimony of thanks for the men and women who worked tirelessly to save their father's life.

Dr. Gustavo DuBois, the pulmonologist who worked so tirelessly as his patient battled ARDS and other complications, later recalled the party. The presence and words of the Vigneulle family touched him. He enjoyed the evening for many reasons, but especially for the glimpse of what he called *the other side of medicine.*

"I thought it was a tremendous privilege to come into his home, along with my wife, and to see Rev. Vigneulle in the context of his family, restored to his loved ones and enjoying life again. It was moving to have been part of the medical team that was responsible for his recovery. He was no longer just a patient in a hospital gown."

Then he added, "The evening with the Vigneulles uniquely showed me that the other side of medicine is the recovery not just of the patient but of the entire family."

After his family members spoke, Dick stepped forward and took his place before all his guests. The invited crowd remained hushed as Dick stood and, turning his head left to right, looked them all in the eye. Without the aid of a wheelchair or cane, and not even a chair to lean on, the preacher summoned his own strength and stood as if a pulpit was before him and he was back in church. God had given him a message to share, and he was eager to oblige this God-given opportunity.

Pointing to his beloved cardiac surgeon, Dick proclaimed, "Dr. Lamberth, you held my heart in your hands! And, Sir, God's hand held yours."

Adding to his family's earlier salute, Dick went on to give a tearful thanks to the men and women of medicine who cared for him. But these guests were invited into this preacher's home for another reason. There was a message he needed to share—the real reason for the Christmas season.

"Folks, I want to tell you about the *Gift of Christmas*."

The title of his sermon announced, Dick proclaimed the Good News as he always had done. With brevity and clarity, he echoed the Apostle Paul's explanation of salvation from Romans 6:23, "For the wages of sin is death, but the gift of God is eternal life in Christ Jesus our Lord."

Making it clear that every man and woman needs God's forgiveness, he explained that good works do not save. "For by grace you have been saved through faith, and that not of yourselves; it is the gift of God, not of works, lest anyone should boast" (Ephesians 2:8-9).

When Dick closed his brief message, just as he ended every sermon at SMI, he gave an invitation.

> If you have a *want to* inside you that says "*I want to be saved! I want to know my sins are forgiven! I want to know for sure that Jesus Christ is my personal Savior*" —then I'd like for you to pray this prayer with me:
>
> *Dear God, I know that I am a sinner, and I believe that God loves sinners—so God, You love me. The best I know how, I ask the Lord Jesus Christ, Who died on the cross for me, to come into my life. I ask You, Lord Jesus, to forgive me of all my sin. I really mean it! I trust You now to save my soul. Lord Jesus, You said that whosoever would call upon the name of the Lord would be saved. I've called just now. Thank You, Lord Jesus, that You saved me. I stand upon Your Word. You said it, and I believe it, and I thank You.*

Next, after a moment of silence, Dick again addressed the crowd.

> With your heads still bowed, I'd like to ask you to do something for me. If you prayed that prayer with me just now, as a testimony to what Christ has done in your life, would you just do this: look up and catch my eye. When you do, you are saying, "*Preacher, I prayed this prayer with you, and I meant it, and I want you to pray for me.*"

Quickly, from every corner of the room, heads popped up as men and women caught Dick's eye. By the end of the evening dozens of guests—doctors, nurses, their family members—had prayed to receive Christ as personal Savior.

Dr. DuBois described Dick's presence and impact that evening.

"I could tell Dick Vigneulle was a man of God who is a loving father, grandfather, husband, and above all a man who loves Christ, and who is so close to His teachings. He is a man who acts the way he preaches."

He went on to say, for himself as a religious man and medical doctor, that particular holiday night was a "spiritually significant evening, and once again reinforced God working in our lives in helping us to help our fellow man. Rev. Vigneulle reinforces the spiritual part of medicine. We doctors can get very technical with one another, talking about types of scalpels and so on, but there is a psychological and spiritual part of illness that we should incorporate in the total healing of patients. Dick Vigneulle has shown people what spiritual and mental and physical strength is all about."

With the 2009 publication of this biography, eleven years have passed since the medical crisis when doctors thought Dick Vigneulle had no tomorrow. The miracle man's recovery still inspires many, including the patient himself.

"Every day is a bonus!" he still celebrates.

With begrudging concessions to a few limitations lingering from his 1998 illness, Dick continues to pursue the goals he set for himself upon his 1995 retirement from the pastorate. Retirement did not mean retreat, just new direction. Likewise, he has refused to allow illness to deter his post-pastorate life ambitions.

The gifts, obvious even from his boyhood days in Delaware and later across a South Carolina college campus, still identify the man today: love of people, musical skills, and natural leadership. The charisma and character that opened doors in his young adulthood, as he scaled Birmingham's corporate ladders and later founded a ministry with international impact, enabled Dick Vigneulle to build a legacy. His family and friends insist that Dick's heritage—based on achievements and reputation—continues to bless and inspire others.

He indulges himself with more time for personal pursuits such as family gatherings, hobbies, and travel. The driving force of his life, however, remains the same. From youth to old age, soul-winning remains Dick Vigneulle's greatest passion. He continues to serve on the Boards of evangelistic ministries, including Rick and Mick Vigneulle Ministries and World Reach, Inc. Whether one-on-one or in public gatherings, he still shares the Good News and leads folks to Christ.

After guest preaching recently, as he drove home, Dick asked Peggy, "Did I do all right? I have to rely on my notes now, not like in the old days! And I can't even read the notes half the time!"

His wife smiled and assured him, pointing out, "Honey, nearly a dozen people got saved. I think you did just fine!"

In a few short years, Lord willing, Dick will reach octogenarian status. While his steps may be a bit slower at times, his mind remains tough and his spirit strong. The zeal of the Memory-O-Matic salesman and the drive of the City Federal banker are still with him. Dick Vigneulle continues to set goals for himself, always raising the bar of his family's expectations for Big Daddy.

At the risk of breaching a confidence, one of his sons repeated his father's end-of-life goals.

"First, Dad wants to finish well—that is the capstone to his entire life. Like the Apostle Paul, he wants to remain in the race and not rest on past laurels. There is more for him to do. Second, he wants to continue to reach the lost any way he can. He still shares his faith and wants to make sure folks are saved. Third and last, Dad hopes to establish a fund that, even after he is long gone, will help ministries to spread the Gospel."

Even from heaven, Dick wants to be a witness on earth.

As Dick reflects on his life, and gives an account of God's calling and faithfulness, he still points to the Bible verse that has guided him since college days. Back then he was a young man in his twenties with a wife to support. College graduation loomed just a few days away, yet he had no clue as to what God wanted him to do. With a deep hunger to make his mark and accomplish something for God, Dick found comfort and direction from God's Word. He claimed a Bible promise that he still holds on to today.

Thou wilt show me the path of life: in thy presence is fullness of joy;
at thy right hand there are pleasures for evermore
(Psalm 16:11/KJV).

Dick and Peggy - 2009

That same verse guides him still.

"Our lives are in God's hands," Dick affirms. "As long as we are submissive to His will, He will show us the path of life."

Although a lifetime of accomplishments already afford a legacy that would settle many, Dick firmly believes the best is yet to be. There is still a work to do for God. He knows because the Bible still promises him so. He is still walking the path, still experiencing the fullness of joy.